# KEEP *or* SELL *your* BUSINESS...

## HOW TO MAKE THE DECISION EVERY PRIVATE COMPANY FACES

### MIKE COHN

#### WITH JAYNE PEARL

**DEARBORN**™ **TRADE**

A **Kaplan Professional** Company

For Lee,
my best friend, spouse, and business partner
and
Jenoa and Michael,
for keeping me balanced.

Acquisitions Editor: Mary B. Good
Senior Managing Editor: Jack Kiburz
Interior Design: Eliot House Productions
Cover Design: Studio Montage

© 2001 by Mike Cohn
Published by Dearborn Trade, a Kaplan Professional Company

Printed in the United States of America
01 02 03 10 9 8 7 6 5 4 3 2 1

**Library of Congress Cataloging-in-Publication Data**
Cohn, Mike.
    Keep or sell your business : how to make the decision every private company faces / Mike Cohn with Jayne Pearl.
        p.      cm.
    Includes bibliographical references and index.
    ISBN 1-57410-139-0 (pbk.)
    1. Corporate divestiture—Decision making. 2. Liquidation—Decision making. 3. Family-owned business enterprises—Succession—Decision making. 4. Sale of business enterprises—Decision making. I. Pearl, Jayne A., 1954- II. Title.
HD2746.6 .C64 2001
658.1'6--dc21
                                                                00-010336

Dearborn Trade books are available at special quantity discounts to use as premiums and sales promotions, or for use in corporate training programs. For more information, please call the Special Sales Manager at 800-621-9621, ext. 4514, or write to Dearborn Financial Publishing, Inc., 155 N. Wacker Drive, Chicago, IL 60606-1719.

# Contents

**Part IV: After You've Decided to Keep or Sell**

# Preface

Since 1976, I have worked with closely held companies and family-owned and -controlled businesses on succession issues. The challenge of succession planning in private companies still fascinates me and probably always will, perhaps because I grew up in a family business and worked in it from age eight through high school. In 1984, I began to work exclusively with family business owners who were debating whether to keep their business or sell to an industry consolidator. Even then, the issues were emotional as well as financial. Business transitions are always complex, regardless of the size of the company, and can bring out the best and the worst in people. A transition becomes the focal point where power and authority, business value, legal and tax issues, family dynamics, and trust (or lack of it) all come together at a point in time.

Over the past 16 years I have worked in a wide variety of situations regarding succession: the healthy families who want to build or continue a legacy, the dysfunctional families who play out their problems inside the family business, the entrepreneurs with big ideas, the caretakers who are reluctant to take risks, those who resist letting go in spite of overwhelming evidence that they should, and those who let go and then coach the successors to greatness. For those who have sold their companies, some are happy in their new activities (some have started new businesses), and some are ambivalent and still second-guess the decision to sell.

My clients are sometimes inspiring, often frustrating, but never boring. I have been hired to structure transfers for those who wish to keep their companies and for those who wish to sell. I often work with two (sometimes three) generations: the successor generation who is taking over (or hopes to) and the senior generation who is withdrawing (or promising to). Sometimes successors are well prepared but the senior generation is reluctant to let go. At other times, current owners are ready to withdraw, but the successors are unsure and reluctant to take on the responsibility and risks of ownership and management. Some clients have been smart enough to keep their company as an investment and to hire professionals to run it for them, when there were no competent (or interested) successors in the family or in the business. Others haven't been that smart.

For some, selling the business is the right way to go. When the company has no energy or capital for growth, owners are burned out and financially dependent on the business, and there are no successors, the decision to sell is easy. It's the timing that's difficult. I've negotiated with buyers, sometimes led by management, but more often strategic buyers in the seller's industry. On several occasions, the financial results realized were greater than the client's highest expectations, but the client became depressed with the sale of the company, his "baby."

In 1990, I wrote a book on succession planning (with a second edition in 1992), called *Passing the Torch* for first-generation entrepreneurs who were dealing with succession, retirement, and estate planning. From 1994 through 1999 I worked more with multi-generational family businesses—some in their second, third, and fourth generations, and I learned that the dynamics of each generation were different. As a result, I also learned that choosing a planning strategy that will work depends on whether the generation is willing to address the transition issues. These issues differ for each generation involved in the planning so the solutions that work differ by generations as well. For example, the strategies and discussions about partnering that seemed applicable for second-generation businesses were not as relevant to cousin-controlled third or fourth generation companies with 30 or more stockholders. For these cousin-controlled companies, governance, stewardship, and learning to be smart owners were the primary goals. This led me to develop generation-specific strategies for my clients.

As I was focusing on the keep side of the Keep-Sell decision, several clients (after working on succession planning) opted to sell their businesses. For some, the offers were too attractive to ignore. For others it had become clear that the next generation didn't have the talent or passion to lead the business. For these, it was the best decision for the family and the business.

Opportunities to sell the private company will continue to be a fact of life. Making the decision to keep or sell will continue to be a tough and complex issue for many who are torn between the financial rewards of selling and the desire to keep their business for future generations.

There are lots of books about how to buy a company and plenty of advice about how to sell yours. But as I worked with clients on the various issues described in this book I realized there wasn't a book that took a balanced approach to help undecided business owners make their decision. That is what I have done here.

## Who Should Read This Book

This book is intended for owners and their families, board members, and executives of private companies who wrestle with issues about the future of their business. This book should stimulate discussions about succession plans, corporate strategy, and developing leadership to meet today's challenges. After reading this book you should have a game plan to go forward whether it is to keep or sell the company. Board members of closely-held businesses who read this book should feel more confident about the contribution they can make to the company and its owners. This book is also for the executives and members of industry and trade associations that are comprised of closely-held companies. Many of these trade associations are changing as consolidators and others systematically acquire members. Association members will know their options with the help of this book. Advisors, such as attorneys, CPAs, financial and insurance professionals who work with closely-held business owners on succession and estate planning issues will find helpful advice and information. Understanding the options and challenges your clients face can help you do a better job with them. This book is also for the families of business owners; working through the issues in this book as a family can help everyone make a better decision.

## How This Book Is Organized

The book is divided into four parts. Part I takes you through an analysis about whether you should keep or sell your company. As one client describes it, you start with the view from 30,000 feet up in the air where you can see the mountain of issues. But then you have to land and start hiking up the mountain. Getting to the top of the mountain and making the right choices are what the first three chapters are about. Chapters 1 and 2 zero in on the health of the company and the commitment and skills of current and future owners. By the end of Chapter 3, you should be ready to decide which path is best for you. But that's only the first step.

Part II is about keeping your company. In my experience, there are three models for ownership of the private business. Deciding which model is right for you is an important decision. Owners need to consider generational differences. Chapters 4 through 7 take you through these three models of ownership and outline how they work from a structural and a management perspective.

Part III is about selling your company. If this is the path you have decided to take, Chapters 8 through 10 take you step by step through what you need to do to prepare for the sale, as well as the negotiations and the legal documents needed.

Part IV addresses post-decision issues, whether you have decided to keep or sell the business. In both cases there are lifestyle issues, investment choices, estate planning, and wealth transfer decisions to be made. These have been outlined in Chapters 11 and 12.

There are two appendixes: one contains information that I believe will be helpful in the Keep decision, and the other contains sample documents that should be helpful in the Sell decision.

My goal is for you to be able to make an informed decision about what you should do with your company. I respect and admire those who have built their companies into something that could be continued for one or more generations and have taken the steps to educate and prepare their successors, top managers, and family as to these challenges. I also respect and admire those who know when the time is right to sell and do something differently with their wealth. Whichever path you take, I hope that this book will help you and those who work with you make the right decision for you, your company, and your family.

—Mike Cohn
Phoenix, Arizona

# Acknowledgments

A lot of people have helped me put this book together in a relatively short period of time. For all of them, I am especially grateful for their friendship and support. I have worked with some extraordinary clients over the past 15 years and have had the fortune to grow with them as they and their businesses have expanded and changed over time. They have wrestled with complex problems of succession and have made tough decisions about their companies, the capabilities of family members, and dealt with their own issues about letting go. I greatly admire these people for having the courage to deal with these difficult issues. In the course of working with these clients I have also worked with some outstanding attorneys and CPAs who are dedicated in helping their clients make the right decisions and who have welcomed a collaboration with me and my firm. The collaboration has almost always produced a better end result for the client. I have also been fortunate to have cultivated a network of experts throughout the United States who bring additional skills to the process of working with closely-held and family-controlled companies—many of these relationships were started through our affiliation with Family Firm Institute, an international organization of advisors and researchers to family businesses.

I want to especially thank Jayne Pearl who has been an extraordinary partner on this project. She spent more time than she planned in organizing and thinking through this material. This is my second major project with Jayne and she has the unique ability to always bring out the best in my writing. For her contribution, her friendship, and her talent, I am especially thankful.

I also want to thank Mary Good at Dearborn for her vision and support. She helped us focus our thoughts from initial submission and has kept us on track throughout the project.

I have drawn on many associates whose expertise enhanced different portions. They include Gail Bradley and Monica Tucevich of Northern Trust; Craig Cantoni of Capstone Consulting; Jeff Davidson of Deloitte & Touche; Leslie Dashew of Human Side of Enterprise; Jim Dwyer of Management Planning; Mark Feldman of Arthur Andersen; turnaround consultant John Furman, Jim McMahon and Alec Berkman of the Executive Compensation Division of CFG Business Solutions; Jim Murphy of deVisscher, Allen, and Olson; Peter Karoff of The Philanthropic Initiative; and Gary Ringel of Ringel Valuation Services. Several attorneys have also helped directly and indirectly with this book and include David Weiss of Snell and Wilmer, Larry Brody of Bryan Cave, and Neal Kurn of Fennemore Craig.

Numerous clients have contributed in many ways—directly by allowing me to interview them for portions of this book and indirectly by letting me help with their planning over the past few years. They know who they are and for their friendship and support, I thank them. I have been fortunate to have a business that lets me do what I enjoy: working with (and learning from) challenging and successful individuals and helping them work through complex problems about their business, their family, and their future.

Finally, the staff of the Succession Planning Division of CFG Business Solutions, LLC has provided great support. Chuck Rains has been a recent addition to our firm and has made several major contributions that were invaluable. Lee Cohn helped me on several chapters; her insights and logic are so important for me. Sandy Amidei is the best retired secretary I have ever worked with and this project would never have been finished without her. Lois Carden, Nate Werner, and Karen Collett all took care of our clients and our business while I was working on this book—they each stepped up in major ways that were invaluable. Lois Carden deserves a special thank you for her daily support, her dedication, her friendship and humor, and her tolerance of me.

# About the Authors

## Mike Cohn

Mike is the managing director of the Succession Planning Division of CFG Business Solutions, LLC. Mike has been a family business consultant for 15 years, working nationally with some of the largest family businesses in the United States. He has written two books on the topic of family business succession: *Passing the Torch: Transfer Strategies for Your Family Business* (1990, Liberty Hall Press) and *Passing the Torch: Succession, Retirement, and Estate Planning in Family-Owned Businesses*, second edition (1992, McGraw-Hill, Inc.). Mike was the editor of the "Family Business Case Study" series in *Nation's Business* magazine from 1992–1994. He was president of the Family Firm Institute, an international organization that serves family businesses, from 1996–1998, and served on its board from 1992–1998. Mike currently serves on the editorial advisory board of *Family Business Professional*, a monthly publication of Harcourt Professional Publishing. Mike is also a board member of the Arizona Community Foundation.

Mike holds an MA and BA in psychology and approaches business issues from both a family dynamics (process) perspective and from a transactional (content) perspective. For the past five years, he has been working exclusively with multi-generational family businesses that have been wrestling with the issues explored in this book.

## Jayne Pearl

Jayne Pearl is author of *Kids and Money: Giving Them the Savvy to Succeed Financially* (Bloomberg Press, 1999), a finalist for the Publishers Marketing Association Benjamin Franklin Award for best parenting book. Jayne was launching senior editor of *Family Business* magazine, which is published by MLR Publishing in Philadelphia. Jayne provided research and editorial assistance for Mike Cohn on *Passing the Torch: Succession, Retirement, and Estate Planning in Family-Owned Businesses*, second edition (1992, McGraw-Hill, Inc.) She created and edited the CFG Business Solutions client newsletter, *TRANSITIONS and traditions*® for several years. Jayne continues to contribute to CFG projects in addition to her other freelance writing and editing, including her regular commentaries about kids and money on PRI's Marketplace Radio.

Jayne has more than 20 years experience in financial journalism, including working on the staff at *Forbes* magazine, as editor of a half-hour daily business news show syndicated by American Public Radio (now PRI International), and as creator and editor of Tom Peters' (of *In Search of Excellence* fame) newsletter, *On Achieving Excellence*.

## About CFG Business Solutions, LLC

CFG Business Solutions provides planning services to private and public companies throughout the United States. Our services are delivered through two divisions, with offices in Phoenix, Los Angeles, and San Diego. If you would like more information, please contact us at <cfg@cfgllc.com> or 800-422-3883.

| Succession Planning Division<br>Mike Cohn<br>Managing Director | Executive Compensation Division<br>Alec Berkman<br>Managing Director |
|---|---|
| • Advise on keep or sell strategies | • Nonqualified plan design and administration |
| • Ownership succession: multi-generational planning | • Executive pay: incentive and performance-based designs |
| • Wealth transfer and estate tax strategies | • Compensation consulting, industry and geographical surveys |
| • Family meetings, family governance | |

PART

I

# Keep or Sell?

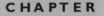

# Where Do I Go from Here?

You've been a successful entrepreneur with a well-established business. All around your industry and local business community you see private business owners selling their companies for fortunes, large and small. Now you are weighing your options. What should you do with your company? Sell or keep it?

There is a fundamental shift occurring in the ownership of private companies. Businesses are merging and consolidating, not due to a lack of planning as the business press has surmised in the past. These sales are due to financial and market opportunities undreamed of before—immediate wealth for entrepreneurs running young, dynamic companies and opportunities to "monetize" illiquid assets for aging owners facing retirement. We have all read about the Internet megamillionaires' tales of quick riches. Less public but more profound, is the sale of thousands of private companies each year—established, mature brick-and-mortar, boring businesses that command significant premiums and create new liquidity for their owners.

The issues that bring you to this decision point about your company often go beyond financial considerations. You may have an overwhelming sense that everything you know is rapidly changing. For some, selling the business is an attempt to slow down the speed of change. For others, it is a way to embrace change through the alchemy of transforming illiquid assets into portable, fungible wealth.

Stan Davis and Christopher Meyer, in *Blur*, describe what we are experiencing this way: ". . . instantaneous communication and computation are shrinking time and focusing us on speed. Connectivity is putting everybody and everything online in one way or another and has led to 'the death of distance,' a shrinking of space. Intangible value of all kinds, like service and information, is growing explosively, reducing the importance of tangible mass. . . .connectivity, speed, and intangibles are blurring the rules and redefining our businesses and our lives. They are destroying solutions, such as mass production, segmented pricing, and standardized jobs, that worked for the relatively slow, unconnected industrial world. The fact is, something enormous is happening all around you. . . ."[1]

For some owners who don't have a clear vision about the future of their business, are worried about competition, and don't have the management strength they need, the necessity for constant change may become "the final straw" that motivates them to sell their company. For others, the opportunity to cash out and move on will be the compelling factors, based purely on financial considerations and timing.

More buyers are in the marketplace today than there have been at any other time in recent history. Companies that have never seen suitors are receiving attention from a variety of buyers. In 1998, *Mergerstat* (which tracks deals in excess of $1 million) reported more than 7,928 business combinations. In 1999 that number increased by 17 percent to more than 9,200.[2] These 17,000 deals of $1 million or more (public and private companies) over the two years represented more than $2.6 trillion of value—exceeding the volume for all of the 1970s and 1980s combined!

Furthermore, buyers are paying more for companies today. In 1992, buyers were paying five to six times earnings before interest expense and taxes (EBIT) for mid-sized businesses. In 1997, the ratio had increased to six to nine times EBIT, according to the Arthur Andersen Center for Family Business.

A Wells Fargo/NFIB study published in their 1998 "Series on Business Starts and Stops" notes that sellers tend to be either in the 25 to 34 age bracket or over 55, indicating two potentially different motivations. The younger seller who "builds to sell" may start (or buy) and sell several companies during his/her lifetime, just as one might periodically turn over an investment portfolio. The older seller may be motivated for different reasons: no successors and no planning, coupled with a dependence on the company for financial security—for these, selling may not be the first choice, but the last choice.

Without a succession plan for your business there is a greater chance you will be a seller. A U.S. Trust Survey of affluent Americans indicates that only 36 percent of affluent business owners (net worth of $3 million+, or gross income of $200,000 or higher) had a well thought-out, fully developed succession plan. The study also found that 53 percent had thought about a succession plan but had not implemented one, while 11 percent had not given succession planning much thought. A 1997 "American Family Business Survey" by Arthur Andersen/Mass Mutual found that of 3,000 respondents, 35 percent were either undecided or intended to sell their business.

According to Mergerstat, only 2 percent (or 200) of the 1999 transactions were the mega-mergers that got national newspaper attention (e.g., MCI WorldCom/Sprint, Pfizer/Warner Lambert, Qwest/U.S. West)—88 percent of all deals in 1999 were for companies whose value was below $100 million. Typical is one client's company, which was appraised at $4 million by a well respected national appraisal firm in mid-1998. Two years later, the client was offered $16 million for one division (representing two-thirds of the company's operations) in an all-cash, unsolicited offer. This client had decided in 1998 that his company would remain in family hands for another generation; now he and his family are rethinking that decision.

Where do these buyers come from? Some may be well-known consolidators active in specific industry and trade associations. They may be public companies or private firms that want to go public. Or brokers or investment bankers may call, wondering if you are interested in selling to an investment group. The industries in 1998 and 1999 with the most sellers: wholesale distribution, construction contractors, broadcasting and communications, and of course, computer suppliers and software manufacturers.

Some buyers may approach owners from the perspective of a strategic combination, such as an electric utility company that buys a mechanical or electrical contractor so electricity can be sold to customers before new construction begins. The potential deals often sound enticing. The idea of selling and walking away with a pile of cash appeals to many owners. Some sell, and then stay on to run the company for the new owners.

You know you will have to take some calculated risks in the future, and the business will have to change, just to survive. Maybe you're better off letting someone else take those risks, with their money, not yours. That's what the seven Hotard siblings and their parents, former owners of Hotard Coaches, Inc., the New Orleans, $18 million (sales) charter bus company, decided when they sold to Laidlaw, Inc. in December 1999. "Every day I worried about how every decision I made was going to impact my entire family," says Eva Hotard, CEO. Her fears were not unfounded. A major bus accident earlier that year that involved a different New Orleans bus company pointed out the tremendous potential liability in that business. "We probably could have grown faster if I wasn't worrying about wiping out the family." All seven siblings who owned and managed the business before the sale continue to run it under the new ownership.

Perhaps you should keep the company, let current management run it, turn it over to family or bring in professional management to carry it on, and create or preserve your family's legacy. There may be unrealized opportunities that you haven't fully capitalized on—maybe keeping the business and borrowing the money to expand is the route to take.

The business has probably been a good corporate citizen for years, employing people from the community, and making or distributing a product or service that you, and your family, are proud of. Selling the company would likely mean a relocation, a consolidation, layoffs, and probably a different way of doing business in the future. Are there key people who can take the business to the next level, or are there family members who are competent or capable of growing the company in the future?

Either way, change is in the wind.

## Transitions and New Beginnings

Noel Tichy, in *The Transformational Leader*, describes companies trying to figure out their future as being in a transitional state. "This is a time when there is a need to leave the past productively—a process of death and rebirth. . . . We tend to think of change as something to be added to the present state, a new frontier, an improvement over the past. . . . There is an attempt to deny that every change process involves a process of destruction."[3]

William Bridges in *Transitions* describes change as a predictable psychological process. "When life transitions occur, they trigger deep emotions. He describes a neutral zone that is like standing in the middle of a busy highway with the traffic going in both directions. It is a frightening experience but psychologically that is what people involved in change must do—simultaneously experience the forces from the past and those pulling us toward the future. During this period there may be a great deal of conflicting emotions and inconsistent behavior. One day a person may be excited about the prospects the future holds and the next day be quite pessimistic that things will not work out."[4]

Both Tichy and Bridges contend that people must successfully work through the processes of change to have a new, successful start. Without working through these stages of change business owners tend to repeat the same mistakes or simply yearn for the past so much that they are unable to make new lives for themselves.

Keep or sell? Both decisions involve endings and beginnings. Endings are always difficult. Whether you keep or sell, the decision means change and an ending. As Bridges notes, endings often begin unexpectedly, such as something going wrong. We often do not choose when or how our endings occur. An ending may be an event that happens suddenly, such as the diagnosis of an illness or accidental death of a friend or family member. For others, it may be a state of mind. It is the rare individual who chooses an ending and moves on to the next phase in their life. It may be losing a key customer, or a decline in profitability. For one client, when a manufacturing process needed to be reengineered with a large capital commitment, the owner decided it was time to sell rather than incur more debt and risk. For another, losing the sales manager who was the heir apparent triggered a sale to the nonfamily CEO. For a third, a heart attack became the motivator to focus on leadership development for key execs. For Maynard Sauder, chairman of Sauder Woodworking Co. in Archbold, Ohio, it was when his 92-year-old dad, who had founded the company, died. "That's when I knew it was time for my brother and me to start working on our succession plan," recalls Maynard.

Beginnings start with an inner idea, an image, an impression. Bridges calls it a "resonance at the lower edge of consciousness, like a half-formed daydream." From there, it moves slowly into awareness—like a picture coming into focus on a large screen. For one client the idea to sell his business first occurred when he bought his brothers out in 1995. He recalls thinking naively it would be nice for someone to buy him out rather than him buying out his brothers. For the next four years he built his mechanical construction company with two ideas formulating in his mind: one to let his daughter run the business and the second to be open to a sale if someone approached him. As the business grew in size and complexity he realized his daughter could continue the business but it would be a tough challenge. The two key executives were the same age as the owner. When a buyer (unsolicited) came along with an attractive offer, the second "picture," (i.e., to sell the company) began to come into focus. All of the vague questions about what to do, and who would run the business, became clarified during the discussions with the buyer and the client's advisors in a way that was attractive to this client. He decided to sell after he and his family discussed the options and everyone's "picture" about the future supported the sale.

The process also involves trust—trust in your own ability to make the right choice, and trust (or lack of trust) in others. Beginnings depend on an inner realignment, a new motivation, an unknown future. If you decide to keep the business, it means a commitment to the succession process. And if you decide to sell the company, it means a commitment to a new type of life without ownership of the business.

Between the ending and the beginning is the transition, a period of confusion, while you explore your options. Each path has risks and rewards. This book will fully explore these issues. Your decision will be based on more than financial reasons alone—you will also need to factor in soul-searching and strategic thinking about what you want for yourself, your company, and your family.

**CHAPTER**

**2**

# Critical Analysis

The status quo won't cut it anymore—you know what you
need to do but do you have the right management team?
Your friends are selling their companies. Before you can
consider your options, you'll need to do a close critical
analysis of the business. Casual budgeting, lax policies, unexplored opportunities, and under-utilized human, financial, and
physical resources can undermine a company's value. Assessing
your business' current strengths and weaknesses, and then fixing those weak spots will not only help you realize maximum
value should you eventually decide to sell, but also poises the
business for unimagined success should you ultimately keep the
business. Before considering the decision to keep or sell, you'll
first need to scale a mountain of issues so you can clearly evaluate and maximize your choices.

The Muselman family of central Indiana addressed these
issues as part of their succession process in deciding to become a
third-generation company. The second generation had grown the
company's commercial printing business but had also successfully
expanded into publishing by acquiring three companies. When

the third generation began their critical assessment, they realized: (1) commercial printing was their "history" but profit margins were shrinking; (2) publishing had become the growth part of their business and continued acquisitions in this area represented their future; (3) continued ownership as a private company was an advantage; and (4) they would need capital to continue to acquire publishing companies. They decided the best strategy was to recruit and hire the best non-family managers they could find to run their business while retaining ownership. The next generation agreed it was in their best interest to step out of day-to-day management. In addressing this challenge, the owners adopted a policy of "noses in, but fingers out." They wanted to develop procedures to keep themselves informed as owners (noses in) but to give their managers the ability and freedom to run the companies subject to mutually agreeable criteria and expectations (fingers out). Out of the assessment came a restructuring of the organization, new positions, and new reporting relationships and a new, performance-based compensation program.

You need to assess the current state of your company, its strengths and weaknesses, before you can determine whether the best strategy for realizing its potential is by continuing to own/run it or choosing to sell. You may need to challenge basic assumptions about your business and its future. Don't assume that the future will be a continuation of the past. The assessment and "future thinking" should include critical "others" such as key management, advisors, and perhaps potential successors and other new voices to avoid blind spots and traditional approaches. Keep them in the loop as the process evolves so your ultimate decision does not catch them off guard and create unnecessary negative reactions.

Explore different scenarios, and understand the trends that are occurring in your industry, so you can create a plan to address various possibilities that may occur. By trying to anticipate unlikely events, you will begin to prepare for change.

If you eventually decide to sell, having a plan will help you maximize the value of your business since it will help support your financial projections for future earnings. If you keep the business, the strategic plan, including alternative scenarios, will provide a road map for addressing future opportunities and threats. This book will not describe how to create a business plan—there are plenty of books and consultants to help you do so. But Figure 2.1 poses critical questions and issues that you will need to consider for such a business plan, and also for cutting through all the pros and cons on each side of the keep or sell equation.

For each business issue in Figure 2.1, list your current strengths and weaknesses. Then consider and rate whatever internal financial, management, and emotional resources you have to address those business issues, on a scale of one (lowest) to five (highest). Then compute the average score for each resource column. If your financial resources score below 3.5, you may want to consider the potential benefits of bringing in outside owners, or selling your business outright. If you have strong internal financial resources, but score low on internal management resources, you might benefit from keeping the business but bring in professional nonfamily managers to help breathe new life and experience into the company. Strong management resources but weak financial resources indicates you might want to continue managing the business, but bring in financial partners to strengthen your capital position.

If the business scores low on the third column—internal emotional resources—you and your management team may have the expertise, but not the heart or will, for running the business with the energy and enthusiasm it requires to remain competitive. It may be time to either sell the business, or keep it and promote or hire others to run it.

One client who had a long-term distributor relationship with John Deere decided to represent a new UK-based equipment manufacturer that promised greater support, faster delivery, and new territories. Terminating the John Deere relationship after 40 years was a difficult decision. Market share with John Deere had been stagnant; with the new manufacturer, market share is growing rapidly. Being realistic about old and new relationships allowed this client to pursue alternatives.

What future technological changes will impact you? One client who made screw machine products was surprised to learn that his largest customer would seek bids for jobs over the Internet. The value of 20-year relationships with the customer's VPs disappeared overnight,

## FIGURE 2.1—YOUR PRODUCTS, MARKET SHARE, AND MARKET POSITION

| Issue | Current Strengths/ Weaknesses | Internal Financial Resources | Internal Management Resources | Internal Emotional Resources |
|---|---|---|---|---|
| **Products**<br>• Product development capabilities<br>• Current product line<br>• Manufacturer/supplier relationships | | | | |
| **Costs**<br>• Compared with the industry | | | | |
| **Market Share**<br>• Current<br>• Potential<br>• Sales growth—increasing or slowing down<br>• Industry trends<br>• Future assumptions | | | | |
| **Marketing/Sales**<br>• Distribution channels<br>• Pricing strategy<br>• Key customers/dependence on key accounts<br>• Motivated sales force | | | | |
| **Services**<br>• Customer service systems in place<br>• Is customer service supported by company culture? | | | | |
| **Competition**<br>• Are they getting ahead of you in e-commerce?<br>• Are they able to charge lower prices?<br>• Global or nontraditional | | | | |

| FIGURE 2.1—CONTINUED | | | | |
|---|---|---|---|---|
| **Issue** | **Current Strengths/ Weaknesses** | **Internal Financial Resources** | **Internal Management Resources** | **Internal Emotional Resources** |
| **Leadership** <br> • Is management team all over 50, or is there a blend of young and old? <br> • Is the team homegrown, or are there experienced outsiders? <br> • How are decisions made? | | | | |
| **Resources** <br> • What's the biggest bet you can afford to lose on a new idea? <br> • Is the capital base sufficient to grow and take risks? <br> • Have you outgrown banking relationships? <br> • Do you innovate on a regular basis? | | | | |

while the client found that bids were coming in from Japan and Taiwan.

What are your new product-development capabilities? Will your products and services today be relevant in five to ten years? How much new thinking goes into new product development? And how much of the current budget?

Does the corporate culture support new ventures? One sign of trouble is when new ideas constantly get shot down. Or, do you support creativity and try new ideas? One client on the Ohio River owns quarries and produces construction aggregate material for roadbeds and foundations for large commercial sites. To improve customer service, he worked with clients to get his product to the customer's site at a lower cost by going into the river barge business. This allowed him to deliver products more quickly via river barge and at a fraction of traditional trucking costs.

## Your Costs

What will impact your supply sources and what could you do to reduce risks? Are you a member of a buying co-op or part of a larger group that buys products with volume discounts from manufacturers? One manufacturing client started a R&D division, staffed with design engineers to create equipment that would improve the efficiency of its manufacturing process. Another client who manufactures recreational vehicles invested in a textile business to lower carpet and furnishings costs. If your external costs for raw materials or supplies suddenly escalated, what would you do? What alternatives would you pursue? How long would it take to react?

## How Well Does Your Company (and Board) Function

What assumptions are you making about how your business functions that may be outdated? In marketing and sales, you will need to evaluate your current distribution channels and pricing strategy. Consolidation in wholesale distribution will affect all lines of trade within the next few years. In one 1997 study, there was a significant decline in 42 of 54 wholesale distribution lines due to consolidation, acquisition, or business failure.[1] Wholesale distributors have learned not to subscribe to the "it can't happen to us" mentality. In manufacturing, you will need to analyze product costs (raw materials, labor, and overhead), the availability of materials, develop operational forecasts, and review the condition and capacity of your manufacturing facilities from a long-term perspective. Analyze your company's financial position and needs—estimate the company's future working capital and capital investment requirements through cash forecasts, and analyze profitability using breakeven scenarios and ratio analyses. Finally, evaluate your management to determine future personnel requirements, current talent and expertise, and transferability of skills. Consider having a profitability "audit"—an outside consulting firm that will advise ways to improve operations and resulting profits. But, before you take this step, be careful about protecting "sacred cows" that are likely to get skewered by an outside consultant.

Are board members chosen strategically? Or, do they constantly agree with the owners and serve to rubber stamp decisions? Is the board part of the problem or is it part of the solution?

## Services

Do your customers want more "value-added" as they are asking you to drop your prices? Do you have the technology and systems to provide customer service? Does your company culture support customer service or is new thinking needed? How would your customers rank you on service if they were asked? Historically companies thought that they could provide low prices or customer service—not both. But the Japanese taught us that to remain competitive we need to provide *both* lower prices and customer service. If you suddenly lost your largest customer, what would you do? Are most of your sales concentrated with several large accounts? If so, what plans should you make for reducing your dependence on these customers?

## Competition

How will your competition change in the future? It may be an e-commerce company that doesn't exist today. How are your competitors addressing these issues? Thompson Newspapers, one of the largest newspaper chains in the United States, put all its newspapers up for sale in early 2000, announcing it was going to focus the company on providing Internet services. What opportunity does a changing landscape of competitors provide to you—and what risks? The environment for business in the future will emphasize innovation and will be highly competitive. Is your company positioned to respond quickly to changing circumstances?

## Leadership and Management

Look around. Is your management team all 50 and older, or do you have a blend of "young turks" who can shake up the thinking and experienced "gray hairs" who can provide depth of management and discipline? How are decisions made? Is the management team home grown or are there some experienced outsiders who can bring fresh ideas? Is there a mentoring plan in place to groom future management? Do you send your key people to programs to learn leadership skills? Is there operational resource sharing or are people protecting their turf? Is it time to do some team building with key managers?

Does new thinking get shot down, or is there a process to try new ideas? Some companies have a *skunk works* department just to test new concepts. Tom Peters, in *In Search of Excellence* (Warner Books, 1982), defines this as, "bands of eight or ten zealots off in the corner, often out-producing product development groups that numbered in the hundreds." One way to measure the experience and maturity for a prospective successor or key manager is to let them "run with an idea" structured as a specific project. For one client in the brick manufacturing business, the project was to research whether the company needed to build a new manufacturing plant. This required the potential successors to work together, sharpen their analytical skills, critique each other's contribution to the project, analyze the financial risks and rewards, and finally present it to senior management. Senior management decided to go forward and put the next-generation team in charge of implementation.

## Resources and Capital

What is the biggest bet you can afford to lose on a new idea? Is the company's capital base sufficient to grow and take risks without the current owner feeling he/she is putting their retirement assets at risk as well? Is additional capital needed to stay competitive? Have you out-grown traditional banking relationships? What level of capital will you need in the future and where will it come from? Are there inactive stockholders who will be willing to forego distributions and/or take on additional debt to meet future capital needs?

## Systems

Information is one key to success in the future. How successfully has your business integrated its operating units? Does information flow efficiently from sales, to manufacturing, to distribution, to customer use? If not, what will it cost to get these systems online? How will you compete with e-commerce companies?

## Use of Consultants, Outside Advisors, Internal Task Forces

How does the company and its owners get information on new practices and policies? Is the advice of consultants and advisors implemented or ignored? Are there internal task forces or ad-hoc committees that can address and solve problems? One Nashville client had to move his manufacturing facility when the Houston Oilers decided to move to Nashville and the city purchased an industrial area (where his plant was located) to build the new stadium. He assembled a task force to design the new building. The task force worked so successfully that he put the group in charge of construction and ultimately the move to the new facility. Employee morale increased dramatically since all employees felt an involvement in the project.

## Financial Commitments to Shareholders

Is the company's cash flow and future earnings "mortgaged" to pay off previous owners? Or, will the price for current owners to let go exceed the company's ability to pay? One client in his late 60s had been paying off stockholder redemptions for 20 years to cousins and uncles and expected his sons to provide for his retirement in the same way. When the two sons disagreed about mortgaging their future, in an increasingly competitive business environment, the client decided that selling the company was the best solution. For a car dealer client, it took the creation of subordinated debentures to balance the increasing needs for capital in the business with a withdrawing owner's need for income.

This assessment will undoubtedly identify areas for improvement. Giving deep thought to these areas can also influence your decision about whether you keep or sell the business. Addressing and solving needed problems can provide more value to a buyer and a higher sales price for you if you decide to sell. Alternatively, solving identified problems may convince you that keeping the business is more advantageous than selling it.

## Why Planning Is Important

In either case, the act of planning is recognized by many as a key part in the ultimate decision of whether you should keep or sell your business. Many entrepreneurs resist the process of planning and by doing so, inadvertently foreclose on their options. Some think planning and a commitment to a plan of action constricts flexibility and reduces options. Actually, the opposite is true. Not having a plan, to sell or to keep, means that over time, there is less and less opportunity to make small mistakes. For many entrepreneurs and business owners, selling the business is the last option—often a default solution because time has run out.

Consider this statistic: most (69.4 percent) business owners surveyed in 1997 did not have a written strategic plan for their business—and there were significant correlations between the existence of a written plan and a variety of other planning and actions necessary for business success.[2]

You may need to reframe your assumptions about planning:

| Perception | Reality |
|---|---|
| • Limits flexibility | • Expands flexibility |
| • Is useless with so many uncertainties | • Helps firms anticipate and cope with uncertainty |
| • Requires owners to share sensitive information | • Empowers the organization with more responsibility |
| • Exposes management's mistakes and incompetency | • Allows managers to improve skills |
| • Implies change, which can threaten the past | • Helps owners/managers base decisions on current and future circumstances, not on past factors |

By carefully planning and by evaluating various scenarios, you may conclude that your objectives can be met through alternative strategies without selling the company. As Craig Aronoff and John Ward point out, "How one defines what initially brought the company success can limit future success...many firms are trapped by their past success. Their early strategies are so powerful and so deeply ingrained that change is all but impossible. Entrepreneurial founders are often highly creative and charismatic, which can easily melt successors' self-confidence to fight for dramatic change."[3]

## Inhibitors of Change in Private Companies

One of the key benefits of undertaking a critical assessment is to find out where you are versus your expectations and your perception of other companies like you. One additional part of this assessment involves how open you and your company are to change. While you may be able to identify key problems and obstacles in growing the business, one factor that is more difficult to spot, but will influence the decision to keep or sell, is whether change is difficult to implement in your business. For example, some entrepreneurs do not have a clear understanding of what has made them successful—they are afraid that changing any aspect of how the business operates will threaten the company's success. The business often gets bogged down in policies and procedures that ensure the company does not veer from its original path. Sometimes deviating from the original path is healthy for the company. Ward and Aronoff describe seven inhibitors to change in private companies:[4]

1. Institutionalizing operating details and certain behaviors
2. Deeply entrenched values
3. Long tenures by each generation of leaders
4. Long-term loyalty to managers and advisors
5. Autocratic/paternalistic management style
6. Insulation from changing conditions outside the business
7. Tendency to be risk-averse and debt-averse

These traits have advantages, but they can also inhibit change. Entrepreneurs who have invested everything in their company may be reluctant to change once they experience success. Instinct makes owners want to cling to their winning strategy and structure. But what brought the business its early success may not ensure its future.

Ward and Aronoff describe how one company made a tradition out of strategic change by constantly adapting its products and processes as changing technology made existing products obsolete. Along the way, the company became a pioneer in developing alliances between manufacturers and supply chain distributors. The Warren Featherbone Company in northeast Georgia was founded in 1885 after Edward Warren realized that turkey quills, bound by thread, could be used in women's dresses as a cheaper and more pliable stay than the commonly-used whalebone, which became brittle and cracked over time. Mr. Warren coined the term "featherbone" and introduced it to the market in 1883. The company prospered and using the same principles of featherbone construction, expanded into the manufacture of buggy whips. With the outbreak of war in 1914, the company received government contracts and began to produce belting and elastic materials for the U.S. Army. As plastic corset stiffeners began to compete with the featherbone products, the company worked with B.F. Goodrich company to produce the first plastic baby pants in 1937, replacing heavier, hotter rubber pants. This early alliance led to the manufacture of plastic bibs, ladies' and children's rainwear and other items.

When disposable diapers began to cut into market share, the company responded by concentrating on developing a full line of toddler wear and is now the sixth largest children's apparel maker in the United States. Ward and Aronoff note that the company distilled its business experience into seven fundamental values: creative thinking; finding a need and filling it; focusing on value for customers; focusing on people at all levels of the process; working hard; maintaining enthusiasm; and maximizing the company's ability to adapt.[5]

## Personal Assessment

A critical analysis of the business can reveal where the business needs attention. Another set of important questions to ask is about the emotional readiness of you, the business owner, in preparing for change.

Too often, men in their mid-to-late 70s are still holding on tightly to their company—afraid to let go, and afraid not to. Gail Sheehy, in *Understanding Men's Passages*, describes how men are often unprepared to make changes in their lives. Men cannot live the same way their fathers or mentors have lived—not when there is increasing life expectancy. She notes that "...society has not prepared [men] for this potential bonus stage of life, and few have developed the skills and inner resources to manage it well."[6] Over the past few decades, a link has been scientifically established between exposure to loss and a host of physical and psychological illnesses. "Exit events" begin to pile up in the second half of life, such as departure of grown children, and sudden deaths of friends. Individuals under high stress, especially men, are often unaware of how these stresses impact one's life. For men who see themselves as eternally strong and able to overcome any obstacle, the issues surrounding the continuity of the business are often linked to unfulfilled personal accomplishments and fear of letting go. The experiences you have had with endings in your life will influence how you address these issues. One client in his 60s had seen sisters exit the business, disengage from the family, and ultimately get cut off from family affairs. This client associated his possible ending with his company as a cut-off from his family. Holding onto his company was his way of staying connected with children and grandchildren. When he realized this, he was able to refocus his activities on maintaining "family glue" outside the business.

Sheehy describes a Second Adulthood in *Understanding Men's Passages* as a period where men revisit their basic values and become reenergized about their life. A man's second adulthood, according to Sheehy, is about getting back to early values—not about coasting or giving up. For example, it may be when a CEO remembers his early days as a visionary entrepreneur and begins to transfer operating responsibilities to others instead of micromanaging. Men will probably live longer than expected due to improved medical care, diet and exercise, so there is plenty of time to reinvent yourself for a second adulthood. Some will continue going down the same path they've been on and will miss the signals for a second adulthood. For these, Sheehy notes, aging will not be fun.

Men will need to be attentive to when this period of second adulthood begins. Women have menopause as their signal, at about age 50, that rings down the curtain of first adulthood. Men do not have such a marker. There is no generally accepted point in a man's career cycle when men say *I've done my duty. I've proven myself. I'm not going to do the same thing anymore.*[7]

How do you know when it is time? Often there are internal signals. Perhaps you have plateaued, or taken a "psychological retirement" while still going through the motions. Maybe you're just not there—unplugged emotionally. Perhaps your relationship with your work has changed. Through our work we express ourselves, we practice commitment, and we test our ideas and vision. Dan Levinson, in *The Seasons of a Man's Life*, describes how men going through these transitions begin to question themselves. Instead of using business successes and accomplishments as a scorecard, new questions arise. You may ask yourself: what do I give to and receive from my work? These new questions are often about measuring satisfaction with work against internal signals instead of external measures.

## Trust and the Vision "Thing"

What role does trust play in the decision-making process about one's company? For the business owner, there is an important distinction that needs to be made: trusting key executives (or family members) to carry on the business in an honest and ethical fashion is generally a "given." But that is not the type of trust that needs to be nurtured. The second form of trust is about the decisions that will need to be made in the future—does the current owner believe that the successors (whoever they may be) will make the right decisions for the business to survive and grow? Trust is created when individuals meet or exceed expectations. Trust is cultivated over time, and maintained based on the framework of business culture. The challenge for succession is how to build and maintain trust in a context of change.

There is a delicate balancing act to encouraging change and maintaining continuity of important core values. For companies with a clearly articulated vision, it may be easier to create (and test) a succession process—the founder's (or previous generation's) vision acts as the framework for future change and continuity. Changing strategy or tactics may be necessary but the company is still committed to its purpose. Without a compelling vision, it may be easier to let go of the business, because there is no clear path to be followed. Francis Fukuyama observed that it is particularly easy for an individual to identify with the aims of an organization over one's own self-interest if the purpose of the organization is not solely to create profits. For example, working for a company whose purpose is to "push the frontiers of information technology . . . rather than maximize stockholder's return on equity"[8] creates a sense of pride, a belief that one is part of something larger than oneself.

Having a vision for the future is a critical part of the planning because it articulates the owner's philosophy that gives employees and the company direction. It is a compass that allows strategic change as needed while maintaining certain core values. Without this directional guide, succeeding generations may not be able to navigate the conflicts and crises that will occur, and may lose sight of the big picture. The challenge is to articulate a shared vision and then demonstrate how the vision can satisfy diverse interests over time.

Having a vision for greatness in whatever form—for customer service, excellence in engineering, for creativity in design, for solving problems, etc. can influence one's decision to keep or sell. In *Built to Last*, Collins and Porras noted that those who understood their purpose used it to guide, inspire, and motivate others. What is your business purpose (besides making money) and philosophy? Take a few minutes to write down the fundamental reasons for your company's existence. As Collins and Porras note, "the primary role of purpose is to guide and inspire . . ." One of the core values at Sauder Woodworking is a commitment to community—not just the people in Archbold, Ohio but the larger community of 3,500 employees and their families, their customers, and their suppliers. For the Muselman's printing and publishing companies in Indiana and Texas, it is a commitment to support creativity, an openness to new ideas, and to constantly improve their products and services.

Identifying and articulating the core values may not be enough. Current owners have to trust that the next generation of management *lives* those values in how they approach their work: with respect for history but with permission and ability to craft their own future.

## Meeting the Competitive Challenge

While most business owners have a good feel for what the competition is doing, they often have not conducted an objective study of the marketplace. The competition study would go beyond identifying which companies present a threat. It would identify where the competition excels, where the business owners products or services are vulnerable, and how the competitors prices and services compare. Even after going through this analysis, you should ask an additional question: "How well do you know your customer?" Many business owners are reluctant to conduct customer research for a number of reasons—no time, too expensive, not important, etc. However, gathering information about customers can be extremely informative and enlightening and the research required doesn't have to be expensive. A well-designed research plan can help answer important questions, such as:

- What is most important to the customer in deciding who to buy from?
- How well does my company perform?
- How well does the competition perform?
- In which area can my company do a better job, and does it need to improve in all these areas?

You will want to conduct this analysis with your top team as well as your actual or potential successors. Their thinking skills, and responses to these issues, will be important in your decision process. Your confidence (or lack of confidence) in others as well as your enthusiasm about addressing these issues will help guide your thinking. The next chapter takes you a step further by asking you to think through reasons to keep, and reasons to sell, your business.

# 3

# Keep or Sell— Which Route Is Best for You?

Private company ownership has long been a path to wealth. Owners of small businesses (with fewer than 500 employees) represent about 20 percent of the $20 trillion in private wealth in the United States according to a 1998 study by Oxford Information Technology Ltd. If that's the case, why is everyone rushing to sell?

The benefits of private company ownership range from freedom to set one's own compensation—and other deductible perks, including employing family members—to rapid decision making, risk-taking, and enjoying the fruits of hard work. For some, it is the ability to realize one's dream, to create a successful business, and to see it grow and evolve. For those who inherited or continued a business started in an earlier generation, it is the opportunity to take a company to a new level, to grow a business from an existing foundation, or to put one's own stamp on the company. For others, it is the ability to keep family assets in one operating business as a way to protect future generations. It may be a way to create a legacy (i.e., building something bigger than oneself that lasts beyond one's lifetime). For some entrepreneurs it's a way to prove that the idea, product, or service really does work.

In the past, entrepreneurs started out with the challenge of building the business and didn't think much about a future transition of ownership until a buyer came along, or children entered the business. They are called *owner-managers*. But there are two other options that many owners have not considered. One increasingly common choice is to keep ownership in the family, but hire nonfamily professional managers to run the business. These are called *owner-investors*.

A third, newer type of entrepreneur, launches a company with the idea of selling shares to the public or a larger company within a year or less. They may use the proceeds to launch a new business and sell that one just as quickly. They are a new breed of *portfolio entrepreneurs*.

Either way, the message is clear: ownership in a successful private business provides a comfortable lifestyle and family wealth. Which route is best for you? The decision hinges on how you assess how well your company's internal resources are poised to handle new economic realities.

This chapter will help you make that assessment. Each section ends with one or more questions. Figure 3.1 will help you track your answers. Photocopy the table and check off your answers as you read the following sections. At the end you can evaluate which options may best suit you, your company, and your family.

## Historical Advantages of Staying Private versus New Realities

When owner-managers describe the benefits of future ownership, they may assume the future will be a logical extension of the past. That isn't likely to happen. Just as change will impact business operations in the future, it will also impact ownership—there will still be plenty of private companies around but the successful ones will have a new discipline, a new focus, and will embrace change. It may be helpful to start with a fresh perspective on the historical benefits of ownership in a private company.

| FIGURE 3.1—HOW WELL POSITIONED ARE YOU TO KEEP OR SELL THE BUSINESS? | | Yes | No |
|---|---|---|---|
| **Trusting relationships** | Would you characterize your business culture as high trust? | | |
| **Privacy** | Are you comfortable sharing sensitive information with key executives, family shareholders, and others involved with the keep-sell issues? | | |
| **Pride/legacy** | Have you and your successors cultivated interdependent, mutually supportive relationships? | | |
| | Does the next generation embrace your vision of the plan? | | |
| **Long-term perspective** | Have your successors learned the balance between acting quickly and making thoughtful decisions? | | |
| **Compensation/perks** | Does the company pay market rates for family and nonfamily employees? | | |
| | Is family compensation based on performance and experience? | | |
| | Are family employees qualified for their jobs and performing well? | | |
| **Wealth consolidation** | Have you begun educating the next generation about handling wealth responsibly? | | |
| | Are there opportunities for family shareholders to get liquidity when they need or want it? | | |
| **Decision making** | Are decisions made by consensus of management instead of unilaterally? | | |
| | Do owners tend to embrace new ideas? | | |
| **Wealth generation** | Will your future assets be worth more by keeping the business versus selling it? | | |

### *Trusting Relationships*

Many private business owners say that one of the biggest advantages of having a private firm is having long-term relationships with partners, key executives, loyal employees, and family members who work in the company. Indeed, in *Future Shock*, Alvin Toffler argued that family-owned firms of the future would have advantages over other companies because of the speed of decision making and trust among the owners. But that assumes that decision making rests in the hands of one or two authority figures who can be trusted to make decisions for all. Today the experts believe that no one person has all the answers; that employees can develop their own ideas and collaborate with others to solve problems.

If your business has cultivated a high-trust environment then it is reasonable to expect that trust in others will continue as decisions and autonomy are pushed down throughout the organization. But a high-trust environment does not occur by accident—it must be cultivated and nurtured as part of the company's culture. When a transition is contemplated (or occurs), and the issues around keeping or selling the business are debated, anxiety and uncertainty are usually part of the process. In a high-trust business climate those involved in the keep or sell discussions have already learned to rely on others, to be open, and to take risks in exploring new relationships. Also, in a high-trust environment, stockholders are more willing to set aside their individual self-interests for the sake of the company—they will want to find the right decision for all the stakeholders.

In a low-trust environment, there may already be conflicted relationships with no process to manage or address the conflict. There may be little collaboration among key people, insecurity, and a tendency to put one's personal needs ahead of the business. Debating the issues around keeping or selling the company in a low-trust climate brings out old fears, unresolved issues, and generally everyone's worst behavior.

One 70-year-old client was motivated to do succession planning after being diagnosed with cancer. His diverse business operations included hotels and fast-food franchises, equipment sales and leasing distributorships, and developing and managing commercial real estate. The company ownership was transferred to the founder's three adult children: one who had been CEO for the past five years, and two daughters both active in the business. The next generation took over while Dad fought the cancer. Although the three siblings had gotten along fairly well growing up they had never worked together as owner/partners. Soon they reverted to old sibling behaviors as a result of navigating the stressful new business responsibilities and awaiting the outcome of their dad's cancer treatments.

Nine months later, Dad's cancer was in remission but now Dad missed the action and making decisions for the business. He was no longer an owner, and couldn't officially step back in. But he was able to be active by manipulating his children behind the scenes. He began to undermine the three children's trust in one another by telling each child how the other two were not acting in the best interests of the business. Since the sibling's relationship was not a high trust one, it was easy for Dad's barbs to find targets; trust among the sibling owners declined and suspicions grew. After the siblings realized what Dad was up to, they agreed to work on repairing trust and creating a new relationship of collaboration.

| C O N S I D E R | Would you characterize your business culture as high trust? |
| --- | --- |

## *Privacy*

Not having to release information to anyone is a dangerous practice. Of course, this one was never entirely accurate because the bank usually had plenty of information about the business. Keeping information close to the vest may work when you're running a poker game, but doesn't work in today's businesses where key people need to understand goals, strategies, operating ratios, and profit targets. Providing information on a need-to-know basis leads to nobody having information they need to work effectively. Success in the future will depend on open systems, shared information, explicit accountabilities, and mutually agreed-upon performance goals.

Privacy in today's Internet world is a misnomer. Your credit information is shared, your purchasing preferences at the grocery store are tracked, and you leave calling cards when you log online through "cookies" that track your visits. Today's successful companies are sharing instead of hoarding information, which can lead to better decisions, less misunderstanding, and improved performance—all of which are intangibles that lead to improving business profitability and stockholder value. In addition, cutting-edge firms know the value of information, which can be packaged and sold to customers, vendors, or other industry players.

---

**C O N S I D E R**

Are you comfortable sharing sensitive information with key executives, family shareholders, and others involved with the keep-sell issues?

---

## Pride of Ownership and the Legacy Factor

As businesses mature and owners age, the entrepreneur begins to take pride in the various accomplishments. Providing a valuable product or service, employing people in the community, supporting local charities, and making money by doing something well are all measures of entrepreneurial success. Why shouldn't the owner keep the business? With a clear vision, a corporate culture that is collaborative and participative, and committed leadership for the next generation, it would appear that all the ducks are in order. However, for the company to continue and prosper, next-generation owners need to bring their own skills to the table while appreciating what the founder has created.

In 1986, Gibb Dyer identified the importance of *interdependent* relationships between current and future leaders as one of the key factors that differentiated successful from unsuccessful business transitions.

"The leaders must be willing to spend the time to teach and train their successors—without resenting the fact that they will eventually be turning over the reins of power. They must be willing to delegate appropriate and significant responsibility to the next generation in order to allow them to gain experience and to demonstrate that they are competent. The successors, for their part, must learn patience, must be willing to listen and learn from the leaders. They must also think about the kind of skills and abilities that the company will need in the future, so they can plan their education and training. Open communication is crucial to build trust and create a climate where both parties can work closely together. These kinds of relationships do not just happen; they are a product of a great deal of time and effort."[1]

Business continuity can then be viewed as a work in progress, never quite finished, but always changing and evolving. As relationships change over time the one constant that is needed is the commitment to the process.

| C O N S I D E R | Have you and your successors cultivated interdependent and mutually supportive relationships? Does the next generation embrace your vision of the plan? |
| --- | --- |

## The Long-Term Perspective

Private companies can take risks and invest for long-term results without accountability to outsiders. Public companies have a shorter-term view since earnings are reported quarterly to stockholders who expect each quarter to be better than the last. Therefore, the thinking goes that private companies don't suffer the same scrutiny and stockholder wrath for botched decisions. However, many private companies are addressing succession by transferring ownership to trusts for the benefit of future generations or to family members not involved in senior management or perhaps not involved at all in the operating business. These next-generation owners may share the long-term view of the entrepreneur but the definition of long-term may have changed. In today's world long-term may mean six months instead of three to five years. While private companies can enjoy going for the home run instead of hitting singles and doubles, and investing for tomorrow, future stockholders will lose patience if management is not performing. Patience will need to be rewarded and managing shareholder relationships will become an important skill set for future CEOs to have.

> **C O N S I D E R**
>
> Have your successors learned the balance between moving on a dime and making thoughtful decisions?

## Compensation, Deductible Perks, and Employing Family Members

CEOs of public companies make far more in total compensation, when including stock options, than owners of private companies. How often do you hear of private companies rewarding their CEO $40 million in stock options as an annual bonus?[2] In a 1998 report of private company compensation, CEOs of private companies averaged 75 percent of public company CEOs base pay, but only made 33 percent of public company CEOs incentive pay.[3] While owners of private companies do, in fact, set their own compensation, it is usually balanced with the needs of the business. The perks such as the Hilton Head or Vail condo, the airplane, and the cruise on the Silver Shadow permit a comfortable lifestyle for some private company CEOs. But, for most CEOs the condominium is rented from someone else, the company plane is Southwest Airlines, and the cruise is an incentive trip paid by one of the company's suppliers.

What will change in the future? New performance-based compensation policies may actually raise the level of compensation in the future for high-performing private companies. Lackluster private companies surviving on past successes will be under increasing pressure as key nonfamily executives feel underpaid and under-appreciated and choose to move to high performing companies. Leadership and management talent are already moving to the exciting businesses—the Darwinian selection process will allow new-generation private companies who have a compelling vision, passion, and culture to attract the best and the brightest talent in the marketplace.

Maynard Sauder's vision for Sauder Woodworking Company was to be "the best place to work" when he and his brother took over the furniture manufacturing business near Toledo, Ohio in 1975, from their dad. According to Maynard, Sauder was the third best place to work in Archbold in those days, behind LaChoy Food Products and Dinner Bell, a privately-owned meat processor. Since then, LaChoy has been sold three times and Dinner Bell is no longer in business. So, Sauder hired every good manager they could from those other local companies. LaChoy is a fraction of its former size, while Sauder Woodworking Company has grown from 370 (in 1975) to 3,500.

Family members will still have opportunities to work in the private company, but they will come in with a portfolio of experience, a college or graduate degree and will be able to make a contribution to the business from day one. The company cannot afford to provide a safety net for children who flunked in the world, or to employ the dozens of cousins who need jobs. Leadership will be earned by family members who compete for available positions with outside and inside candidates. And in today's scarce market for qualified employees, private companies will have to compete with outside companies for both family and nonfamily employees.

As one client described it, "I knew [potential family successors] were bright and capable. What I had to find out was whether they *really* were interested in running the company. I was sure they had the ability; I had to find out if they had the desire."

In many cases, family members will learn to become smart owners and will let qualified managers run their companies. The business will become an investment for its owners—they will still be connected emotionally to the company but will increasingly find other career opportunities more satisfying.

> C O N S I D E R
>
> Does the company pay market rates for family and nonfamily employees? Is family compensation based on performance and experience? Are family employees qualified for their jobs and performing well?

## *Wealth Consolidation*

One benefit of keeping the business is to consolidate family wealth in one entity for multiple generations. Some owners tend to be overly cautious in their approach to sharing family wealth. Their thinking is to underpay family members (and key people), and to emphasize the deemed opportunity associated with owning stock in the company—distributions are only made for tax payments due, and all profits are reinvested in the company. By avoiding tough discussions about the family's need for liquidity, underpaying (and thereby discouraging) qualified family members from joining the company, and keeping stock concentrated in trusts (or subject to restrictive shareholder agreements), these owners inadvertently discourage the next generation from continuing on as owners. Overly restrictive provisions designed to protect family members from the negative effects of the family's wealth may backfire when the next generation resents these efforts and works instead to unravel the previous generation's plans. Instead, owners should spend time educating family members about their responsibilities regarding family wealth, including how to make smart decisions about investments, and using wealth wisely.

> C O N S I D E R
>
> Have you begun educating the next generation about handling wealth responsibly? Are there opportunities for family shareholders to get liquidity when they need or want it? ‹

## Decision Making

Rapid decision making, no committees, no bureaucracy are all seen as pluses in keeping a company. The fallacy of rapid decision making is that many aging owners are quick to say "no" to new ideas so decision making is rapid, but may be more knee-jerk than thoughtful. One group of successors figured out when and how to make presentations to senior management. Their suggestions are as follows:

- Never present new ideas on Mondays
- Never present radical ideas
- Look for precedents
- Let senior management think it was their idea
- Define sunk costs as investments
- Demonstrate rates of return on the investment required
- Always show how the new idea is more efficient than something they are already doing

The need to make unilateral decisions will be a detriment in the future when decision making and authority need to be shared with professional managers. An aversion to bureaucracy may mask a reliance on "how we've always done things" and discourage innovation and creativity.

One client, a successor in a firm who has decided to stay private, explained his attitude toward decision making this way: "One thing I've had to learn as a new leader is that even though I'm not afraid to take risks, I don't need to solve problems overnight. When I first got into this job I thought I had to solve everything today. I figured I got there because I was good at making decisions and, therefore, I should

> **C O N S I D E R**
>
> Are decisions made by consensus or management instead of unilaterally? Do owners tend to embrace new ideas?

make the decisions immediately. I would take it on and solve it right away. Now what I've learned from the former president is I don't have to solve everything today. I should take time to process the problem, let others process it, and take more time in making decisions."

## Wealth Generation

The wealth generating potential of the business may be the single most important issue in deciding whether to keep or sell the company.

To make this analysis, you have to start with certain assumptions. The first is that the company is successful and will continue to be successful in the future. If you're already worried about the future viability of the company, you either need to get clear about your vision and restructure the business so it can succeed or plan to sell it to someone who can make the hard decisions that may need to be made for the business.

The second assumption is about risk and rates of return—whether you keep or sell your business. A risk-free rate of return is defined as the rate earned from investing in short term Treasury bills—currently about 6 percent for a one year maturity. For example, if you sold the business, paid the taxes, and wanted ZERO investment risk, you could put your money in T-bills and sleep like a baby. That is, you could sleep until you realized there were other risks you needed to worry about—and those might keep you up at night. For example, T-bills are subject to reinvestment risk. That is, when you reinvest after the one year, you may not get 6 percent. You'll get the current rate of interest at the time. Another risk is inflation—your purchasing power in the future may be less than it is today. With low inflation in year 2000 (when this book was published) the projected loss of purchasing power over time is a low 2 to 3 percent. But inflation can change. Also, that assumes general inflation is what will affect you—it doesn't take into account your personal lifestyle and spending habits, costs of healthcare in the future, or what you spend and where you spend it. Your need for purchasing power in the future may be greater than the 2 to 3 percent inflation rate.

Another assumption is investment rates of return. *Beta* is an investment term that measures relative risk. For example a Beta of 1.0 is average risk. A Beta of 1.1 is a slightly above-average risk and a Beta of .9 is a slightly below-average risk. A Beta of 0 is the same as a T-bill. Let's take the Standard and Poore's (S&P) average over the past 20 years of 12 percent—that's equivalent to a risk premium of 6 percent on top of the risk free rate of 6 percent. Assuming you can earn 12 percent over time on a portfolio of securities, you can begin to calculate what the effect would be of selling the business and reinvesting the after-tax proceeds.

Finally, there is a lifestyle factor to be determined and included in the analysis. If you have been drawing say, $150,000 from your business (including perks, etc.), and you sell the company, you will have to consume a portion of your investment earnings each year to maintain your lifestyle. Or, you may want to invest part of the sale proceeds in income producing securities (for current income) and part in growth-oriented securities (for the future).

In Figure 3.2, some additional assumptions about capital gain and income taxes have been made. We have not factored in portfolio turnover (how often you buy and sell securities), or management fees paid to investment advisors, etc. Therefore, although this is not a comprehensive model, it may be a helpful and easy way to begin the comparison.

---

**FIGURE 3.2—SELL AND INVEST THE PROCEEDS**

Sale price: $2 million all cash; zero basis, 20% capital gain

Withdraw $150,000 annually. Seller's age: 54

| Rate of Return Assumed | Account balance after 15 years | Proceeds last for __ years | Proceeds last through age __ |
|---|---|---|---|
| 8.0% | $87,103 | 15 | 69 |
| 10.0% | $579,657 | 19 | 73 |
| 12.0% | $1,263,353 | 29 | 83 |
| 15.0% | $2,773,473 | more than 40 | |

In Figure 3.2, if you sold your business for $2 million, and invested the after-tax proceeds at 8 percent, you would run out of money in 15 years, (if you pulled $150,000 out of your investment account each year to live on). If you earned 15 percent annually on your investments, you could live comfortably. But how realistic is it to assume you could consistently earn 15 percent on investments?

Now consider the alternative of keeping the business.

Assume a $2 million business value (because that's what you would have sold it for in the above example). But included in that is compensation to you of $150,000.

Assume you continue to own and run the company, and that it grows at an 8 percent, 10 percent, 12 percent, and 15 percent rate of return as described above. At certain points in time, as illustrated, the business value would be as outlined in Figure 3.3.

Now, assume you hire someone to run the business for you and you pay *them* the $150,000 you were receiving previously. Assume the business grows at the same rates, but you also withdraw $150,000 as a dividend or distribution from your company to maintain your lifestyle. Again at certain points in time, the business value would be as outlined in Figure 3.4.

---

**FIGURE 3.3—KEEP THE BUSINESS—WHAT WILL IT BE WORTH?**

Current value: $2 million (after owner's compensation)

Withdraw $150,000 annually as compensation. Current age: 54

| Rate of Return Assumed | Value of business after __ years, age __ | | |
| --- | --- | --- | --- |
| | 10 years age 64 | 20 years age 74 | 30 years age 84 |
| 8.0% | $4,317,850 | $9,321,914 | $20,125,314 |
| 10.0% | $5,187,485 | $13,455,000 | $34,898,805 |
| 12.0% | $6,211,696 | $19,292,586 | $59,919,844 |
| 15.0% | $8,091,115 | $32,733,075 | $132,423,544 |

**FIGURE 3.4—KEEP THE BUSINESS—HIRE AN EXECUTIVE: WHAT WILL IT BE WORTH?**

Current value: $2 million; pay $150,000 annually to CEO
*and* withdraw $150,000 annually as a dividend (S corporation). Current age: 54

| Rate of Return Assumed | Value of business after __ years, age __ | | |
| --- | --- | --- | --- |
| | 10 years age 64 | 20 years age 74 | 30 years age 84 |
| 8.0% | $1,971,027 | $1,908,476 | $1,773,434 |
| 10.0% | $2,557,810 | $4,004,625 | $7,757,291 |
| 12.0% | $3,263,509 | $7,187,776 | $19,375,953 |
| 15.0% | $4,588,724 | $15,061,557 | $57,430,006 |

Marshall Paisner, a retired business owner in Massachusetts, analyzes the issue this way: "Let's assume the business' market value is $10 million—that's the amount investment bankers have told you the business would be worth to a third party. The company's book value is currently $5 million, annual after-tax earnings are $500,000 (the company earns 10 percent on assets after taxes) and the reinvestment rate is 50 percent of annual after-tax earnings each year, or $250,000." Paisner argues that with that reinvestment rate, the *book value* of the company would be $15 million in 20 years, or in one generation. "During that period, the business could provide family members with employment, provide a respected standing in the community, and satisfaction to you."[4]

Alternatively, if the business is sold for the $10 million (assume a low basis in the stock), after 20 percent capital gains tax ($2 million), the owner would have $8 million for investment purposes, some of which would be needed to maintain the owner's current lifestyle. So, if investments generated a 6 percent after-tax return (or 10 percent pretax) on the $8 million, and the owner consumed 4 percent (or $320,000 annually) out of the investments each year, that leaves only 2 percent for investment growth. After 20 years, the $8 million would be worth about $12 million. Twelve million dollars from a sale, or $20 million from keeping the business…hmmmm.

Then there are estate taxes. The business owner who kept the business could take advantage of various estate-freezing and asset-shifting techniques to almost eliminate estate taxes. Meanwhile, the retired seller's family with the $12 million (in 20 years) might pay 55 percent in estate taxes (another $6 million), leaving the family with $6 million—not chump change but not as good as an operating company worth 15 million bucks.

| C O N S I D E R | Will your future assets be worth more by keeping the business versus selling it? |
|---|---|

In Figure 3.5 we have summarized some of the reasons to *keep* as well as to *sell* the business. You may be able to identify additional reasons to keep or sell.

---

**FIGURE 3.5—COMPARISON OF KEEPING OR SELLING THE BUSINESS**

| Keep | Sell |
|---|---|
| • Trusting relationships | • Opportunity with qualified buyers |
| • Privacy—not having to release information | • Waning personal interest in the business |
| • Pride of ownership/build a legacy | • Strategic decision, competitive pressures, consolidation in the industry |
| • Long-term perspective | • Reduced capital gains tax |
| • Control your compensation and perks, employ family members | • Fear that the window to sell may close |
| • Keep family wealth consolidated in one entity for multiple generations | • Financial reasons—insufficient retirement assets, diversification, and reduce risk |
| • Rapid decision making, no committees, no bureaucracy | • No successors, or unsure of successor's competencies and leadership skills |
| • Wealth building potential of keeping the business versus selling | • Wealth building potential of selling the business versus keeping |

## The New Face of Future Owners of Private Companies

Let's say that you've decided to keep your company as a private, independent firm. Perhaps even pass it along to family members to enjoy some of the business' rewards. You wonder if future owners will be good owners—committed to the company, not demanding excessive dividends or distributions, respectful of management. Or will they fight over business decisions and destroy the golden goose? Well, the good news is that future owners will be smarter and the bad news is that because they are smarter they will demand much, much more from management.

The private companies of the future who succeed will be global players, technologically sophisticated on all levels—from responding to customer needs to driving redundancies out of the system by constantly improving the efficiency of manufacturing, production, and distribution processes. Firms will partner with other businesses, form joint ventures and alliances, and share resources. Ownership in these new businesses will be more sophisticated as well. These new organizations will incorporate the best of the fifth discipline/learning organizations, which enjoy the intangible benefits of being a private firm with a unique culture and a connection to people and community.

The shareholders of these new companies will be different as well. They will be more knowledgeable, they will expect more, and they will be vocal about their expectations. In many ways, the private company of the future will act like a public company accountable to its shareholders. Increasingly, shareholders may not be involved in day-to-day business operations.

Privately-held companies that will be successful in the future will need to meet a number of conditions to keep shareholders engaged. Figure 3.1 asked questions to assess factors that impact current management's ability to keep the business. Figure 3.6 will help you assess future management's and owners' ability to handle new challenges.

### *Patient Capital*

Financial capital is provided by shareholders willing to trade a current return on their business investment for the future return that a

| FIGURE 3.6—HOW WELL ARE FUTURE MANAGERS AND OWNERS PREPARED TO RUN THE BUSINESS? | | | |
|---|---|---|---|
| | | Yes | No |
| **Patient capital** | • Is additional capital needed to support growth initiatives?<br>• Are there sources to increase the company's capital?<br>• Are shareholders patient concerning liquidity and long-term results? | | |
| **Risk management** | • Does your shareholder's return correlate with the risk they bear?<br>• Do you consciously seek to take measured risks to stimulate the business? | | |
| **External forces** | • Have future owners and managers assessed industry forces (consolidations, globalization, etc.) and their effects on future profitability?<br>• Have you considered, and agreed upon, what it will take to meet these challenges? | | |
| **Management of internal resources** | • Is management challenged to take risks?<br>• Does management involve others to help solve problems?<br>• Is leadership consciously cultivated?<br>• Is the board actively involved in the succession process? | | |
| **Cohesiveness of owners** | • Do owners collaborate on finding solutions to problems?<br>• Do successors work as a team?<br>• Does the senior generation assist successors in learning how to partner?<br>• Does your compensation structure pay different salaries to owners based on responsibility and performance? | | |

| FIGURE 3.6—CONTINUED | | Yes | No |
|---|---|---|---|
| **Wealth consolidation** | • Are there entities formed and functioning to hold family assets?<br>• Were the adult members of the next generation involved in the decisions about those entities? | | |
| **Decision making** | • Are major decisions limited to one or two people at the top of the company?<br>• Is decision making pushed down into the organization?<br>• Are there specific limits of authority given to others?<br>• Is accountability by others encouraged? | | |
| **Liquidity** | • Is there a way to provide liquidity to shareholders who wish to sell a few (not all) shares?<br>• Is there regular reporting on the value of the business?<br>• Is business performance compared regularly to other peer companies? | | |

long-term strategy is likely to generate. The tradeoff creates potential conflict between shareholders who want the long-term wealth creation potential offered by the private company versus other shareholders who prefer the liquidity and diversification other types of investments provide.

The nature of capital is also changing. Historically, capital referred to the accumulation of productive capacity. The infrastructure (factories, equipment, and warehouses along with the money to update and replace equipment and facilities as needed) must be built and maintained to support the production of a stream of goods and services. In *Blur*, Davis and Meyer describe a new form of capital that is mobile (a flow not a stock), which is just-in-time instead of permanent inventory or equipment, and is intangible (such as brand, customer relationships, management skills, processes and systems).[5]

Future shareholders will be patient with capital that flows (e.g., salespeople who are closing deals, managers who are turning inventory), but impatient with capital that is stagnant or earns below-market rates of return. One client company had a history of tying up significant capital in inventory, which they were not able to turn quickly. Stockholders eventually became impatient and forced a sale of the company, resulting in a sale of inventory at a discount. No one realized full potential value of their shares.

If your shareholders seem restless, this is a good time to make sure you understand their expectations and they understand what to expect concerning future earnings and dividends. If they seem impatient, try to work together to align business and personal strategic priorities.

| C O N S I D E R | Do you measure results by a return on capital deployed? How patient are shareholders concerning liquidity and long-term returns? If you define capital to include intangible assets such as quality of information and investment in people, what additional capital needs would you have in the future? |
|---|---|

## Risk Management

If shareholders believe they are shouldering a lot of risk, they will expect high returns on their investment. Alternatively, if they are confident in the business' prospects, understand the company's strategy, and are confident in management's ability to execute, they will accept lower current returns. Shareholders' expectations and perception of risk can actually have an effect on the company's financial performance. When shareholders demand a high current return in the form of dividends or distributions, growth will need to be financed by outside sources. Working capital will be diverted, not just to pay dividends, but also to pay the interest on the debt. When shareholders are willing to leave their profits in the business as retained earnings, growth can be funded internally. Even when outside borrowing is used, the company's base of retained earnings will influence the lender's perception of risk and, therefore, the interest rate and terms.

Calculating your company's risk is an arduous task. Even if you are leaning toward keeping the business, this might be a good time to call in an appraiser, who can help quantify this.

You'll need to have a "big idea" or vision to keep shareholders focused, subordinating current returns (dividends and distributions) for the sake of something bigger than themselves that they can believe in. The vision at Sauder Woodworking is, "Be the best place to work; be 100 percent ethical in all that we do; and be the preferred supplier to top retailers in the United States." At Sauder, this means creating opportunities for employees to be proud of the work they do and the people with whom they work, and to feel fulfilled in their work. As a result of this vision, and management's ability to deliver results year after year, the company's 125 shareholders consistently vote to support the board and to support management's initiatives. Risk? Of course. The company even offers a buyback program for shareholders who wish to sell their stock—but only a few take advantage of the offer, and then only for a few shares at a time.

| C O N S I D E R | Have you calculated your company's risk-reward ratio? Have you communicated this to shareholders? |
| --- | --- |

## External Forces

Understanding the environment in which the company operates is another component of risk. Technological change, global competition, and increasing demands from customers all put pressure on the profitability of the private company. The response to these challenges may require a significant investment of capital, in the form of equity (from shareholders) or debt (from third-party sources), with an unknown return to the shareholders. A realistic view of these issues and the risks they entail is necessary for shareholders to share the responsibility for the investment required with management.

> **C O N S I D E R**
>
> Have future owners and managers assessed external forces and the effect the forces may have on future profitability? Have you considered, and agreed upon, what it will take to meet these challenges?

## Management of Internal Resources

Managing human resources as an asset is as important as managing other assets of the company. Shareholders will expect management to exhibit extraordinary levels of motivation, provide emotional strength to manage change, show a willingness and ability to involve others (employees, advisors, and consultants) in problem solving, and an ability to share power and control with others in the organization.

> **C O N S I D E R**
>
> Are management and employees sufficiently motivated and capable of managing change? Does management involve others to help solve problems? Does management share power with others in the organization?

## Cohesiveness of Owners

A collaborative effort balances tension between owner/family culture and bottom-line results. The cohesiveness and commitment of shareholders as a group can be a powerful factor, which can work in the company's favor or to its disadvantage (when it results in a "we versus them" attitude). With common expectations and goals, shareholders can provide support and a sense of security to management. Performance and measurable results can be delivered without compromising the advantages (and the culture) of being a private company.

These variables will need to be maximized as shareholders of private companies (1) move from an entrepreneurial management style to a more professional style, and (2) change from an owner-manager model of ownership to an owner-investor model. Those who are unwilling to address the challenges of ownership may find the attractiveness of selling the business to be more compelling.

One thing is clear. Owners of private companies will find that information will become less private and more public as stockholders want to know more about the business, key management's compensation is driven more and more by bottom-line performance, and board members demand greater accountability from corporate officers.

| C O N S I D E R | Are there clear boundaries between the owner's family and the business with rules of entry for family members who want to work in your company? Is there a policy of hiring "the best and the brightest?" Can owners be investors without working in the company? What steps should you take for family members to become smart owners? |
| --- | --- |

## Reasons to Sell

There may also be compelling reasons to sell the company.

A strategic buyer who has purchased 17 companies describes the motivation of sellers this way: "There are a number of issues. It's the lack of family members to assume responsibility. It's an issue about owners reaching retirement. It's an issue of work versus risk—for the first time the owner tries to rationalize the financial investment that has been made in the company. The owner looks at his or her business and says, 'My God, I have this huge investment—what do I do to protect it?'"

Do you recognize any of the following in yourself? Personal burnout, not enough confidence in successors, unsure about the future, and a readiness to try something new in life. If so, it's time for a change. The question is whether the malaise can be cured by selling the company. Also, there may be a timing gap between intellectually knowing you should sell the company and emotionally being ready to do so.

Here are some additional signals that it might be time to sell:

**Have you developed an aversion to risk?** Private companies tend to use owner's equity or traditional financing to fund growth instead of seeking creative ways to partner with others. Leverage is risk from a financial standpoint. If you're getting increasingly reluctant to guarantee the next round of financing personally, find yourself delaying decisions to purchase needed equipment, or spending more time managing your securities portfolio, then it may be time for a change.

**Would others say you're becoming more and more inflexible?** Of course you're not—they're all wrong. But just in case, when was the last time you said "yes" to a new idea? Or, have the people in your company learned how to go around you or manage the presentation to get a "yes" instead of a "no"?

**Have you developed a narrow perspective and do you avoid new ideas?** When engaging consultants, is there a tendency to shoot the messenger rather than implement needed change? Is change happening all around you while you are barricading the doors? On a scale of 1 to 10 (1 being a killer of new ideas and 10 being a supporter), where would others rank you?

Deciding to sell the business doesn't have to be driven by some negative event. For many, there are powerful and positive reasons for selling the business. A few reasons are as follows:

- *Opportunity*. The booming stock market has created cheap currency for acquisitions by public strategic buyers. The financial strength of today's buyers is stronger due to many years of good profits, and senior lenders have been more aggressive about financing acquisitions for their clients. The opportunity to sell at today's prices may be a short-lived opportunity.

- *Waning interest*. There may be reduced family pressure for the next generation to join the business, so without family members involved, and without a compelling reason or vision to keep the company, selling it may be the right option for you and the business.

- *Strategic decision*. If you are in a consolidating industry where large companies are trying to reduce costs through economies of scale and seeking access to new markets and new technologies quickly, you may find that if you don't sell, you'll be left behind and unable to compete.

- *Reduced capital gains taxes.* Paying 20 percent tax on a sale of stock, or even less through creative structuring, can put more after-tax money in your pocket than at any time in recent history.

- *Fear that the window may close.* Everything moves in cycles and seasons and the past few years have been great ones for sellers. If the buyers suddenly find they can't profitably digest all the deals they are doing, or the proposed synergies don't work as planned, or the stock market corrects, the window of opportunity may close and who knows when it will open again.

## The Dream

Ivan Lansberg, in *Succeeding Generations*, describes the importance of a shared dream in maintaining continuity of the company. For those who wish to keep the business, developing a vision for the future is important in planning the continuity of the company. Importantly, the lack of a shared dream can also be an important contributor in deciding to sell the business.

> The Shared Dream is a collective vision of the future that inspires [those involved] to engage in the hard work of planning and to do whatever is necessary to maintain their collaboration and achieve their goals. It shapes the choices made at every point in the succession journey, from the company's strategic plan, to the selection of future leaders, to the type of leadership structure it will adopt in the next generation. The Shared Dream emerges from the family's fundamental values and aspirations. It defines who they are, who they want to be, what kind of enterprise they wish to build, and how they wish to be perceived in the world.[6]

Here's how one Arizona business reinvented itself to sustain its dream. Kaibab Industries started in 1893 as a sawmill and timber-cutting operation in Utah and in 1952 moved to Arizona. At one point,

Kaibab was one of the largest privately owned businesses in Arizona with more than $200 million in revenues from 13 sawmills and timber-cutting operations, 39 gas stations, and more than 500 employees. By 1998, Kaibab had shut down all of its sawmills, sold off its gas stations, and laid off the 500 employees. But third-generation Bruce Whiting did not want to simply shut down the company and walk away from what two generations before him had built. Commented Whiting, "What we learned—and it's a true principle—is that change will happen, and you can either change with the times or get left behind . . . my conscious decision was let's take our resources and do something else with them." Whiting launched a private business incubator to help other entrepreneurs develop their ideas. Whiting maintains that privately owned Kaibab is still harvesting natural resources. They are just different from the ones his grandfather harvested. Today, he's cultivating ideas, money, and response time instead of logs and petroleum products.

## Involving Others in the Decision

Finally, the decision to keep or sell cannot be made unilaterally. Others are effected and should be involved in the decision because it will have a profound impact on family members and key people in the future. The spouse who says, "I married him for better or worse, but not for lunch," children who may (or may not) have envisioned themselves coming into the business someday, and key management, will all be impacted. Lansberg encourages those involved to have a "continuing, open-ended discussion through which family members [and others] clarify their aspirations and expectations about the future, to themselves and to one another."[7]

## Selling May Be the Smartest Move After All

For families that own an interest in a closely held company, there often comes a time when it is in the best interest of the owners to sell the business. If the next generation has no involvement in the company professionally, emotionally, or financially, or doesn't have the skills to run or own the business, then selling the company may be the smartest move for the owner to take. Without a compelling vision, capable and passionate successors, and a good business plan, then planning to sell may be the best next step to take.

## Ignoring What Logic Tells You

Even if all the objective factors indicate you would be better off selling the business, you still may want to keep it. And that's okay. But after reading this chapter, you should now know where some of the weaknesses in your businesses are, and you can begin to address them so you can keep the business in a way that will maximize your financial and emotional opportunities and goals. The chapters in the next section of the book will help you do just that.

PART

II

# Deciding to Keep Your Business

# Three Models for Keeping Ownership—

## Deciding Which Is Right for You

**N**ow you have evaluated the criteria for keeping or selling your business. If you are inclined to keep it, there is another critical decision you need to confront. Who is best suited to run the business? Just because you own it doesn't mean you have to lead it. There are three main options:

1. *Owner-manager model*, in which only active employees can own shares.

2. *Owner-investor model*, in which you and family members retain ownership, but do not run the company day to day.

3. *Hybrid model*, in which ownership can include management, employees, and inactive shareholders.

This chapter will help you identify which option best suits you. Deciding which of these is right for you, your business, and your family is the most important first step to take once you decide to keep the company instead of selling it. Your decision will impact many future business options, such as how to cultivate leadership, structure compensation, build teams, and educate stakeholders.

For example, say you envision that the family may keep the business but professional managers will run the company. That decision will have an impact on your hiring practices, your succession plan, and the education of family members as owners. Each model also requires different ways to structure an ownership transition to best assure the business a chance of success.

You may not know at this time whether you want family as owners. Perhaps you have young children and it is too early to decide. Or, you may have already decided that only those (family or others) who work in the company should be owners. Some clients who have many children, but only one or two involved in the business, struggle with being fair to all children when it comes to estate planning, while at the same time wanting to recognize the contribution of those who have been working in the business. That often causes the business owner to procrastinate.

Without proper planning and communication with others, the impact of these issues may not be known until after the entrepreneur retires, or dies, and is no longer around to act as referee or to call the shots. In such cases, some advisors suggest selling the business to avoid potential conflict among family and the business in the future. But that is generally a short-term solution: family conflict, if it is going to happen, will happen whether you own a business or not. The challenge of structuring ownership is to have the company run the best way possible with checks and balances on family ownership, senior management, and the involvement from family members.

It is important that the owner explore the three models openly with board members, family, potential successors, and key executives in the company, just as the owner should consult with these stakeholders about the question of whether to keep or sell. Which ownership model best meets your personal, family, and company goals? As you bring others into the discussion, the issues can become less emotional and the answers can be based on practical and objective criteria.

## Decide How Ownership Will Be Structured

For many entrepreneurs, ownership of the company is the same as running the company on a day-to-day basis. For these same entrepreneurs, the benefits of ownership are derived from compensation and benefits that provide tax deductions to the company. Ownership and control of the business are so intertwined that it may be difficult to imagine a different way for ownership to be held successfully in the future—yet that is exactly what must be done. Whether equity is shared with key executives or ownership is extended throughout the family, it is increasingly difficult for successful companies to keep ownership consolidated in one person. Therefore, successful private companies are finding methods to separate the management function from the ownership function so that each group understands their roles and their responsibilities to each other.

The owner-manager model is based on the premise that the best owners for the business are those who work in the business. Ownership is therefore restricted to those who have dedicated their careers to the company. As owners retire, or die, their interests are typically repurchased by the company so that ownership stays consolidated in the hands of those who run the business. Benefits of ownership are primarily derived from the ability to set one's own compensation, pay extraordinary bonuses to oneself and others, and receive tax-deductible perks from the company. This model tends to look to inside sources for information on how to best run the company. Owner-managers may rely on industry data, but not go deeper than that. There is no outside pressure to change management systems or structures.

The owner-investor model is based on the premise that owners look to the company as a long-term investment. Owners may or may not be employed by the company. A governance structure is important to this model so that owners and managers have a process to articulate and address each other's goals and objectives. A significant difference between this model and the owner-manager is that owner-investors often view their ownership as a form of stewardship, such as, having a responsibility to others (e.g., children or grandchildren) to manage assets wisely, increase their value, and to be able to make strategic decisions. For managers this model includes the expectation for operational decision making and authority and a fair compensation system that rewards accomplishments. If owners occupy management positions, they receive fair compensation for the jobs they perform. For owners, there is a responsibility to have realistic expectations about the value and risks of ownership. The owner-investor model attempts to hire the right people to run the business to maximize shareholder value. Owners tend to look to outside sources, like board members, for information and for benchmarking company performance.

The hybrid model often serves as a transitional model while ownership moves from owner-manager to owner-investor (and sometimes from owner-investor back to owner-manager). The hybrid model may be chosen for only one generation or for a shorter term of 10 to 20 years. The hybrid model is often used with second-generation firms. First generation entrepreneurs typically use the owner-manager model, while third (and later) generations of owners tend to be owner-investors. The hybrid model can be the beginning of a governance process, and can be structured so that both active and nonactive shareholders are treated fairly. One advantage of the hybrid model is that it typically lets those who run the company do so without a lot of interference from nonactive shareholders. And yet, the hybrid model can create ways for nonactive shareholders to be involved in major decisions so they retain some "voice." The hybrid model promotes a healthy consideration of the differences between being an owner-manager and an owner-investor. The following are some of the pros, cons, and critical success factors of each ownership model.

## Owner-Manager Model

This is the pure entrepreneurial model. As the business passes from one generation to the next, ownership typically becomes dispersed among the key people running the business. The primary restriction on who can have ownership is conditional on working full time in the company.

### Pros

- Owners are not subject to outside (inactive) shareholders who may have different views and goals than active shareholders might.
- Governance is by those who own the business.
- This model can be used to encourage ownership among a key executive group, perhaps with an eye towards a sale in the future.

- Shares can be sold to executives using an installment loan from the company, financed through the local bank, or distributed as a taxable bonus.

- A phantom equity-based incentive plan, as described in Chapter 6, can be used to reward executives for performance without current taxation, giving them the opportunity to convert to real shares if the company is sold.

- Depending on how far you want ownership to extend in your company, an Employee Stock Ownership Plan (ESOP) also works well with this model. One client spent several years educating his employees about ownership: first implementing a gain-sharing plan so employees would better understand how their individual and department efforts affected profits, and later an ESOP so they would view the company as theirs. The ESOP owns approximately 10 percent of the company and the executive team reports ESOP values to employees as if the company were publicly owned.

## Cons

- Family members may want to work in the company because they have an emotional connectedness to it, but may not be the best for the job.

- Management may resent the interference of children who lack experience or haven't "paid their dues."

- It may be difficult for owner/parents to equalize their estate between children who work in the business and own shares and those who are inactive in the business and will not own shares (in this model).

- It is often difficult for the current owner-manager to give up real authority or control. Without a transfer of authority, however, the owner-manager risks losing qualified successors.

- The owner-manager may create financial disadvantages between children active, full-time, in the business and those who are not active, as active children may enjoy greater compensation and lifestyles than those who are not qualified to come to work in the business.

- This ownership model can create forced partnerships among children who work in the business but may not get along.

- The owner-manager may procrastinate about turning over authority because of concern about conflict among successors.

- Some entrepreneurs view this as a way to ensure that family members retain ownership. But this restriction can backfire when the family-member-successor is not the most competent.

- Because ownership is restricted, those who work in the company are accountable only to themselves, not to outside shareholders. Governance structures are usually not widely used so the checks and balances that come with outside shareholders is lacking. This can be overcome with a board of directors comprised of outsiders who can challenge the owner-managers; or the owner-managers may believe they can best make all the decisions for the business.

- Often internal buyouts with the owner-manager model are priced based on what the owners feel is fair and does not reflect true fair market value for a withdrawing shareholder's interest. This can create conflict for the shareholder or the estate, if they are permitted to sell at a below market price. Furthermore, trying to equalize the owner's estate with inactive children may add to the complexity, indirectly encouraging owner-managers ultimately to sell the business so family assets can be more evenly divided.

**Critical success factors.** Communication with family members is critical to the success of this model for it to work. A family member not involved with the company may feel cut off when denied an opportunity for ownership. Or, family members may gravitate to the business as a career, not because they are competent or passionate about the company, but because that's the only way they can enjoy the fruits of ownership.

Another difficulty with this model is the diversion of capital (away from operations) needed to buy out withdrawing or deceased owners. If business margins have been shrinking, for instance, there will be little cushion for error, and limited funds to pay a withdrawing or deceased stockholder.

Figure 4.1 will help you determine whether this model is likely to work for you, your business, and your family.

## FIGURE 4.1—WILL THE OWNER-MANAGER MODEL WORK FOR YOU?

| Issue | Yes | No |
|---|---|---|
| Family members may want to work in the company because they have an emotional connectedness to it, but may not be the best for the job. Are you prepared to decide whether family can or cannot work in the company or create rigorous policies to help decide? | | |
| Will management tolerate the employment of children if they obtain experience and "pay their dues"? | | |
| Are you prepared to create a career path and mentoring for family members (as well as promising nonfamily employees) who join the company so they can earn the respect of the senior team? | | |
| Are you reluctant to give inactive family members stock in the business? | | |
| If not, do you have financial resources to allow you to equalize your estate between active and inactive family members? | | |
| This ownership model can create forced partnerships among children who decide to work in the business and who have competed with each other throughout their lives. Do you have teambuilding training and structures in your company that will enhance the success of their working relationships? | | |
| Do you have stock purchase or buy-sell agreements to allow stockholders to repurchase shares when they retire, become disabled, or die, thereby preventing stock from falling very far from the company tree? | | |
| Have you reviewed your agreements recently to determine if the pricing mechanism is still fair, or whether provisions need to be amended or added? | | |
| Are you confident that successors can work together productively? | | |

Here is a typical problem scenario for the owner-manager model. If a family member believes she should be running the company, even though she may not be the best candidate, would you

- allow the family member to take over, possibly putting the "golden goose" at risk and alienating loyal key people?
- say "no" and risk alienating family members because they did not understand the decision?
- create a process in which both management and family make a smart decision about future leadership?

## Owner-Investor Model

By permitting family members, or others, to become owners regardless of whether they work in the business, ownership typically remains with the entrepreneur's family, in trusts, or other entities for their benefit. Ownership may also be held by key executives, subject to buy-out arrangements at their retirement or death. This is generally the best model for a long-term keep scenario, but requires a great deal of work with family and key people for it to be successful.

### Pros

- This approach permits broad ownership of the business in family (and/or nonfamily) hands and encourages a governance structure for business decisions to be managed through the board.
- This model gives the family an ability to make decisions about the company that are very investor based.
- Owners can hire the best people for the company, can be very strategic about their goals, and can also have the company run in such a way that it's consistent with the family's values, and therefore can create a legacy that the family can be proud of without all the complications when some shareholders work in the business and some don't.
- As the owning family gets larger, it's a way the family can continue to own the company, which can keep them connected to each other.

**Cons**

- Inactive voting shareholders, who have a majority of voting shares, may oust management for nonperformance or other reasons.

- Management may align with family factions to control the board.

- A consensus approach on ownership issues may foster disagreement about important strategic issues, including tension around distributions versus reinvestment.

- Management may stray from the culture of the founder if focused solely on performance; conversely, remaining too loyal to the original vision may cause missed opportunities.

- Management may not have proper incentives to take prudent risks on shareholder's behalf, instead functioning more like caretakers.

- Liquidity may be needed for estate taxes (on shares retained) or simply for diversification, which may inadvertently force a sale of the company.

**Critical success factors.** This model works best when there is a clear vision for the company and clear boundaries between ownership and management. Ownership sets goals with management and then steps back to let management run the company. The owner-investor model also works best when stockholders view their ownership of the company in a stewardship role.

Senior managers control day-to-day operations of the business while inactive shareholders may elect to place their stock in a Voting Trust or partnership to consolidate the voice of each family's line. The stockholders are involved in major decisions through participation at the board level. When several family lines with multiple generations are involved, ownership may be held in trusts with Trustees, selected by the family, voting the block of shares. An emerging trend is for different family voices to come together in a Family Council, with two or three members of the Family Council actually on the company's board. Family members employed in the owner-investor company are treated the same as nonfamily with standardized compensation and incentive plans. The owner-investor company typically distributes some part of its annual earnings to shareholders in the form of a current dividend (for C or S corporations) while developing a reporting format for shareholders that provides them sufficient information to evaluate how the company is performing. Figure 4.2 explores key issues to help you decide if the owner-investor model is the right choice for your business.

| FIGURE 4.2—WILL THE OWNER-INVESTOR MODEL WORK FOR YOU? | | |
| --- | --- | --- |
| **Issue** | **Yes** | **No** |
| Are you willing and able to work with key executives and family members to create reasonable expectations and a process to discuss differences? | | |
| Are you willing to take a look at your bylaws and amend them to encourage or discourage certain voting practices and create a new governance structure? | | |
| Are you willing to create a policy that balances the company's needs for capital with the family's needs for distributions? | | |
| Are you willing to vest authority in the CEO, to let him or her make tough decisions, without you or other stockholders trying to micromanage the CEO? | | |
| Do you have or are you willing to spend time to develop (with others) a strategic plan for the company that can be used as a roadmap for the future? | | |
| Have you considered the pros and cons of consolidating your ownership in an entity that can last several generations, with trustees selected by family members, to vote the shares? | | |
| Do stockholders understand that they have a responsibility to the company to oversee its management in a prudent fashion? | | |

## *The Hybrid Approach*

This model permits broad ownership (per the owner-investor model) but restricts operating responsibilities to those who run the business (per the owner-manager model). For some companies this will be a transitional model as the company moves from owner-manager to owner-investor or vice versa. Typically the company is recapitalized to issue voting and nonvoting shares. (S corporations can have nonvoting shares without losing their S status because nonvoting is technically not a second class of stock.) After the recapitalization, existing owners are given a new currency in the form of nonvoting shares that can be used for planning purposes. Nonvoting shares can be retained, or transferred to children, grandchildren, or trusts for the family's benefit. Nonvoting shares provide a way to share equity without shareholders having a voice. Depending on the state in which your company is domiciled, there may be voting rights granted under state law to nonvoting shareholders. For example, state law may give nonvoting shareholders the right to vote on major decisions such as the sale of the business. For the most part, however, nonvoting shareholders have limited input. Therefore, you may want to provide put options to the nonvoting shareholders to give them liquidity and the opportunity to sell their shares back to the company at various points in time. Similarly, call options can be structured for the company to redeem the nonvoting shareholders.

Voting shares are reserved for those in charge of day-to-day business operations. With voting shares in the hands of those active in the company, this approach resembles the owner-manager model, but by disseminating non-voting shares to family or key executives, it resembles the owner-investor model. Typically the non-voting shares are given the right to vote on major decisions such as a sale of the business, or changing the capital structure of the company so there are checks and balances between the two shareholder groups. The creation of voting and nonvoting has one important advantage in that the timing of when shares get transferred can be different for voting than for nonvoting. For example, nonvoting shares could be transferred to trusts, a smart estate planning move, while voting shares could be retained until the owner is more assured of who will run the business in the future.

**Pros**

- This model addresses equalization among family members by allowing them to hold nonvoting stock.

- This gives inactive shareholders a voice on major, strategic decisions.

- It gives those who run the company the assurance of knowing they can run it on a day-to-day basis without interference from the inactive owners.

- This provides patient capital—inactive shareholders can be cheerleaders for the success of those who are active in running the business.

- This can be structured to provide liquidity so that inactive shareholders can be bought out if they wish to do so and active shareholders can have an option to buy them out if they wish to do so.

**Cons**

- Inactives have a limited voice as holders of nonvoting shares. There is limited protection under state law related to the obligations (called fiduciary duties) of those who hold voting shares to take care of those with nonvoting shares.

- Compensation and perks for actives may become a source of contention (e.g., when non-actives believe excessive compensation is being paid to those running the business).

- Actives may feel it's their business, and resent the free ride of the inactives.

- Limited checks and balances on those with voting shares.

- With S corporations, if there is no distribution policy (for taxes, at least), the lack of adequate distributions from the company may create conflict, or worse, a freeze-out if taxable income is not accompanied with cash distributions. Because those who hold the voting shares can declare bonuses to themselves for taxes due (on S corporation profits) they can also decide to not distribute funds to the nonactives for their share of the S corporation earnings. Nonvoting shareholders can be protected by amending the company's bylaws to require distributions for income taxes, while further amendments could require the consent of the nonvoting holders.

**Critical success factors.** The goal is to include all family in ownership even though some are active and others are not. The hybrid model attempts to balance fairness for all family (through sharing equity) while recognizing that those who are active have made career choices and commitments in favor of the business. This model works best in a high trust environment where some family members are competent to move into executive positions (or will be in a few years) and other family members have developed careers outside the business.

The hybrid model helps next generation owners articulate differences between active and inactive shareholders and develop a plan to address those differences in a way that works for the business and the two groups of stockholders. The questions in Figure 4.3 may help you determine if the hybrid model can work for you.

| FIGURE 4.3—WILL THE HYBRID MODEL WORK FOR YOU? | | |
| --- | --- | --- |
| **Issue** | **Yes** | **No** |
| Would you consider giving nonvoting stockholders a voice on major decisions effecting the business? | | |
| Would you be willing to implement a compensation policy based on market rates for the jobs and accountability for performance? | | |
| Do you have education and systems in place to prevent conflict from occurring between active and inactive shareholders? | | |
| Do those with nonvoting shares have (or are you prepared to give them) one or more seats on the Board, possibly with limited voting rights, to create checks and balances that everyone could agree was fair? | | |
| Do you have a written distribution policy in the company's bylaws (or are you prepared to create one) that would prevent those with voting shares from declaring bonuses to themselves for taxes due (on S corporation profits) while also deciding not to distribute funds to inactive shareholders? | | |

Once you've completed the questions, you should have a pretty good idea of which model is likely to work best for you, your business, and your family. However, you may find that even though you rate higher for one particular model, you feel emotionally more comfortable with another model. That's okay, at least for today. But remember you're not just keeping your company for today, but for the future. As you look toward the long-term viability of the business, you may find in the future it is smart to make a change in the ownership structure.

As you read the next few chapters, keep in mind there are four Cs to be addressed: capital, competition, consolidations, and competencies (Figure 4.4). The reward of making smart decisions in these four areas is the ability to keep ownership of the company.

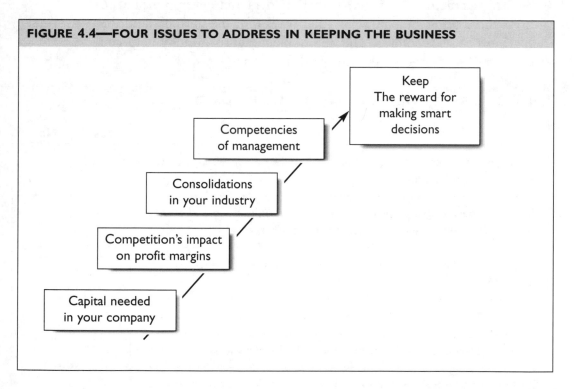

**FIGURE 4.4—FOUR ISSUES TO ADDRESS IN KEEPING THE BUSINESS**

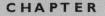

# Making Each Model Work Structurally

S mith Packaging (not the real name) is a $50 million revenue, second-generation, S corporation in Atlanta, Georgia. CEO Alfred Smith, now in his late 60s, is partially retired, having delegated day-to-day management to a nonfamily executive, Joel. The family wants to keep the business. Once they choose whether to follow the owner-manager, owner-investor, or a hybrid approach, they need to take a fresh look at the business structure, to make sure it best supports their ownership model.

Alfred's daughter Sarah, 33, and her brothers Pete, 26, and Steve, 29, each own 15 percent of the company. Alfred owns 55 percent. Sarah, who works as a freelance graphic designer in Boston, and Pete, who's working on a PhD in anthropology, and Steve, who dropped out of high school and is floundering, are all paid salaries even though they don't work for the company. Sarah has been on the payroll for 16 years, also collecting distributions to pay for taxes. She doesn't feel good about collecting money for work she hasn't performed. She's also uncomfortable with her role as a part owner. She has valid concerns about the way the company is run. "Five of our customers make up 75 percent of our business. It's been a tremendous part of our growth in the past three years. Our largest customer is Hewlett-Packard. We also make packaging for Olivetti, Dell, and Gateway, besides H-P. We've recently opened a third plant." When Alfred retires in five years, Sarah knows that she cannot take over. The board of directors insists she would have to go back to school to earn an MBA, which she has no intention of doing.

Instead, Sarah says, "What we've tried to work on is how to become educated owners. There's a huge backlog of work that my brothers and I need to do to know what we're doing. We have no power to make decisions and no ability to do so. We don't know enough to make informed decisions. Dad has opted out. He is Joel's cheerleader, but not ours. He hasn't encouraged us to become smart owners. He has a terribly difficult time relating to us kids as other than a daughter and sons. I feel like a complete fraud. I don't really have a viable role in the business."

Sarah and her brothers acknowledge they do not play a meaningful role in the company, and are overpaid for the jobs they do perform.

As an owner-manager company, Alfred could eventually sell his (and the family's) stock to Joel in some form of a leveraged buy-out. With a solid growth plan, Joel could probably find financing to buy out Alfred's interest. A competent management team is already in place, which would make the deal more attractive to an investment banker. But is Joel interested? With a $1 million annual salary, Joel may not want to take the entrepreneurial risk that is involved. Meanwhile it may be emotionally difficult for Alfred to sell this second-generation business and terminate the family's involvement.

What about an investor-owned company? This seems more likely because a board is already in place. Joel and his management team don't seem like they are eager to buy the business. One challenge is to educate Sarah and her brothers about what is involved in being a smart owner. How about starting with Alfred, and explaining to him how an investor-owned company is different from an owner-managed company. If the family agreed on the owner-investor role, benchmarks should be created so the family could have comparative information to see how their company was performing against other companies. Joel and his team should be included in setting the benchmarks. The performance expectations created by the benchmarks would also be the foundation of a new compensation program for Joel and his team. The company might become less family-friendly but could also be part of the family's portfolio of long-term investments. Equity sharing for Joel and some of the other key people could also be considered.

Finally, what about a hybrid model? The family is not likely to only be involved as nonvoting shareholders and give Joel the voting power. But a variation of this could be created with voting shares placed in a Voting Trust by Alfred. The Trustees of the Voting Trust could be a committee comprised of Joel, one or two board members, Alfred, and a family representative—perhaps Sarah, or one of her siblings, or someone they chose to represent their interests. Nonvoting shares could be held separately by Sarah and her siblings so that distributions made from company profits could financially support the family's needs, while voting control was held in an entity such as the Voting Trust.

In any case, this company should distribute some part of the company's earnings to the shareholders to give them a sense of getting a return on their investment—something in excess of what is now being distributed for taxes. And, Alfred, Sarah, Steve, and Pete should all fire themselves, moving Alfred to Chairman and Joel to CEO.

Whichever ownership model Alfred may choose, he will confront critical structural management and governance issues. Here are the specific structural issues for each ownership model.

## Structural Issues for Owner-Manager Companies

- *Leadership development*. This and teambuilding are often needed with a specific timeframe for a change of control contingent on mutually agreeable performance targets or other accomplishments being realized. While the next generation often looks to the current owner-manager as the ultimate decision-maker, this paternalistic style can fail when the referee is gone. A process will be needed to resolve differences among the next-generation team. Appointing a qualified individual as President/CEO works if he/she has earned all the other executives' respect. Limits of authority during a transition period need to be clearly understood.

- *Shareholder agreements.* A shareholder's option agreement can resolve the owner-manager's equalization issues with inactive children by permitting transfers of stock and then requiring inactives who have received stock gifts to sell their shares back to the company or to the active siblings at the parent's death (or sooner). The inactives can thereby participate in growth in stock value for an interim period as a temporary shareholder.

- *Equalization language.* The use of equalization language in parents' estate planning documents can provide additional distributions to inactive children comparable to the value received by the active children in family business stock.

- *Installment sale.* This is the best ownership transfer strategy by the current generation to the next generation of actives, in order to resolve fairness issues. In other words, the next generation (family or key people) buy stock from the current owners; the cash or note can then be estate planned to treat all children fairly. This is often coupled with some form of deferred compensation or supplemental pension arrangement from the company to provide additional retirement income for senior family members. Another option is to use an installment sale with a Self-Canceling Installment Note (SCIN) transaction that automatically cancels any amounts still owed at the death of the seller. If the note is cancelled, this can also reduce estate taxes since the note (from the sale of stock) is no longer in the estate by virtue of its cancellation.

- *Debenture.* If your company is an S corporation you may have an Accumulated Adjustments Account or "AAA": previously taxed but undistributed earnings. You should consider withdrawing the AAA (or part of it) in the form of a non-taxable debenture. Properly structured the debenture will qualify under the safe harbor rules of S corporations and will not be treated as a second class of stock. By withdrawing your equity on a non-taxable basis, it will be easier to then transfer the remaining value to new owner-managers. Interest paid by the company on the debenture is deductible to the business and taxable to you as interest income.

- *Employee Stock Ownership Plans (ESOP).* These can be an effective method to reward employees with ownership while providing a way for a withdrawing owner-manager to be cashed-out on a nontaxable basis. As long as the ESOP owns 30 percent or more of the value of the business, the selling shareholder can use the ESOP proceeds received to then purchase qualifying securities and avoid the capital gain tax from selling stock in the business.

## Structural Issues for Owner-Investor Companies

- *Recruit and hire professional managers.* Professional managers (typically nonfamily) hired to run the business, while the family learns to be smart owners is key to structuring an owner-investor company. The first step is to determine competencies for the jobs needed and then recruit people whose values align with the owner's values. The talent may already be on the payroll. If not, then the owners will need to form a search committee, and interview both internal candidates as well as external applicants after forming a clear set of expectations about what is to be accomplished.

- *Board of directors.* The company's board of directors may need to be reorganized to include experienced outsiders. The current owner, with help from the management team, should start by drafting a memo that outlines the company's three-to-five-year strategic plan. This should be consulted when recruiting outsiders, to make sure they have what it takes to help implement the plan.

- *Family council.* This can help educate the family, facilitate communication, and address family issues (such as family philanthropy or career counseling). The family council can serve to separate business issues from family issues. While all family members may be involved in the family council, generally only one or two from the family council serve on the board of the company.

- *Consolidation of voting rights.* Either a trust (for S corporations) or a family partnership (for C corporations) can be formed to hold the family's voting shares and consolidate the family voice on company voting matters. This may be especially important in multigenerational companies with many family members as stockholders. One entity per family line can represent multiple generations of that family's lineage with the succession and selection of Trustees (or general partners) clearly outlined in the governing documents.

- *ESOP.* An employee ownership plan may be attractive to provide liquidity for family members who wish to sell, and a fair method for pricing the shares.

- *Generation-skipping transfer trusts.* Leveraged gifting strategies via GSTT work here. For example, a sale of voting or nonvoting shares to a defective trust (intentionally designed to be defective for income tax purposes) structured with generation skipping provisions, can freeze value in the senior generation's estate while transferring appreciation to future generations.

## Structural Issues for the Hybrid Model

- *Recapitalization.* This is designed to create a new nonvoting currency that can be transferred to nonactive family members or trusts for their benefit. Those who work in the business receive/acquire voting shares by gift or purchase.

- *Special voting rights.* Designed for new nonvoting shares, this can help create a governance structure, with appropriate checks and balances. Inactive shareholders would still have a vote on major decisions such as a sale of the company (or its assets), a change in the capital structure of the company, changes in the company's bylaws, corporate borrowing in excess of a stated amount, or acquisitions or divestitures, to name a few.

- *Shareholder agreements with special provisions.* This is for inactive shareholders who wish to sell their shares: put options so inactives can sell shares on a periodic basis (a put feature) back to the company. Put features typically are accompanied by a call option so actives can call shares held by inactives at certain triggering events.

- *Tag-along (or crawl back) provisions*. This can be used as part of a shareholder's agreement to provide adjustments, for a limited period of time (e.g., five to ten years) to shareholders who previously sold, if the business is sold to a third-party in the future.

- *Leveraged gifting strategies*. This strategy combined with non-voting shares works here (e.g., GRATs, and Sales to Defective Trusts), since annuity requirements and/or interest payments can be funded with S corporation distributions.

## Structural Issues for All Ownership Models

### Family Policies for Building Trust

With the owner-investor and hybrid models, governance structures should evolve along with written policies and procedures so owners have a clear understanding about their company. These include educating inactive owners who hold stock about business value, the risks confronting the company, fair compensation for senior management, and other important issues.

Written policies that need to be developed, include:

- Financial disclosures about the company and education for stockholders about historical results, future opportunities, capital needs, competition, and risk.

- Annual business valuations based on fair market value determinations—these can be used to help shareholders understand the impact of management decisions on bottom-line earnings and resulting company value.

- Profit/earnings distribution policy—a policy that balances a current return to shareholders with the company's need for reinvestment and for longer-term results.

- Ethics policy and conflicts of interest—a policy of full disclosure for key officers and board members that maintains the integrity of the private company and avoids conflicts of interest in business affairs.

- Family employment policy that articulates what is required from family members who wish to work in the company.

- Shareholder agreements that clearly lay out whether shares can be transferred to family members, or if sold back to the company, under what conditions, and how the value will be determined and paid.

- Articulating specific financial goals for management, such as return on equity (ROE), return on assets (ROA), or other measures.

- Acquisition policies and guidelines for acquiring other companies or expanding into new lines of business.

- Compensation policies for key executives that the define company's compensation philosophy.

## How to Step Out without Selling

When one client needed capital to grow the company and also to buy out some family shareholders, they turned to deVisscher & Company for a leveraged recapitalization. Leveraged recapitalizations and other techniques are gaining popularity with private companies, along with the leveraged ESOP. There are numerous capital formation options for private companies seeking liquidity. For some of these solutions, you may need the help of an investment banker. In some cases, your commercial bank can help you and of course, some solutions are paid entirely out of existing assets and/or future earnings of the business.

## Internal Solutions Requiring No Outside Capital

- *Stock buyback program sponsored by the company*. Each year, the company can announce to shareholders that it is willing to purchase shares for a 60–90 day period. The company determines the total amount it is willing to spend that year (say, $100,000). Based on a current determination of the value of the stock, shareholders can take advantage of the liquidity opportunity if they wish to do so. Whether one, or several, shareholders wish to sell some of their shares, the company only spends the amount it has announced it will spend. The available pool of funds (i.e., the $100,000), is then allocated among the selling shareholders. The sale of a few shares by a shareholder may be treated as a dividend to the selling shareholder (as a partial redemption) instead of qualifying for capital gain treatment. However, sometimes having the opportunity to sell is an advantage regardless of the income tax consequences.

- *Exchange of stock for corporate assets.* A redemption of stock can be funded with corporate assets (property, etc. that can be leased back) rather than cash. If the selling shareholder sells all of her shares, and is no longer employed by the company as an officer or director, the property received by the shareholder may qualify for favorable capital gain tax treatment. The property can then be leased back to the company with rents paid to the shareholder for the use of the property. If the property has been depreciated by the business, or has appreciated in value, there may be an income tax liability to the company when the property is distributed. When property is transferred in this way, the value of the property (including depreciation) in excess of the company's basis is treated as a gain to the company for income tax purposes.

- *S corporation distributions.* Often, distributions are limited to the amount shareholders need to pay their income tax liabilities. By increasing distributions in excess of this amount, shareholders can receive a current return on their equity investment in the business. Distributions must be made prorata to all shareholders.

- *S corporation debenture.* An alternative to increasing distributions is to issue a debenture to a shareholder of an S corporation. Properly structured, the debenture will meet the safe harbor rules of S corporations and may not be taxed to the shareholder if the debenture is equal to or less than the shareholder's share of previously taxed, but undistributed earnings of the company. Interest on the debenture is paid by the company creating interest income for the shareholder. Furthermore, the debenture may be discounted in the estate of the shareholder at the time of death.

- *Special dividends.* Special dividends can be declared at any time; they are not deductible to the company and are taxable to the recipients so they are the least efficient way to provide liquidity from a tax perspective. However, sometimes nontax reasons can override tax considerations.

## Solutions Requiring Outside Capital

- *Bank loan to finance buyout.* Commercial banks have become more aggressive and creative as they have watched clients obtain venture capital funds. Your bank might be willing to negotiate more favorable pricing and terms if they can have a piece of the future action. It pays to shop around especially when a regional or money-center bank can be involved.

- *Private placement of debt.* Don't overlook opportunities to package and place your debt with an investment banker who can negotiate a better deal for you with an institutional investor such as a pension plan. Some pension plans such as a State Retirement Fund are required to invest a portion of their billions in socially responsible investments. Your private company, with a large employment base in that state may meet their qualifications for responsible investing. A matter of a few basis points in the interest rate charged can make a big difference in your cash flow.

- *Leveraged ESOP.* Employee Stock Ownership Plans (ESOPs) are very flexible tools that provide a way to sell privately-held stock to your company's retirement plan and receive tax benefits. Since 1997, S corporations could also establish ESOP plans. For C corporations, there are special benefits of using a newly created convertible preferred class of shares for an ESOP transaction. Basically, the ESOP borrows funds from a lending institution and purchases shares from the seller. If the ESOP owns at least 30 percent of the value of the company after the acquisition of shares, and the seller purchases qualifying securities with the proceeds, the seller may be able to defer the taxable gain from the sale of stock to the ESOP. Your company makes tax-deductible contributions to the ESOP plan (to fund retirement benefits for employees) and the plan uses those funds to repay the lending institution. As the lending institution is repaid the shares are released to the retirement plan for the benefit of the employees. Therefore both the principal and interest on an ESOP loan becomes a deductible company expense; normally only the interest portion of the loan would be deductible. The added tax benefit to the company reduces the overall cost of purchasing the shares, while the tax deferral to the seller can help the seller realize her goals. As the company's stock appreciates in value, the portion owned by the ESOP helps enhance employee's retirement benefits.

- *Leveraged recapitalization.* A recapitalization is a partial sale of a company to a financial buyer such as a leveraged buyout group. A recapitalization can provide liquidity to all or only certain shareholders. In addition, a recapitalization transaction can combine shareholder liquidity with access to growth capital. In a recapitalization the existing management/shareholders (the Rollover Shareholders) typically retain a significant ownership position in the company as well as their management responsibilities.

At a later date, the company can be sold, taken public, or recapitalized again, providing liquidity to the financial buyer and a "second bite at the apple" for the Rollover Shareholders. Jim Dwyer at MPI Securities, Princeton, New Jersey, provided the following example (Figure 5.1) of a leveraged recapitalization.

---

**FIGURE 5.1—LEVERAGED RECAPITALIZATION**

| | | | |
|---|---|---|---|
| **Assumptions:** | Sale valuation of the company | $100,000,000 | |
| | Acceptable debt load | 60,000,000 | |
| | Shareholder wants to retain 20% ownership | | |
| **Results:** | **Sources of Funds** | | |
| | Debt | $ 60,000,000 | |
| | Equity invested by financial buyer | 32,000,000 | |
| | Rollover equity amount | 8,000,000 | |
| | **Total** | **$100,000,000** | |
| | **Uses of Funds** | | |
| | Cash to shareholders | $ 92,000,000 | |
| | Rollover amount | 8,000,000 | |
| | **Total** | **$100,000,000** | |
| | **New Ownership Structure** | | |
| | Financial buyer | $ 32,000,000 | 80% |
| | Rollover shareholder | 8,000,000 | 20% |
| | **Total** | **$ 40,000,000** | **100%** |

## The Private Company as a Platform

The most compelling reason to keep the business is probably defined by those who have reinvented and changed their companies over the course of time. The business provides opportunity, challenge, and a variety of ways to keep wealth consolidated (some see that as a big plus)—for others, those reasons are exactly why they want to sell.

For business owners who want to preserve the platform the business offers and are willing to let go—either by bringing in family as successors or hiring professionals to run the business—keeping the business may be the path chosen. Even in the face of compelling sell offers.

Most second-generation companies agree that having an existing business to build from is better than starting from scratch. One client joined his dad's small ($650,000 in sales, one location) distributorship in 1967, when he was 25. Dad died unexpectedly three years later, so at age 28, this young entrepreneur took over the business. Over the next 30 years, he grew it to over $100 million in sales with eight warehouses. "The advantage of coming in as a second-generation even though it was a much smaller company, is that you have a 'jump-start.' You can begin building from a base rather than starting fresh and you have continuity. I had employees who had 20 years of experience when I came to work."

One client outlined their goals for keeping their company as a private firm as follows:

- Maintain a positive, proactive, problem-solving outlook on family relations.
- Avoid procrastination.
- Generate the right kind of leadership.
- Manage risk.
- Raise capital and keep control.
- Give the amount of time needed to ensure effective family involvement.
- Innovate consistently.
- Attract and keep the right quality of nonfamily management.
- Put the needs of the business first where necessary.

- Trust the process of family consensus.
- Build and maintain inter-generational teamwork.
- Plan long term, maintaining energy, commitment, and vision.

# Family Ownership Education

Family members who are owners of a family business often have little idea what knowledge they should have in order to be effective owners. Leslie Dashew is an organizational consultant and coach for private companies. She recommends a range of knowledge is needed in four areas as follows:

1. *Knowledge of the business as an investment*
   - Ability to evaluate the company in terms of return, and financial strength.
   - Understanding debt/equity ratios, the company's return on investment (ROI) or return on equity (ROE).
   - Knowing the market value of one's shares and how the value of one's holdings change each year.
   - Income/share and earnings trends.
   - Investment return as compared to other types of investments.
   - Diversity of the overall portfolio (e.g., emerging as well as mature businesses).
   - Understanding the company's cash flow and how it is used.

2. *Knowledge of the business' operations and its industry(ies)*
   - Evaluating management effectiveness, trust in company leadership.
   - Strategic direction of the business and position in your industry(ies).
   - Awareness of the relevant industry trends, returns, challenges, and opportunities.

3. *Personal planning*
   - Personal career planning.

- Financial planning (including estate planning).
- Ability to evaluate investment opportunities against own plans (amount of risk, exploring returns, etc.).

4. *Role of ownership*

- Boundaries between ownership and management; understanding where the line exists between wanting to know and overstepping boundaries.
- Role and operations of Boards of Directors.
- Responsibility for decision making.
- Effective team participation and leadership.

## Summary: What Do I Need to Do to Keep My Company—and Keep It Successful?

From discussions with clients and others who have decided to keep their business (for now), former owners who have sold their company, and consolidators and other buyers who have purchased more than 500 private companies, several steps unfolded. The points outlined below can help you create a road map through this process.

### What You Need to Know to Make Smart Decisions

- Define the role of your board in the process—let them know this is a question you want to answer and ask them for input and help in getting answers. For example, if you keep the company and promote yourself to office of chairman, what would you be doing differently?
- Hire someone to do a profitability audit of your firm. That is, where are you leaving money on the table? Interview two or three companies who have experience in doing these kinds of audits in your industry. Talk to clients they have worked for and find out what results they have accomplished. You may already know some areas where you could make improvements. For example, one client that manufactures wood furniture created tons of wood waste as a byproduct. Even after building their

own power plant to burn the sawdust, they still had tons to dispose of. Rather than paying someone to haul the wood waste away they began exploring alternatives, and found that by filtering the waste through a screen, and packaging it into different sizes, they could sell it for a variety of uses to others for $40 to $100 per ton. A projected $1million expense (the cost to haul the waste away) turned into an actual $1 million profit.

- Realistically assess your company's performance against traditional investment criteria. For example, what is your ROA? ROA is determined by the following formula:

$$\text{ROA} = \frac{\text{Pretax earnings}}{\text{Equity} + \text{Long-term financing}}$$

For example, assume your pretax earnings this year (adjusted for extraordinary owner's compensation) are $250,000. Your equity (retained earnings plus capital stock) is $1,000,000 and long-term debt is $300,000. Your ROA is 19 percent.

$$19\% = \frac{\$250,000}{[\$1,000,000 + \$300,000]}$$

Also, determine your ROE, and then benchmark against peer companies. In this case, your ROE would be 25 percent.

$$\text{ROE} = \frac{\text{Pretax earnings of } \$250,000}{\text{Equity of } \$1 \text{ million}}$$

- Define competencies needed to run the company in the future, establish needs for General Manager, President, CEO roles, begin an assessment of internal candidates and management strength.
- Will the family be involved as owners? If so, you may need to create boundaries between the family and the business. See Chapter 6 for policies you may want to consider implementing. What about family employment, or compensation (if active in the company)? Does the family need education about the business, or the industry in which you operate?
- Should you have an appraisal of the business to determine its market value (for sale or for benchmarking purposes)?

- Quantify the risk of continuing to own the business. An appraiser will develop a capitalization rate to use in discounting future cash flows. The capitalization rate reflects the risk factor as determined by the appraiser. For example, a capitalization rate of 15 percent would reflect the appraiser's perception of the comparable return you would need to realize with an alternative investment.

- What do you need to be financially independent of your business? Have your CPA or financial advisor review your investments, retirement assets, and your standard of living to quantify your financial dependence on the business.

- Bring key people into the process. What role will they play in the analysis of keeping the company? Do you need to address communication skills and teamwork with your key group?

- Conduct a compensation review and determine where your key executives stand in comparison to your peers (industry and geographical). Then add a performance based component, if necessary, or equity sharing for key executives.

### Transition Your Perspective to Holding This Business as a Long-Term Investment

- Establish specific goals for the CEO position, then promote yourself and become chairman. Begin the search process to hire, or promote someone to take over the CEO's responsibilities.

- Articulate your values and long-term mission for the business. In other words, if a new CEO came in what are the unchangeable values you want maintained, what are the key reasons you have been successful to date, and what are the two or three most important long-term goals for the company.

- Start thinking strategically. Develop a plan to address the challenges your company will face in the future. Identify the key initiatives for facing those challenges, and form an executive team to prioritize and assign accountabilities. Implement the plan and monitor results.

- If you plan to grow by acquisition, consult with investment bankers and those knowledgeable in your industry, identify potential targets, understand who the other buyers are in your industry, and develop a plan.

- Assess your current board and reorganize if necessary. Create a board book with an outline of your plan for the company. Search for the right board candidates to help you accomplish your plan.

- Implement leadership development plans in the company to begin to grow leadership.

- Address capital needs for the business and decide how you will meet those. One company addressed their capital needs and after realizing their business needed $10 million of new plant and equipment, decided to sell the company rather than put their money at risk.

- Transition from entrepreneur/CEO to chairman. Manage the process of change, lead the growth plan, explore financing for capital needs and growth, and most importantly, begin to let go of the day-to-day responsibilities. Educate family owners, implement succession and modernize estate plans.

## Bring on the Successor—GM, Then President, Then CEO?

- Create a timeframe for implementing needed changes. Involve others in creating the timeline so that you have their emotional buy-in into the process. Then spend your time checking performance against the goals outlined.

- Identify skill sets/competencies that others need to accomplish the goals. Then help key people gain the needed skills, or hire people with the experience that you seek.

- Be clear about the owner's expectations and risk tolerance. Articulate the limits of authority where others can and cannot go.

- Articulate the culture of your company. If management opposes change because "we don't do it that way here" then you may need to do some teambuilding so that you can preserve the important values of the company while emphasizing the need for others to be flexible and adaptable.

- Transfer authority and accountability for results to others and then check their progress.

## Evaluate Results

- If early results appear favorable, you may want to begin transferring stock to the next generation of family members, or to key people. Begin to work on stock transfer strategies—these may involve creating stock option plans for nonfamily members and ownership succession plans for family members.

- Coordinate ownership succession with your estate planning and address family issues to head off any future conflict or confusion about your goals.

- Monitor, monitor, monitor.

# Maximizing Management Strength for Each Model

In Part I, you reaffirmed your decision to keep the business—at least for now. What do you have to do operationally to make that decision work for you and the company? A lot of the literature dumps on the owner-manager. They say you can keep the business, but you can't stay there. That's not necessarily true. Face it: If you're not ready to let go, you shouldn't. And you don't have to. But it would be wise to consider developing the management of the company to ensure its continued success.

A successful business must have three vital pieces that fit together for the whole organization to function well. First: *leadership* must be in place with the ability to carry out its goals, along with a process for future leaders to develop in the business. Second, there should be a *compensation structure* that rewards management for realizing results. And, third, key people who are expected to work as a team should learn how *successful teams* function. This chapter explores these three important components, and discusses them in light of the three ownership models.

## Leadership Transition Issues

There are two time horizons you need to consider concerning leadership of your company: today and tomorrow. What are the immediate leadership improvements you should tackle? And how can you begin to pave the path for future leaders and create a comfortable exit strategy in anticipation of your future retirement? Begin to work on the following immediately.

### *Professionalize Management*

Many companies have enjoyed success because of the entrepreneurial nature of a founder, who took risks, constantly "bet the farm," and ultimately succeeded—often without the structure, systems, or people to manage a growing and complex organization. Today's chief operating officer or general manager spends significant time on human resource issues, systems, technology, and planning—not the areas of expertise of most entrepreneurs. In fact, some management experts suggest the following skill sets will be the most important in the future: strategic thinking, implementing policy, building teams and alliances, and creating a motivating corporate culture. Many entrepreneurs who spend their time *doing* would find these skill sets somewhat foreign—and boring.

Even owner-manager companies whose CEO plans to remain at the helm indefinitely, will need to change from an entrepreneurial style of management to a more focused, more disciplined, and more complex organization. Many of today's entrepreneurs, especially young people launching dot-com companies—sometimes before they are out of college—rely on venture capitalists who are only willing to shell out millions of start-up equity if there is a seasoned management team on board.

So if you are not good at or not interested in tackling the planning and policymaking that your growing, more sophisticated company most likely needs, it is wise to train existing and hire new managers who can do those tasks for you.

### *Establish a Real versus a Rubber-Stamp Board of Directors*

The board's function is often minimized with the owner-manager model—the owner-manager is reluctant to seek advice (or listen when advice is given) from others. The board of the owner-manager company is often comprised of insiders or those who are most likely to rubber-stamp the owner's decisions.

The board of the owner-investor and hybrid company, however, often plays a key role in articulating goals, representing the owner's interests, but then letting management run the day-to-day operations.

---

**EXAMPLE OF TRANSITIONING THE LEADERSHIP ROLE**

The following list outlines how one client wrestling with moving from CEO to chairperson defined her new role—can you guess which ownership model she has chosen? (Answer follows the list.)

- In coordination with CEO, develop clearly articulated visions for operating companies reporting to CEO; establish short- and long-term goals consistent with the vision.

- Lead and encourage the CEO by establishing mutually agreeable short-term and long-term performance goals, monitor progress on a regular basis, attend top team meetings as necessary, meet with CEO regularly to discuss progress. Lead decision-making related to major operating issues in conjunction with CEO.

- Review, analyze, and critique annual business plan from a micro and macro perspective. Coordinate with CFO in developing budgets and capital expenditures to support plan goals. Help build and maintain relationships with banks and other financing sources. Monitor performance against plan goals on a regular basis; review plan modifications as necessary.

- In conjunction with CEO, create and maintain compensation policies that support corporate objectives, establish target quartiles for pay practices, review industry and peer group compensation data, form and maintain compensation committee of the board to review and approve compensation practices, establish bonus goals with CEO.

- Formulate acquisition policies for business growth; coordinate with operating goals, needs, and financing, initiate acquisition activities and related financing consistent with the policy; present information and recommendations to Board, and assist with post-closure merger activities.

---

**EXAMPLE OF TRANSITIONING THE LEADERSHIP ROLE, CONTINUED**

- Develop, implement, and maintain governance policies for family members' ownership of operating companies, including timely and accurate financial reporting, presentations at family meetings as necessary, acting as ombudsman for family shareholders, and providing an interface between family, board, and operating company executives, as needed. Help balance family issues with sound business decision making.

- Create and maintain environmental scans in the industries in which we operate, assist with integrating that information into operating plans, strategy discussions with CEO, acquisition and financing activities, and presentations to the board and Family Council as needed.

- Recruit a Board of Directors for the company with a minimum of three outside, non-related members. Review strategic needs with CEO to develop criteria for board membership. Recruit prospective board members and orient them to corporate goals.

- In cooperation with CEO, interface as necessary with operating executives to provide support and consulting advice, and to assist them with meeting their operating plan targets.

Did you guess correctly that this new chairperson has chosen to become an owner-investor type company?

---

## Recruit

Owner-managers tend to recruit from within, while owner-investors may prefer to recruit new talent from outside the organization. Whether recruitment comes from within or outside the company, owner managers should look for key executives who have both management and leadership skills.

Another common scenario is that the business owner mistakenly chooses a capable manager who can run the business and later learns the manager can manage but cannot lead; he/she cannot rally the staff, inspire others, or take the business to a new level of performance. The explanation may be that the manager was reluctant to take risks with the owner's capital when the real story was that the wrong person was put in charge of the business. This would be a typical story in an owner-manager company. In *Transformational Leader*,[1] the authors describe the skills needed to transform a company as being like the architect who takes an existing structure, perhaps dated and outmoded, and then remodels and renovates it to meet today's needs. Transforming an organization requires new vision and new frames for thinking about strategy, structure, and people. While entrepreneurs can start with a clean slate, successors start with what is already in place. Successors who try to renovate or transform a company may not know the condition of the company's infrastructure. And changes may be complicated by the fact that existing employees are living in the building while it is being remodeled. Owner-investors give permission for the remodeling. Owner-managers say it's okay to repaint, but then often insist on choosing the paint color.

A 1977 *Harvard Business Review* article describes the differences between managers and leaders as follows: "Managers . . . maintain the balance of operations in an organization, relate to others according to their role, are detached, impersonal, seek solutions acceptable as a compromise among conflicting values, and identify totally with the organization. Leaders create new approaches and imagine new areas to explore; they relate to people in more intuitive and empathetic ways, seek risk where opportunity and reward are high, and project ideas into images to excite people."[2]

In other words, management may be more involved with the use of existing resources, prioritization of issues and structure, while leadership primarily involves vision, motivation, and commitment. Yet they are interdependent: leaders need managers' support for implementation; and managers have to trust and be inspired by the leaders' vision.

One CEO who made the decision to keep the company private began working on next generation leadership almost as soon as he took over the CEOs job. "Somebody can always do something better than me," this client confided. "So I saw my objective as finding those people, giving them opportunities, encouraging them, and getting the team to work together." Obviously, this CEO was building an owner-investor type of company.

You may have latent leadership talent within your organization that hasn't been given a chance to evolve. One of your first steps is to define what you need, assess your internal candidates, and then determine if you need new energy or talent from outside your organization.

Mike Zwell, a CEO search consultant was asked what are the major obstacles in recruiting outside CEOs for a private company. As you read this, ask yourself if he is describing an owner-manager style or an owner-investor style. His answer:

> Often these clients are looking for a good general manager who has the following traits:
>
> - a good strategic thinker
> - can build a team
> - a good communicator and can let others know direction
> - can set realistic, but challenging organizational goals
> - can make tough decisions
>
> Where we encounter obstacles in the hiring process it is generally from a reluctance to turn over power and authority to the new CEO. Or, the owner promises to turn over authority, but that doesn't turn out to be the case. Another obstacle often occurs in the selection process. We have one client where the owner had three presidents over 12 years. When we began to look at the selection process, we found that none of it was analytical. All of the presidents were hired on chemistry and there were no criteria to evaluate performance—no accountability. Amazingly, there are often no specific criteria for CEO performance in the private company.
>
> It's not an issue of money. The issue is that the founder knows how to create a company but doesn't know any good models for organizational leadership. Most founders had a good idea and passion, and they often are not good managers. Because of their passion and drive they could grow something.
>
> Generally you need two or three executives to replace the entrepreneur. If the founder is an engineer, you may need an engineer and a CEO to replace him. If the entrepreneur is sales oriented, you may need a sales VP and a CEO. If she had a product development background, you may need a product development person and a senior sales person.

We find equity participation is a matter of course these days—in the form of stock options, stock appreciation rights (SARs), or phantom stock. In terms of total compensation, it generally breaks down as follows: cash compensation may be 70 percent salary and 30 percent performance bonus, but that's not total compensation. On top of cash compensation may be another 5 percent equity in the business over time (e.g., 1 percent a year for five years).

## Build Stronger Teams

Craig J. Cantoni heads Capstone Consulting Group, a strategic planning firm. He advises, "teambuilding is about helping teams get the work of the team done as effectively as possible by improving openness, honesty, and trust. It is not about liking each other. It is not about being touchy-feely. It is about getting the task done. Period."

Although Cantoni acknowledges the importance of communications, coordination, and relationships—the "soft" side—in other words, he believes these are only important in terms of how it affects the "hard" side of the business. "Teambuilding that is disconnected from the real work of the team and the business is a form of therapy or personal development, but it has little to do with team development and running a business. The problem with trying to build effective teams by having managers climb ropes and poles together is that the real work of business teams is not climbing ropes and poles. A football team wins the Super Bowl by learning teamwork on the football field, not by playing basketball. Likewise, the real practice field for a business team is the office or factory, not a ropes course in the mountains of Colorado."

That's why teams are frequently great on the ropes course but lousy in the boardroom. Cantoni describes one executive group that would take an annual ropes course, during which the participants would superficially exhibit mutual respect, trust, and supportive behavior. But hiding beneath the surface were some long-festering interpersonal issues and disagreements about the direction of the business. These unaddressed issues eventually drove the company into the red. The chief financial officer, one of the most fearless people on the ropes course, finally admitted he was terrified of sharing these issues with the

CEO. For this particular team, the ropes course had turned into a form of play-acting, a convenient way of avoiding the real problems affecting team performance.

Says Cantoni: "Strong leaders have the courage to admit fallibility, to be open to feedback, and to get outside help in addressing the tougher issues affecting team performance, especially if the issue is their own behavior. They have the confidence to keep teambuilding at the office where it belongs, and the wisdom to keep pole climbing at the telephone company where it belongs."

Leslie Dashew provided the following example of effective teamwork:

Tom and Jim started a small construction business and did it all: Jim found the land, Tom sold the house, and together they decided what design to build. Tom was the one who understood how to build the house and oversaw that process as well. Over the years, they built a successful business, constructing several hundred houses. They had offers to sell their business, but still enjoyed the process. Their first challenges came as they hired managers to oversee the business of the business—finance, sales, purchasing, etc. There was confusion over authority—who made what decisions—and the managers found themselves zigzagging and wasting huge amounts of time as a result of changing direction from one owner to the other.

The problem became severe enough that they brought in help to see if they could come to an agreement and give one set of directions to the other operating managers. They couldn't, and decided it was time to part company. They considered selling the company and even entertained offers. Jim was becoming more risk averse and wanted to take his "chips off the table." However, Tom still enjoyed "the game" and wanted to stay in. So he bought Jim out.

In the next phase, Tom used outside assistance to build a true leadership team and he empowered the team to operate the business. He elevated one manager to General Manager and he retained the position of President. The team did strategic planning and developed the approach to achieving Tom's vision. They worked with a single direction for the first time. The team worked well for a time, but they hit another snag as they grew to yet the next size. They had doubled in size and grown throughout the region. Control across that span was more difficult and Tom realized he was entering territory he had never been in before. He asked a group of his friends and advisors to serve on a board of advisors. He found they offered him valuable advice.

The success of this organization illustrates the three levels at which teamwork is so essential. At the *ownership level*, at the *operating level*, and at the *board level*. The key elements of successful teamwork include:

- Shared vision and a commitment to the future enhances commitment, focuses energy, and is a compelling vision that is shared by the major stakeholders in the organization.
- Genuine appreciation that the vision requires the input of all key players (what we call interdependence).
- Atmosphere of trust and openness.
- The realization that I have something to contribute, that my contribution will be valued, and that I can develop while in this position.
- Recognizing and accepting differences and allowing them to help the company grow (fostering the creativity and sense of commitment).
- Ability to problem-solve and manage conflict constructively.
- Communication: structure, safety, and skills.

It is important that a team have a clear mission or purpose for being. This creates the focus, and assures that the boundaries of the team are clear. One leadership team defined its purpose as follows:

- Run the company according to our mission statement.
- Assure the continuity of the company.
- Assure full involvement of all key personnel and perspectives in decision making.
- Assure communication across the company.
- Implement the strategic plan and continue to establish the direction of the company.

- Establish company-wide policies and practices, including compensation, etc.

Developing objectives and measures of success should help clarify how the team will accomplish its mission and define some of its major activities. For example, a list for the leadership team might consist of the following:

- Develop strategic objectives for the company.
- Analyze opportunities for company growth and well-being.
- Establish guidelines on new directions in product development.
- Develop strategies for company-wide process improvement systems.
- Make strategic or operational decisions that impact the company as a whole.

It is important to clarify to whom the team is accountable and who defines the boundaries of authority for the team. For example, one client has a top team that meets each Monday; the chairman of the company sits in on the meetings when she is in town. When out of town, the company's president runs the meetings.

Forty years ago, Douglas McGregor wrote a watershed book entitled, *The Human Side of Enterprise*.[3] In this early management book, he described the characteristics of effective teams that are still valid today.

- The "atmosphere" tends to be informal, comfortable, relaxed. There are no obvious tensions. It is a working atmosphere in which people are involved and interested.
- Discussions are focused and pertinent. Everyone participates, but if the discussion gets off the subject, someone will bring it back in short order.
- The task is understood and accepted and the members are committed to its objectives.
- Members listen to each other! Ideas are given a hearing; but discussions do not jump from one unrelated idea to another. People feel safe enough to do creative thinking even if it seems fairly extreme.

- There is disagreement. The group is not afraid of conflict and does not try to keep everything on a plane of sweetness and light. Disagreements are not suppressed. Reasons are examined, and the group seeks to resolve them rather than dominate the dissenter. Also, there is no "tyranny of the minority." Individuals who disagree do not appear to be trying to dominate the group or to express hostility. When disagreements cannot be resolved and action is necessary, it will be taken but may be subject to later reconsideration.

- Most decisions are reached by a kind of consensus in which it is clear that everybody is in general agreement. Individuals who oppose the action do not keep their opposition private and let an apparent consensus mask real disagreement. Formal voting is at a minimum.

- Criticism is frequent, frank, and relatively comfortable. There is little evidence of personal attack, either openly or in a hidden fashion. The criticism is constructive and oriented toward removing an obstacle that faces the group and prevents it from getting the job done.

- No pussyfooting; there are few hidden agendas. Everybody appears to know how everybody feels about any matter under discussion.

- When action is taken, clear assignments are made and accepted.

- The chairperson of the group does not dominate it, nor does the group defer unduly to the chair. Leadership shifts from time to time, depending on the circumstances. Different members, because of knowledge or experience, may act as resources for the group. The members utilize them in this fashion. There is little evidence of power struggles. The issue is not who controls, but how to get the job done.

- The group is self-conscious about its own operations. It may stop to examine how well it is doing or what may be interfering with its operation. Whatever the problem, it gets open discussion until a solution is found.

If a team leader feels that teambuilding is warranted, the leader may want to consider outside help. The following are guidelines provided by Craig Cantoni for selecting a teambuilding consultant. Retain a consultant who

- insists on conducting a diagnosis before facilitating a teambuilding session. A diagnosis consists of interviewing all of the team members to ascertain what issues are getting in the way of team effectiveness.
- believes that events like ropes courses alone will not build a team.
- asks how team issues are affecting the business.
- knows how to conduct a teambuilding session in conjunction with some task facing the team. Typically, the task will be a planning session in which the team has to make tough decisions about business goals and resources.
- trains the team to do its own teambuilding after the initial teambuilding, so the consultant will not be needed on an ongoing basis.

## Mañana (Tomorrow)

For most private companies, leadership is one of the most important qualities for a successor to possess. Yet, many owners are either unable or reluctant to develop leadership skills for others in their business. Then when it is time to explore one's options for succession, surprise! Without experienced leadership in place, the owner is more likely to sell the company. Or, the owner may hang on to the business longer than he/she should, with the rationale that "I'm waiting for leadership to emerge" as if leadership were hiding somewhere in the plant waiting for the right moment to pop out. Here are some of the typical transition issues owners must face, and the implications for different ownership models, where applicable.

### Planning an Exit Strategy

Owner-managers are the last to see that problems in the business might be solved by their thinking and planning to transfer some control and responsibility to others. In other words, they might be the problem. They are used to doing things themselves and don't realize there are energy, knowledge, and skills right in front of them, waiting for their chance to tackle organizational needs and make tough changes necessary for the company to remain competitive. With an owner-investor model, these forces may be created from external demands by owners for higher performance. Some owners would rather sell the business than adapt to these new challenges. While many post-World War II entrepreneurs still have trouble planning their exit strategies, today's Internet entrepreneurs write their exit strategy—to go public or sell to a larger company within a year or so—into their initial business plan.

Having an exit policy for the CEO suggests an ongoing evaluation of the CEOs performance, and by definition includes succession planning. If the job is for a finite period, or not beyond a certain age (e.g., age 70), then three to five years in advance of the CEOs transition or retirement, training for a successor should begin. While most owner/entrepreneurs would not want an outside evaluation of how they are doing as CEO, they generally endorse the evaluation process when someone else is in the CEO position. Therefore, to avoid one of the entrepreneur's traps, try to separate your investor role from your owner-manager role. As an investor in your business, and also as chairperson of your board, you would want the best person leading the company. An exit policy is one way of assuring all shareholders that from time to time new leadership will be brought in to reinvigorate the business. And, having an outside evaluation of the individual's performance, can provide the benchmarking you need to compare your investment to how others are doing.

## Succession Planning

One entrepreneurial trap is to think that the responsibility for choosing the successor is entirely up to the current CEO. That thinking is changing. Today, the company's board often takes on that role with public companies and it should be a task for the board of the private company as well, ranging from interviewing internal candidates for the top spot, to hiring a search firm to compare inside talent against outside possibilities.

The *Harvard Business Review* echoed this responsibility in a 1999 article: "One of the key functions of a board, [according to *HBR*] is to help with the succession planning process. The article identified key tasks in the process: First, the board should identify potential successors early on and review their performance at regular intervals. Second, the board should make succession planning part of an overall management development program for the company. Third, there should be regular and direct contact between the board and the candidates. Fourth, board members should discuss succession planning without the CEO present."[4]

Here are some additional ways the board can be involved. The CEO and the board should review, at least once a year, who would take over in a crisis, reviewing choices as company strategy changes or shifts. The board can help identify a group of potential CEO candidates and then educate them about challenges, business plans, and strategies across the company. Potential CEOs should be encouraged to accept an outside board assignment and get exposure to lenders, vendors, and major customers.

If you don't think your board is up to this task, then maybe it's time you reorganized your board to get the insights you will need to help you in this process.

Meanwhile, the CEO should nurture a succession culture so that promising executives are given jobs intended to broaden their skills.

## Assessing Potential Leadership

Implementing a leadership-development program should also include some method to evaluate its effectiveness. What will success in the program look like? What new skills will successors have and how will they demonstrate their new competencies? Will you use outside consultants, board members, or advisors to measure success? A timeframe and mutually agreeable goals should be established up front for candidates.

Some beginning questions are as follows:

- Are there potential successors in-house? If so, list their strengths and weaknesses.

- Would you be willing to develop a mentoring program? Outline what you would expect from such a program.
- Can your potential candidate(s) motivate others?
- Does the candidate understand the big picture of how the company operates? Does the candidate understand the company's history? And has he/she been through a down cycle in the business?
- How will you determine someone's readiness to assume more responsibility?

> **Try this Experiment**
>
> Assign a project to potential successors. Have them meet as a group to tackle the task. Let them grapple with their own leadership issues (e.g., who assigns jobs within the group, etc.). Set a deadline for project completion. Provide a small budget if necessary for research. Permit the group to use outsiders for help if necessary (including people within the company). Insist that the presentation be a formal one; that is, a written report or PowerPoint® presentation (to you and your board) including financial projections and impact on the company. Ask tough questions. Ask for a recommendation for action. If appropriate, assign implementation responsibility to "the team."

- How would the candidate respond to the three biggest challenges facing your company today?
- How would others in the organization view the candidate?
- How would your top three customers view your candidate?

## Mentoring

Mentoring goes back to the Greek classic of *The Odyssey*—when Odysseus went to fight in the Trojan War, he entrusted his son's upbringing to Mentor. Mentor's job however, was more than raising Odysseus' son; it was to prepare him for the responsibilities he would assume during his life. In the context of succession planning, mentors are senior people in an organization who help mentees develop their skills. The mentor serves as career advisor, friend, counselor, and tutor and grooms the mentee for a leadership position. The mentoring relationship seems to work best when mentor and mentee mutually agree to work together, rather than one being assigned to the other. The mentor provides a sounding board, can challenge assumptions, and encourage original thinking. The mentor is a cheerleader for the success of the mentee, and provides an opportunity for a younger individual to learn from someone who is respected and experienced in the organization. The mentor may be involved in the business, but not as a direct supervisor to the mentee. The mentor should also consider the future needs of the business and identify the knowledge, skills, background and experience needed for the mentee to be successful. In some cases when additional management skills are needed, the mentee may be advised to work on strategic planning, problem solving, teambuilding, or communication skills.

One successor, whose mentor was a senior executive in the company, described his relationship with his mentor: "He would set up opportunities for me to succeed. He put me in charge of a start-up division and asked, 'what can you do with it?' He gave me the power to hire and fire. He said, 'let's see what happens.' He kept giving me slack and encouragement. He was involved and he was approving—he encouraged me every step of the way. I grew the division from $0 to $50 million in sales in the time I had it. I'm sure that had things gone wrong he would have stepped in, but I never had the sense he was overbearing. But I did know he was there if I needed him. He was like the proud parent in the bleachers at the Little League game, beaming as I hit the home run. He was actually more proud of me if I hit the home run, than if he hit it."

Ivan Lansberg suggests larger companies that implement a mentoring program usually have a formal, step-by-step process for developing the managerial and leadership skills of successors. In smaller companies, he notes that the process is less formal, based more on the instincts and intuitive knowledge of the owner. In all cases however, mentoring should be tailored to the individual. "Unlike training," Lansberg notes "it is concerned not just with teaching specific skills, but with giving the mentee a broad, comprehensive view of the whole business and its competitive environment. It focuses on instilling the kind of maturity in managing others and developing a vision for the business that is required of those who will ultimately own and lead the company. It is also the process by which the mentee, if he or she passes all the tests, earns the right to lead."[5]

## Doing Things the Gen X Way

But be prepared for the next generation to do things differently. One successor, with an MBA from a prominent business school, describes key differences in how he runs the business as president, from the previous generation.

> My business school training taught me to get mountains of information, boil it to a core, and then decide, in teams, what to do with it. I crunch through a lot of information; I use the computer to run the business; and technology is my right arm. I've introduced budgets, strategic planning, and prioritization of initiatives. I like to have a plan on paper and chart how we're doing against the plan. Also we now have constructive debates. In the past, if the head of engineering needed money for a new machine, no one questioned it. Now we want to understand the assumptions engineering is using, we want to see all the numbers, hash it out, learn from one another and agree on a solution together. This is a cultural change because the people in engineering feel like we don't trust them. I tell them it isn't a matter of trust; I need to understand your assumptions.
>
> I think my generation has added the dimension of better quantitative analysis and planning to the mix. We also aren't afraid of "constructive debate" so the older generation has had to get used to not always having 100 percent consensus in decisions. We tend to be a little less trusting and loyal to existing vendor relationships, perhaps because we've seen how some of the vendors have taken advantage of our "nice guy" image in a few cases. I'm all for loyalty as long as the vendor remains competitive and service-oriented, but if a company has a truly better mousetrap, I'm not afraid to switch. We've formalized the performance review processes and salary and wage structure to better maintain consistency and fairness. We're a little less obsessed with the confidentiality of wages and benefits now that the structure is consistent and explainable. We're also more marketing and technology-oriented. There are many ways in which we are similar and have maintained the culture—our respect for all

people, our giving back to the community and to our employees, and our priority on maintaining the highest integrity.

Workplace values are also changing.[6] The values ranked highest in 1968, and again in 1981 were:

- honesty
- ambition
- responsibility
- forgiveness
- broadmindedness
- courage

By the mid-90s, the most important core values had changed to:

- integrity, fairness
- competence, ability
- teamwork
- communication
- personal growth
- creativity, challenge
- freedom, autonomy

One client reiterated these changing workplace values with the following comment: "Gary introduced team based management principles to the company when he joined the company in 1993. This enables the factory workers to work in teams with less supervision and more autonomy. It's had a certain measure of success, and it has definitely fostered improved communication both up and down the hierarchy."

Future leaders will need to understand, respect, and buy into the vision of the founder to maintain the corporate culture and keep it alive. If there is no vision, no "big idea," then two of the leader's tasks will be (1) to articulate a vision for the future that also respects the company's history, and (2) mobilize commitment from key people to accomplish the goals. One of the challenges will be to create consensus from diverse groups, including stockholders who may not be actively involved in the business. Therefore, communication skills and understanding how to bring groups with different interests together for a common goal, will be an important skill for next generation leaders to master.

Owner-managers will want to develop leadership from within. The key elements will be the following:

- Be clear about your expectations.
- Develop a thorough job description including reporting responsibilities, measurable and attainable goals, and financial rewards for achieving results.
- Establish boundaries and limits of authority so you don't second-guess, undermine, or sabotage results.

### Preserving Entrepreneurial Flair

One hurdle for next-generation owners, of brick and mortar or brick and click companies, will be to preserve the entrepreneurial flair while modifying the existing bureaucracy into a more streamlined organization. Streamlined doesn't necessarily mean fewer people; it means more efficient thinking and planning, improved communication and collaboration. Inherent in the transition from entrepreneur-style to new leadership is potential conflict. The entrepreneur's role is to change direction, and bring new opportunities into the company.

For the founder, every problem is an opportunity. For the professional manager, every opportunity may feel like a problem. Today's successful leaders will have to find balance between entrepreneurial and professional management styles.

### Letting Go

In privately-held, owner-manager companies, CEOs often don't step down, even when they are "long in the tooth" and well past their prime. While CEO tenure at public companies is generally five years or less,[7] tenure at privately-held companies averages 21 years according to a 1995 Arthur Andersen survey of family businesses. With public companies, shortened tenure is the result of institutional shareholders setting tough performance standards for corporate bosses. One of the advantages of being both owner and manager is that no one can force you to step down as CEO.

The paradox is that the owner-manager who cannot let go, and wants to keep the company, is often the one who has to sell out because the management breadth and strength is never developed to carry on the business. Ironically, the owner-manager who lets go is often the one who gets to keep the business.

Many entrepreneurs are their own worst enemy in developing qualified successors. Many entrepreneurs are unwilling to listen to advice, are reluctant to collaborate with others, and are unwilling to recognize their own weaknesses. Yet, as Gibb Dyer notes in *Cultural Change in Family Firms*,[8] one of the keys to maintaining control of the business is to foster a more participative culture based on trust and then delegate authority, often to nonfamily executives. Dyer studied charismatic founder-entrepreneurs. Their positive traits are well known—building a successful business requires extraordinary talent. But there is a dark side that comes into play when succession is being considered: entrepreneurs distrust authority figures, are secretive, controlling, reluctant to delegate to others, and are often seen by others as larger than life.

For most entrepreneurs, the letting go problem will be the biggest obstacle to successfully grooming future successors and turning authority over to them. One client, son of a visionary entrepreneur, successfully expanded the company from $10 million to $500 million in sales and said the hardest problem he experienced was his dad letting go of the business. "Dad was an engineer, very controlling, and second-guessed most decisions. For the business to survive and grow, we had to turn over management, which meant Dad had to get out of the way. He had to have something to do—he was great at creating, starting, and building, so when he began working at building an historical village as a living museum, he put all of his attention on that and finally was able to let go of the company. Thankfully we had the money to allow Dad to build the living history museum the way he wanted."

Another client wanted his son and son-in-law to take over his large and successful electrical contracting company. He transferred his ownership to them, but not any authority. Two years later, he admitted he was having difficulty with the transition. Meanwhile the son and son-in-law were frustrated with their inability to implement needed changes in the company. Finally the client let them buy the rolling stock they needed, change the company's bonus structure, and reorganize the accounting and contracts departments. When the company didn't collapse, as the client feared, he realized that the two new owners were ready to run the whole show.

New styles of leadership evolving in private companies support teamwork and partnering, collaboration, a flattening of the organization, shared accountabilities, greater empowerment, and most importantly, an understanding of change. Consider this comment from one consolidator (after 20 acquisitions) when describing some of his deals: "A 'good' acquisition occurs when the family/seller has already entrusted power to others. Too often, the owner has acted as a patriarch with no one else having accountability. Everyone runs to the owner for all decisions. When we purchase a company, we introduce a high level of accountability, if it doesn't already exist. We want the employees to figure things out for themselves, to learn how to think and how to plan. Owners who haven't figured out how to let others take on some of the business responsibilities are more likely to be sellers. That's one of the things we look for."

The challenge you face is whether you, the owner-manager, have the energy and commitment to help future managers and leaders act in teams, learn to partner and collaborate, be accountable and empowered. If you don't have the energy and commitment to manage this process, maybe this is an indication that you should transition to an owner-investor business and find a CEO whose specific job it is to lead this process.

## Firing Yourself

But once a business begins to transition to an owner-investor or hybrid model, it may make sense for the CEO to resign as CEO, create an office of the Chairman and then move into the Chairman's role. Hire a new CEO, establish clear goals, penalize non-performance, and have an exit policy ready for him or her.

Some believe the ideal tenure for a CEO is ten years; after that time they begin to get stale. New CEOs may have implemented a successful strategy when they were first hired that fits their style and background.

Over time they may get fixated with whatever made them successful. Then they become resistant to change any part of the formula. Some signs that your CEO may be getting a little moldy are

- the CEO doesn't change the company's product portfolio, customer base, or key personnel.
- the CEO becomes remote from organizational affairs.
- the organization starts accumulating excess cash as executives run out of ideas for spending money.

If any of these seem familiar to you, then maybe it's time for someone else to try the CEOs job. If you can successfully bring in a new CEO, you might decide the company is worth keeping for the long term.

### Family Member as Successor—Mistakes to Avoid

Sometimes a family member can be groomed for the CEOs role, or can be recruited to join the business. There is additional complexity when working with family members due to family dynamics. Conflict in businesses that have tried to address succession with family members is well known. Indeed, one popular statistic is that 70 percent of first generation businesses do not survive into a second generation. On the other hand, business owners who can successfully develop a family CEO or COO have accomplished what most others cannot: perpetuating a private company and creating a legacy for family members.

Some of the mistakes start with how family members (and which ones) are recruited to work in the business. Some entrepreneurs have made the following mistakes when involving family members in the business.

**Mistake 1.** Having an open-door policy for all family members who want to work in the company (i.e., any family member who wants to work in the company can do so).

*Try this*: Implement a Family Employment Policy so if family members are qualified (by education and work experience) they can join the business, but only if a position is open. A sample Family Employment Policy is included in the Keep Appendix.

**Mistake 2.** Paying family members the same salary/bonus regardless of position or experience. Equal treatment works in families but usually causes conflict in businesses. Or, business resources are used to support family needs, generally by hiring and overpaying children, or paying them what they need to live a comfortable lifestyle.

*Try this*: Establish a compensation policy for the job and pay what the job is worth, not what family members need. If in doubt, hire a compensation consultant to help you determine a pay range for the job in question. Provide perks and other benefits relative to the job. Reexamine your benefits program if necessary. Consider a performance-based pay plan.

**Mistake 3.** Leadership is bestowed by the founder; the eldest son may be anointed as crown prince, regardless of skill, leading to family conflict among siblings. Or, longevity in the business is seen as more relevant for a potential successor, more so than outside experience and/or qualifications for the job.

*Try this*: Implement a leadership-development program in the company both for family and nonfamily members. Take advantage of leadership-training programs offered by local universities/colleges or your trade association. Set up a mentoring program. Establish expectations for performance in the program. Ask your board to assess the candidates and recommend the best person for the CEOs job.

On the other hand, both owner-manager and owner-investor companies have successfully recruited family members. Characteristics of their treatment of family members in the business are as follows:

- Compensation for family members is based on market rates, responsibility, and performance
- No nepotism—leadership is earned
- Business resources are used strategically for the company—no unusual family perks
- Outside experience is important for family members who want to join the company
- There are clear boundaries between the entrepreneur's family and its business interests

- There are strong outside influences on the board

### Try Co-Leadership

Some companies are adapting a *co-leadership* structure whereby power doesn't reside in a single individual or corner office. In *Co-Leaders*, David Heenan and Warren Bennis argue that "in a world of increasing interdependence and ceaseless technological change, even the greatest of Great Men or Women simply cannot get the job done alone . . . . We need to rethink our most basic concepts of leadership."[9]

With co-leaders, power is dispersed, creating what Heenan and Bennis call "a constellation of co-stars—co-leaders with shared values and aspirations, all of whom work together toward common goals."[10] Would you think this is an owner-manager or owner-investor characteristic?

The Arthur Andersen/Mass Mutual 1997 American Family Business Survey indicated that 12 percent of the respondents already have co-CEOs while 42 percent indicated that co-CEOs were a strong possibility in the future.

Is this something you should consider? One client described important conditions in his company's experiment with co-leadership: "It's critical that we are all focused on the same goals and we have mutual respect for one another. Our styles are different, but we don't compete with one another. We have different roles in the business and we don't overlap; we each have our own responsibilities and authority. There is enough room in the business for us to try this out. What's important is that the company's best interest is always at the heart of our decisions. Our fights are competition and global imports, not one another."

## Compensation Challenges

Too often, entrepreneurs view their employees and executives as expenses rather than as investments. As a result, typical compensation philosophies are to pay executives in the 50 to 75 percent quartile for the industry to which their company belongs. Owners who have decided to keep the business should consider an important question:

"What kind of pay is needed to attract the best and brightest talent and keep them motivated to be productive and creative, in order to make this company perform as a great investment?"

The issue of executive pay becomes more pronounced as the company develops from start-up to fast-growth and then finally to maturity. While the core group of founding management may have handled business operations in the past, the company may now need to hire additional seasoned executives to accommodate its growth, and expansion, and take it to the next level. This pits the company against other successful companies—both public and private—in competition for valuable resources.

Some companies may compete with public companies by paying a relatively high base salary with lower incentive opportunities, while others leverage more compensation to the incentives, enabling compensation to exceed market if performance warrants. One of the disadvantages of paying a high base salary is the use of cash, versus the incentive program, which gives the company the flexibility of deferring that portion of compensation and using equity instead of cash.

One of the difficulties private companies often have is in creating long-term incentives as part of an overall pay plan. Private companies typically do not use stock options or restricted stock as public companies do, because the market value of stock in the privately-held business cannot be readily determined. Therefore, private companies overwhelmingly tend to rely on performance unit plans, phantom stock, and stock appreciation rights instead of stock option plans. While these incentives are comparable to public company pay programs, they have their own drawbacks, ranging from problems with determining the value of the stock to the entrepreneur's reluctance to share ownership in his or her private business.

There have been a number of studies that provide insight into how incentives are handled in private companies compared with public enterprise. A 1997 KPMG Peat Marwick study indicated that in the area of short-term (annual) incentive targets, private and public companies set comparable targets for their executives. For example, both tend to set the CEO incentive target at 60 to 70 percent of base salary and the CFO target at 50 to 55 percent of base. However, compared with public companies, private companies set substantially lower long-term incentives for their senior officers than public companies do. In 1998, M Financial Group and Arthur Andersen reported that public company CEOs are paid 30 percent more total cash compensation than CEOs working in private companies. Base salaries in private companies were 76 percent of what CEOs in similarly sized public companies receive, and incentive payments for the private company CEO were 63 percent of their public company counterpart.[11]

Furthermore, eligibility for long-term incentives is more restricted in private companies. And private companies do not take their long-term incentive plans as deep into the organization—to lower levels of management and rank-and-file employees—as do public companies.

The challenge that entrepreneurs face in using incentive plans is how to turn their executives into emotionally vested stockholders without actually issuing stock. Thought has to be given to determining the stock value and the changes in value over time. For example, stock valuation for compensation purposes may conflict with a business valuation appraisal prepared for estate-planning purposes. When valuing the company for compensation, owners are motivated to show the highest possible value for the stock; for estate planning owners may wish to report the lowest possible value for the stock.

Also, in a private company, since there is no market for the stock, the company must eventually cash out executive stockholders, which may create a substantial cash flow requirement. Some companies have elected to fund this future liability informally—others believe in a "pay as you go" scenario and will fund benefits for executives out of future profits.

## Developing a Market Philosophy

Search a few proxy statements of high-performing public companies and read the statement of philosophy section dealing with executive compensation. The Security and Exchange Commission (SEC) requires companies to include such a statement, although companies are given a good deal of latitude as to how specific they wish to be. A number of companies do, in fact, wish to be fairly specific. One highly successful Silicon Valley company informs its readers that the CEO base salary is set at the 25th lowest percentile of their industry group. And it is not uncommon for companies to mention the composition of the industry group to which they are comparing themselves. Private companies, of course, aren't faced with this requirement, but the exercise of defining your market in this way and deciding where you want to be in that market is the beginning of an orderly approach to compensation decisions.

You can find examples of the statement of philosophy and details of executive compensation online for public companies at <www.freeedgar.com>. The example statement of philosophy is one for an electronics company based in California.

Unless your private company is large and well established, you probably should not depend solely on the compensation levels of public companies when establishing pay in your firm. You should also look elsewhere for comparative data, including using a compensation

---

**EXAMPLE OF A COMPENSATION PHILOSOPHY**

### Compensation Philosophy
### Bell Industries, Inc.
### El Segundo, California

The company's compensation philosophy is based upon the belief that the company's success is the result of the coordinated efforts of all employees working towards common objectives. Its executive officer compensation program is composed of base salary, annual incentive cash bonuses, and long-term incentive compensation in the form of stock options. The committee attempts to set the base salary levels competitively with those paid by others in the electronics and industrial distribution companies comprising its Peer Group. Based upon its most recent survey (December 1996), the committee believes that the compensation levels paid to company executives are in the mid-range of compensation paid by its Peer Group. In determining salaries, the committee also takes into account individual experience and performance, past salary history, and specific issues particular to the company.

consultant to conduct a salary survey. If you are fortunate and belong to a progressive trade association, it may be your best source of <u>data</u>. Most trade associations at some point survey their members about compensation. The quality of those surveys varies considerably, however.

Alternatively, you may wish to commission a custom survey. You can determine who will be invited to participate and what the content will be. Since confidentiality is an important factor, you will need a third-party consultant to assist with the design, collection, and analysis of the data. Don't overlook the fact that your participants will expect to receive a copy of the results. After all, they didn't take the time to complete the survey input for their health.

If there is sufficient interest and you and the other participants find the results to be of value, you might get everyone interested in keeping it going in future years with everyone sharing in the cost.

We'll assume that now you have measured the marketplace and have a pretty good handle on your competitive position. The next decision is to decide where you wish to be. That may vary for different forms of compensation. You will find some good ideas from those proxy statements. As mentioned above, one prominent high-tech company sets the base salary of its CEO at the first quartile of comparable companies. That means 75 percent of the CEOs have a *base* salary equal to or higher than the high-tech's CEO. That is the company policy. The proxy goes on to say that where performance warrants, it wants its CEO to receive total cash compensation at the third quartile. Now the CEO is paid higher than 75 percent of CEOs in the sample. Long-term incentives can bring total compensation to a higher level.

You are then ready to take the next step. It is extremely useful to select key employees and ask them what they think about existing compensation. What's good? What would they change? Would they have an interest in purchasing company stock if the opportunity to buy was made available? Remember to consider their circumstances. It may not be feasible for a $10 million dollar company that has four key people now reporting to the owner to make an investment. Those four people might be paid $40,000 or $50,000 and have growing families with little in the way of disposal income. These are some of the things that you can learn in these interviews. In addition to good information, you are also getting some employee relations points and maybe their buy-in to the resulting program. If you use a compensation consultant, he or she needs to emphasize that the conversations will be kept confidential and that the owners will only learn in summary form how the interviewees feel about their pay.

Compensation professionals typically examine base salary, bonus, and long-term incentives received in the last fiscal year. Developing your compensation plan, or using a compensation professional, you will generally establish a market range for top executives. This range will represent base salaries, bonus, and long-term incentives. If it is below the target market range, then the executive may be under-compensated. Similarly, the executive may be over-compensated or unreasonably compensated if compensation is above the market range. The pivotal element in the reasonableness equation will be the long-term incentive.

Using the salary structure, decide what the relationship between base and bonus should be. Establish targets for each position. Break down the targets in terms of the types of incentive plans you envision. The idea behind multiple plans is that employees will focus their efforts and attention on different measures of business success. Many companies will base the payouts strictly on financial success but some will use both financial results and individual goals that may not be quantifiable.

Plans are often based on three-, four-, or five-year rolling periods. Once the first period is completed there is the potential for a payment each year. If the annual plan rewards employees for increasing sales, as an example, the multi-year plan might reward them for return on assets, capital, or equity.

## Long-Term Incentive Plans

Long-term incentive plans provide executives the opportunity to build their own net worth when a private company's long-term objectives are met or when the company's stock increases in value. By providing executives either ownership opportunities or opportunities to increase their income as the value of the company increases, there is motivation to reach the long-term goals of the company. In addition, the goals of the shareholders and executives are aligned.

Thirty seven percent of the 210 respondents included in the 1998 Private Company Compensation report produced by M Financial Group provided a long-term incentive plan. Eligibility, for the most part, was confined to senior executives (51 percent) and executive/middle management levels (32 percent). Forty-one percent reported limiting their long-term incentive plans to nonfamily employees and 3 percent to family employees. As can be seen in the Figure 6.1, participants prefer using stock-based long-term incentive plans (83 percent) to cash-based plans (33 percent). Over half of the companies with stock-based plans reported using actual shares.

Stock-based plans are often more prevalent in C corporations than in S corporations. This is not surprising, as an S corporation must limit and monitor the number of shareholders participating in a plan (up to 75) and must avoid creating a second class of stock or risk losing S corporation status.

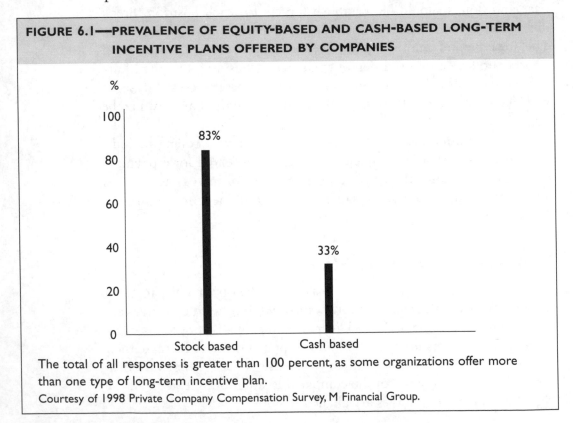

**FIGURE 6.1—PREVALENCE OF EQUITY-BASED AND CASH-BASED LONG-TERM INCENTIVE PLANS OFFERED BY COMPANIES**

The total of all responses is greater than 100 percent, as some organizations offer more than one type of long-term incentive plan.

Courtesy of 1998 Private Company Compensation Survey, M Financial Group.

Stock option plans are the most prevalent type of long-term incentive plans used, followed by performance-based cash plans, based on the Private Company Compensation Survey. One of the variables in granting long-term incentives is whether to grant the incentives each year (i.e., more options at each year's current value), or to grant the incentive as a one-time lump sum. Another choice in plan design revolves around vesting the participant in the benefit (e.g., over time, all at once, or at a specified age).

## Stock Options

A stock option plan gives an executive the opportunity to purchase a fixed number of shares, at a fixed price, over a specified period, after a vesting schedule is met. For example, assume an executive is given an option to purchase 1,000 shares at their current value of $1 per share. The option can be exercised anytime within the next five years. If the stock grows in value by the fifth year, say to $5 per share, the executive could purchase the 1,000 shares for $1,000 even though the shares were worth $5,000 at the time the option was exercised. Assume the executive purchases the 1,000 shares (for $1,000) at the end of five years, and then holds the 1,000 shares until retirement. He or she could sell the 1,000 shares back to the company at retirement (or termination) under a prearranged buyback plan. The executive will be paid the value of the shares at the time they are sold, and pay capital gains tax on the difference between the amount paid for the stock and the amount received.

The most common form of stock options are nonqualified, as shown in Figure 6.2. This means the gains are taxed as ordinary income. Incentive stock options have tax advantages, but numerous conditions must be met in order to realize those advantages. You can find lots of information about stock options at

The National Center for Employee Ownership
1736 Franklin St., 8th Floor
Oakland, CA 94612
510-272-9461; Fax 510-272-9510
Web site: <www.nceo.org>

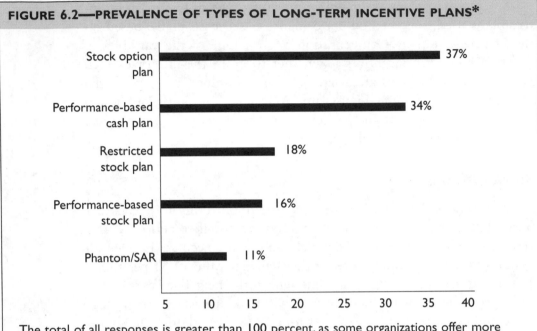

**FIGURE 6.2—PREVALENCE OF TYPES OF LONG-TERM INCENTIVE PLANS***

The total of all responses is greater than 100 percent, as some organizations offer more than one type of long-term incentive plan.

*Reported by companies that provide long-term incentive plans (37 percent).

Courtesy of 1998 Private Company Compensation Survey, M Financial Group.

Employee Benefit Research Institute
2121 K Street, NW, Suite 600
Washington, DC 20037-1896
202-659-0670; Fax 202-775-6312
Web site: <www.ebri.org>

### *Restricted Stock*

Stock granted to employees in a restricted plan is subject to forfeiture unless certain conditions (i.e., restrictions) are met. Conditions typically require the executive to complete a period of employment, say five years, or they can be based on the performance of the company. Once the restrictions lapse, the shares become fully available to the executive. Only 18 percent of companies surveyed in the Private Company Compensation Survey had a restricted stock plan.

## Performance-Based Cash/Stock Plans

Performance-based plans are often called performance unit plans. Executives earn performance units based on reaching performance goals over a specific period of time. The rewards are calculated by the number of units earned times a predetermined fixed value and may be paid in cash or stock. The sole difference between performance-based stock plans and performance-based cash plans is that the awards are paid in either stock or cash. Awards paid in stock are typically subject to a buyback arrangement at the executive's retirement or termination. Typical performance measures used in performance-based plans are outlined in Figure 6.3.

When establishing objectives for performance-based stock and cash plans, some companies use internal criteria such as measuring

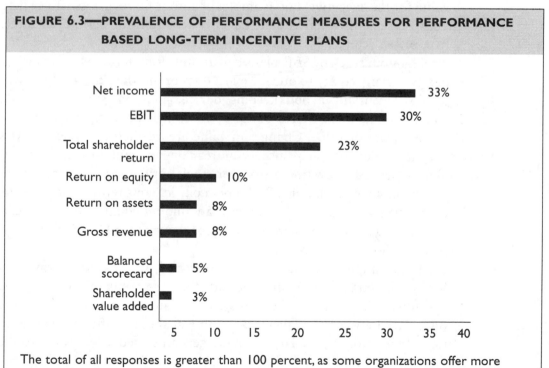

**FIGURE 6.3—PREVALENCE OF PERFORMANCE MEASURES FOR PERFORMANCE BASED LONG-TERM INCENTIVE PLANS**

Net income — 33%
EBIT — 30%
Total shareholder return — 23%
Return on equity — 10%
Return on assets — 8%
Gross revenue — 8%
Balanced scorecard — 5%
Shareholder value added — 3%

The total of all responses is greater than 100 percent, as some organizations offer more than one type of long-term incentive plan.
Courtesy of 1998 Private Company Compensation Survey, M Financial Group.

performance against a budget or plan, others use performance against a peer group or industry data. Some companies use performance against the previous year, or against a publicly-traded competitor. The most frequently used performance measures from the Private Company Compensation survey were Net Income and Earnings Before Interest Expense and Income Taxes (EBIT).

## Phantom or Shared Appreciation Rights (SAR) Plans

Phantom stock and SAR plans are both a form of simulated equity. That means that actual shares are *not* transferred as occurs with Stock Option and Restricted Stock plans. What the executive receives as a benefit is based on a change in the *value* of the stock without actually owning the stock. The main difference between Phantom stock and the SAR plan is based on the period that is used to calculate the change in value for the executive. For example, phantom shares are generally held until retirement, whereas SAR benefits are often for periods of three, five, or ten years.

Phantom stock or SAR plans can address long-term incentives without giving any equity to outside executives or diluting the family's ownership. Essentially a bookkeeping device, phantom stock and SARs consists of fictional shares or rights to which the company assigns a current price or value. Changes in value are credited to the executive's account reflecting their success at reaching certain financial benchmarks. Instead of awarding stock or stock options, the company credits the employee with units. When plan participants retire or their rights in the plan vest, they receive in cash an amount equal to the appreciation in value of the company's stock plus any dividends or distributions paid on those phantom units.

For example, if a unit of phantom stock is worth $30 at grant and $80 at the end of the vesting period, then the company will pay the executive $50 per unit. The executive pays income taxes on $50—the difference between the fair market value at the time the unit is cashed in and the initial price. The company gets a tax deduction equal to the amount paid to the executive.

Phantom stock and SAR plans have certain advantages over traditional stock plans. Companies are able to permit key employees to participate directly in the increased value of the company stock without giving away voting rights. Executives share in the upside potential of the company's value, but the ownership percentage of stockholders is not diluted. When the stock has been valued for estate planning purposes (generally at a lower amount) then phantom stock may be ideal, since a different measure for valuing the contribution of executives may be used that does not conflict with an estate planning valuation of the stock of the company.

A disadvantage of phantom stock is that it can result in a charge against earnings because its ultimate value depends on stock performance. In addition, companies sometimes find it difficult to appropriately value company stock—should they use book value, fair market value, or formula value?

## Other Issues in Compensation

One-fourth of the companies in the Private Company Compensation Survey reported they were thinking about implementing a long-term incentive plan or implementing an additional plan in the future. Performance-based plans are the most prevalent type of long-term incentives companies anticipate adding. For those companies, which did not offer a long-term incentive plan, the primary reason given was that they did not want to grant ownership interest in the company to nonfamily members. Whether you are leaning to the owner-manager or owner-investor model, having some type of performance-based plan may be critical to keeping the kinds of qualified individuals your company needs.

While 41 percent of the companies that did not have long-term incentives stated they did not perceive any significant consequences for not providing a plan, 70 percent believed that executives lacked the focus needed on long-term company performance without a plan. Nearly one-half of the companies also believed they had difficulty retaining, recruiting, and motivating executives without a plan.

## Summary

We are in the middle of one of the tightest labor markets in history. A *Forbes* cover story in April 2000, featured "The $100 million CEO." The article highlighted an important fact for business owners: Internet and e-commerce companies are attracting the best and the brightest with salaries that most private companies cannot afford to match. Furthermore, a large percentage of total compensation is now paid in stock options or ownership of the company that the CEO is being recruited to run. If that shocks you, consider this from *Forbes*: in 1965 a CEO of a public company received 80 percent of compensation in salary and bonus, another 20 percent in long-term incentives such as stock options. By 1999, CEOs were receiving only 30 percent of total pay in salary and bonus, and 70 percent in stock options or other incentives![12]

Stock options are also moving down in the organization—a 1997 Mercer study revealed that 30 percent of the largest U.S. companies have stock option plans for more than half of their employees.[13] Implications for the closely-held business owner are (1) you better start grooming from within because hiring from outside is very expensive, and (2) be prepared to offer equity or equity-type incentives as part of the pay plan.

The point is, if you want your management team to think like shareholders, make them shareholders!

# Transition Turbulence and Traps to Avoid

S o far, you have navigated the process of deciding whether to keep or sell the business. Those of you who have decided to keep the business have explored three models of ownership, and then considered the ramifications of those decisions on your company's structure and management. We have presented a lot of information and ideas for you to try. So how do you get from here (tough decisions) to there (implementation)?

Under the best of circumstances, transitions tend to be difficult. There may be significant differences between your current management style and a new style the business may need for the future. It's one thing for entrepreneurs to say, and believe, they embrace change. It is often quite difficult to actually live with change. You may get off to a galloping start, and then suddenly change your mind. It will be easy to second-guess, and find fault with how others are doing things if you lose sight of what you are trying to accomplish. Knowing where the typical traps lie will be helpful so that you can plan ahead and figure out alternatives if things don't turn out the way you expected.

Dennis Jaffe, a well-known organizational consultant, describes the roller coaster of change as having two components: an emotional and an action component. The emotional component is your personal response as you struggle to deal with new realities. The action component involves moving into relationships and ways of doing things that are different. Jaffe notes that individuals, teams, and organizations go through predictable phases of denial and resistance before they can explore new ways and recommit. Managing change means navigating through these phases, not wishing they didn't exist.[1]

Jaffe suggests that before you begin the transition, you ask yourself three questions:

1. Why do we need to change?
2. What if we don't change?
3. What's in it for me?

## Common Transition Traps

There are numerous pitfalls when transitioning your company. The following are some of the most common ones. Be aware that you may experience more than one of these traps while the structure of your company changes.

### Profit versus Other Priorities Trap

For first-generation owners, profit may not be the primary measure of performance. That's especially true for today's new breed of Internet entrepreneurs, who spent the late 1990s and early 2000 plowing billions of dollars of venture capital, public-company equity, and even revenues into their companies without turning a dime of profit. Eventually, professional managers and MBA-types who have been trained to seek profit as an explicit goal come charging in. In one survey, while most business owners indicated net profit growth as an important indicator of financial performance, there were other priorities they also relied upon, most notably the ability to fund growth from operating profits and sales volume growth.[2] Getting clear about future expectations will help avoid conflict between current owners and top managers, and will create a focus that current owners and the next generation can both support.

| C O N S I D E R | What are the performance measures that top managers and future leaders may want to use that are different from what you have relied upon? What information will be needed to track those measures? |
|---|---|

## Debt Aversion Trap

A typical trap entrepreneurs fall into is the avoidance of leverage as they age and their companies mature. Early-stage entrepreneurs generally have difficulty obtaining bank financing for their new business venture, although today's high-tech company founders are awash in angel and venture funding. Traditional lenders were often leery of the risks. As the wild-eyed entrepreneur ages, two things happen: cash in the company accumulates (or it may accumulate in the entrepreneur's pocket instead), and the rate of growth slows as debt is paid down or paid off. Most family businesses are under-leveraged: 34 percent of family businesses report NO debt other than trade payables and another 34 percent have debt levels below 25 percent of their equity.

Having a moderate amount of medium-term (five-to-seven years) or long-term debt can be helpful in growing the business. Too often, long-term debt is used only to finance real estate acquisition (or construction) or shareholder repurchases. Once those debts are paid off, the entrepreneur helps the company grow with the company's own earnings stream. Growth is limited by what the prior year's profit will support. How much debt should you have? Your Certified Public Accountant (CPA) can help you determine an optimal amount of leverage for you and can develop the necessary cash flow projections for your bank to review.

David Packard once explained how Hewlett-Packard Co. maintained an affordable growth rate in its early days without using outside capital. The company increased its sales 12-fold from 1950 to 1957, which was a 43 percent annual growth rate. They used a financial formula called an *affordable growth rate (AGR)* to manage growth.

The AGR is based on two assumptions. The first is that your company's sales can grow only as fast as your assets. For example, sales can grow 25 percent only if receivables, inventories, and fixed assets increase by 25 percent as well. The second assumption is that your firm has a target debt-to-equity ratio and that your lenders are willing to continue to extend credit at that ratio. In other words, as your equity grows, your debt will grow at the same rate, allowing you to maintain a constant debt-to-equity ratio. The growth rate of sales (your AGR) will therefore depend on the growth rate of your equity.

AGR = Profit retention rate x ROE

Here is an example. Assume your company pays out 10 percent of earnings (after-tax) as a dividend to shareholders. The profit retention ratio (PRR) is therefore 90 percent. If your firm keeps 90 percent of its after-tax earnings, and your business maintains a return on equity of 25 percent, your affordable growth rate is equal to 90 percent times 25 percent or an AGR of 22.5 percent. That means that if you maintain a growth rate of about 22 percent, your financial growth will stay in balance with debt-equity ratios. A faster growth rate would cause the debt-equity ratio to increase and a slower growth rate would reduce the debt ratio.

You may have mixed feelings about financing the growth of the company. As an owner you may be tired of funding growth totally out of earnings. And, you may not want to fund your growth needs from

**C O N S I D E R**

Talk with your CPA and your CFO about the level of debt the company could afford to support growth initiatives and decide on a policy for managing debt—instead of one-shot loans. Talk with your bank to discuss a relationship for long-term financing. If your bank wants personal guarantees, talk to another bank. As the company's equity grows, the bank's comfort level of lending without personal guarantees will also grow.

equity investors who would want to have a say in decision making. Therefore, financing growth with debt may be the best solution, but you are wary about friendly bankers today who could be just as unfriendly tomorrow. The approach described may give you a way to add a measure of debt that never gets ahead of the equity of the company.

## Organizational Structure Trap

Entrepreneurs typically approach organizational structure in an informal way. Planning is often ad-hoc: grab the right people when you need them, have a short meeting, then go do what needs to get done. Next generation leadership may want a more formal organizational structure and may rely more on planning as a process to test ideas, challenge assumptions, and collaborate. Today's younger managers are usually more experienced at working in teams, going back to their high school days when assignments were given to small groups to teach collaboration. Young managers are more likely to be comfortable with process. Entrepreneurs are typically less patient and more autocratic.

A patriarchal culture, common in entrepreneurial companies, often hands out jobs, but not accountabilities, with an informal structure and overlapping and undefined responsibilities. Next generation managers often prefer more formal structures, clear job descriptions, accountabilities, and lots of information made available from which they can analyze decisions. One investment banker who structures transactions for private companies indicated that the inability for the entrepreneur to hold others accountable was one of the major obstacles in assimilating

**CONSIDER**

Try this: Ask your top executives to come up with an organizational structure that would work for them and then compare it with the reporting relationships you have currently. If everyone likes the reporting relationships then there may not need to be any changes. But there may be more efficient ways to push decision making and accountabilities to others, freeing up time for the CEO to focus on strategy issues.

employees after a deal closes. So, if you decide to keep the business, holding others accountable (with penalties for nonperformance) may be a step towards retaining the business as an investment. If you decide to sell, having accountability in your organization can improve the chances of the sale being a successful one.

## Management Development Trap

Entrepreneurs approach development in an ad-hoc style using on-the-job training. Next-generation managers may do their job well, but often are not privy to strategy or other information to help them understand the big picture (i.e., how the whole company operates). Rarely is there a specific path for younger managers to follow to build broad business knowledge. One of the common complaints from both entrepreneurs and next-generation managers is the lack of understanding of the business as a whole. Younger executives want information, authority, and a career path to improve themselves and the company. Entrepreneurs should send them to leadership-development programs offered by training institutes, universities, or their trade association. Then, give them looser reins and support them.

> **CONSIDER**
>
> How much money have you budgeted or do you spend annually on management development? If you haven't focused specifically on developing leadership skills in your management group, consider making that a top priority.

## Commitment Trap

One concern voiced by many entrepreneurs is a lack of commitment on the part of the next generation. It is dangerous, the entrepreneur argues, to turn over substantial authority and responsibility, much less turn the business over, to people whose commitment hasn't been tested. This is often one of the main reasons that entrepreneurs tend to hang on to their CEO role. Next-generation leaders argue that the founder won't discuss or plan for succession, doesn't have a time frame, doesn't have a strong enough board to challenge the founder, has no plan for future leaders to develop, and that whatever thoughts for succession may exist are kept secret by the founder.

| | |
|---|---|
| **C O N S I D E R** | If this applies to you, then it is time to reorganize your board, create an advisory group, or at least bring younger managers and advisors together to discuss reasonable expectations, delegation of responsibility and accountability, and time frames for future leadership transitions. Maybe it's time for a heartfelt conversation with current managers to help identify the underlying issues. If you are sensing a lack of commitment, it could be due to your management style. Or, are you snuffing out their passion by not giving enough authority? If a family member is the focus of your concern, are your expectations for their role overriding their own career dreams—maybe to be somewhere else? Perhaps they don't have the skills—the sooner you begin discussing these questions, the sooner you can begin developing an appropriate action plan. |

## Invisible Goals Trap

Many owners tend to undermine and second-guess the decisions of younger managers. They believe it's easier for them to "just do it" themselves, and are convinced they can do the job better than anyone else. And, as long as they fail to outline the goals they want to achieve, they are right—no one can meet goals they are not aware of. You can avoid this trap by having clearly-described performance goals with quarterly (or weekly) meetings to discuss accomplishments and/or problems. If you are not sure about how to set performance goals, then you should hire a consultant to help you benchmark your company against your peers. You can then establish realistic sales growth goals, operating ratios, profit growth, etc. that can be used as performance targets.

<table>
<tr><td>C O N S I D E R</td><td>Imagine that a qualified and competent individual (other than yourself) was going to run your business tomorrow. What would be the initial limits of their authority that you would be comfortable with? Make a list—financial decisions, personnel, reporting relationships, customer and vendor relations, etc., and outline where your comfort limit would be for someone else to step in for those tasks. If your answer is "none" then you have some real work to do in setting and sharing goals, and letting people you have hired do their job to help you reach those goals.</td></tr>
</table>

## Budget Trap

Entrepreneurs generally do not have defined, explicit budgets. However, budgets are the first step for internal benchmarking and evaluating how you are doing versus your expectations. It is also the first step in external benchmarking; evaluating how your business is performing against its peers. It is difficult to keep a private company as an investment without accurate financial information to determine how management is doing versus how they thought they would do.

The budgeting process, properly done, accomplishes important additional functions. It gets others in the organization more involved, it requires you to share needed information, it creates accountabilities for others to take responsibility for revenues and associated expenses, and it can form the foundation of a compensation policy that is performance-based. Overall, the budgeting process creates a potential team of

<table>
<tr><td>C O N S I D E R</td><td>Do you have a budgeting process that you have confidence in? If not, why not?</td></tr>
</table>

executives who have the responsibility for carrying out the strategy for the company.

One client recently acknowledged that for the first time in 60 years, his company had gone through a formal budgeting process with department heads. Budgeting is now part of a new assignment of responsibilities requested by and willingly transferred to the next generation.

## Risk Trap

Entrepreneurs are often willing to take major risks and are inclined towards major innovations. Next-generation leaders are more comfortable taking calculated risks that yield incremental innovations. Risk needs to be discussed—just as there is risk at jumping at every business opportunity, there is as much risk in being too conservative. A research and development (R&D) strategy, or acquisition strategy for growth, needs to be funded, and expectations discussed as part of an overall plan.

<table>
<tr><td>C<br>O<br>N<br>S<br>I<br>D<br>E<br>R</td><td>How have you and your company experienced innovation in the past? Did ideas or deals find you or do you consciously experiment? Does your business culture support innovation or focus more on how you have always done things? Do you spend money each year on new ideas, new processes? Do you spend time seeking business combinations that are synergistic for you?</td></tr>
</table>

## Culture Trap

Entrepreneurial culture is usually loosely defined as family-oriented. For next-generation managers, a well-defined culture that is generally tighter, more controlled, may be preferred. Respecting the company's culture while at the same time focusing the company on 21st century challenges often requires a tough balancing act for successors. In an earlier example, we saw how one client described her company as being too family friendly. The owner avoided conflict at all costs and in so doing created distrust between the highly competent nonfamily executives and the grown children who owned a large block of stock. A reverse trap is when the entrepreneur feels extremely loyal to long-term employees, whom successors may believe are overpaid and past retirement.

It is important to address these cultural issues and find a balance. If you keep the business, you want to remember what (and who) brought you success. At the same time, you need to create an environment businesslike enough to keep and reward employees (old-time non-family executives and younger family members) who have the skills and experience your company needs.

---

**C O N S I D E R**

Creating a values statement can be a good place to start. You should articulate and discuss core values—how you work with others, how you treat others in the organization, and what you focus on day to day, to form a foundation for the company that provides guiding principles for the future. In *Rekindling Commitment*, Dennis Jaffe writes: "Values form the foundation for behavior; the direction of behavior is formed by the mission . . . . The mission helps people make choices, set strategies, and stay on track, rather than simply react to outside pressures."[3]

---

## Dividend Distribution Trap

Some entrepreneurs want to keep the business in the family but feel that their grown children aren't ready or worthy to handle the responsibilities of ownership. So they inadvertently cultivate a lack of readiness on the part of children and discourage the next generation from wanting to keep the business as an investment. This starts with a "minimal or no distribution" policy. For example, if the business is an S corporation, the company may only distribute sufficient funds for the shareholders to pay their respective share of income taxes. Then, the estate-planning attorney recommends that stock in the S corporation should be gifted to family members. And, it is. Meanwhile the owner convinces adult children that the value of the private company is enhanced by leaving all profits, in excess of taxes, in the company.

Generally there is no benchmarking, so it is hard to quantify whether plowing all the profits back is a smart thing to do. For example if the company value is growing at a 5 percent rate, it may be smarter to diversify by putting some of the profits into a better investment. When the entrepreneur refuses to distribute S corporation dividends to the stockholders beyond what is needed for taxes, there is less likelihood that the next generation will actually perceive the business as an investment worth holding onto. An alternative is to establish a Distribution Policy so stockholders know what to expect. For example, some distribute 50 percent of profits to stockholders as a way of covering their income tax liabilities and leaving a little left over for the stockholders to have a financial benefit from ownership. Since the distribution for taxes may be 40 to 45 percent of profits, distributing an extra 10 percent or so is a way to begin educating stockholders about their investment in the business.

| C O N S I D E R | What do you need to do to begin educating family members about the company? Will they be able to make smart decisions? If no, what will it take to get them ready to understand the business in such a way that they can make tough calls? |
| --- | --- |

## Leader-Successor Trap

Gibb Dyer, a professor of organizational behavior at Brigham-Young University, studied successful and unsuccessful leadership transitions and found consistent attributes of successful firms. One of the traits was an *interdependent* relationship between the current CEO and his or her successor. Dyer identified three types of relationships between founder and successor: interdependent, counterdependent, or dependent.

Owners and successors that have a counterdependent or dependent relationship experience a great deal of difficulty during the transition of management and ownership. The founders either find themselves turning the business over to someone they distrust or with whom they have strong disagreements (counterdependent), or they find that their replacement lacks the necessary skills and leadership to run the business in the future (dependent).

Interdependent relationships create two conditions that favor a successful transition. First the founders and their organizations benefit because the successors bring with them a set of attributes or skills that are needed for the firm's future development. The newcomers make a major contribution. Second, the future leaders feel a need to learn from the current leadership. Thus the leaders of the business are able to inculcate some of their basic beliefs upon the next generation of leaders...both generations benefit from the relationship, and such relationships pave the way for a smooth transition."[4]

> **C O N S I D E R**
>
> Think of a project that you and your successor(s) have worked on together. Would you characterize the process as interdependent? What was the best part of the process; what was the worst? Do you need a facilitator to help articulate and/or mediate differences with successors?

Knowing where the obstacles and landmines are doesn't mean you will miss them all. Keeping focused on the big picture of keeping the company can help you navigate these tough issues.

In the next few chapters we will explore what you will need to know about how to sell your company.

PART

III

# Deciding to Sell Your Business

# Before You Get to the Bargaining Table

As you read through the previous chapters about keeping the business, you may have been quietly saying to yourself, "That's not for me." It takes a new kind of entrepreneur to own a company today and you just may not have the energy and drive. Maybe it's time to explore a sale of the company and get some chips off the table. You could be financially independent, give the kids some money to pursue their own dreams (maybe even sell the business to them) and do something different with your life.

The key issues for this chapter are:

- Who is the most likely company to be interested in buying your business?

- How badly do they need or want the business?

- How many other companies are out there that might also be interested?

- How can you realize maximum value for your company?

- What can you do to prepare the sale of your business to be a successful one?

If you're like most business owners, selling your business will be one of the most monumental events of your life, both financially and personally. Done right, it can create great satisfaction and financial security from many years of effort. Done poorly, it can cause frustration, financial risks, and a disappointing return on your investment.

How do you recognize when it is time to sell? What are the options? What does a seller need to know? This section will outline the steps in the sale of a business, leading up to negotiating the various sale agreements.

Interviews conducted for this book with consolidators and buyers of all kinds of companies have consistently identified common traits among sellers:

- Personal burnout
- Not enough confidence in successors
- Unsure about the future
- A readiness to try something new in life

If any of this sounds like you, then let's start by doing some internal presale housekeeping.

## Presale Housekeeping

Selling the business can provide instant liquidity—especially if your financial "eggs" are mostly in the company, and if you are seeking ways to diversify your investments and potentially reduce your risk. If you are thinking about spending less time in the business, or retiring altogether, and have no clear successor, selling the company can help you meet this goal. Perhaps the business has become too large and too complex to manage personally, or you may be unable to provide the capital you need to expand. By selling to a larger company, you may gain greater management depth, more sophisticated operating systems, or better financing than you could on your own.

### Alternatives to Selling the Entire Company

One alternative to selling the entire business is to consider divesting only part of the business. Often, companies downsize and sell off a subsidiary, a division, a product line, or branches for one or more of the following reasons:

- *Product fit*. Companies often sell off product lines or spin off operations that are no longer compatible with the strategic direction of the business.
- *Liquidity*. Funds may be needed to finance product development or expansion, to meet capital needs, or to provide cash to shareholders.
- *Operating losses*. Obsolete products, limited markets, poor management, and high overhead costs, etc. can lead to a decision to divest a division rather than continuing to support it from other, more profitable, business operations.
- *Management time*. Sometimes problem divisions, or product lines, absorb an extraordinary amount of management's time, which could be used more efficiently in other areas of the company.
- *Limited growth potential*. A product line may have exhausted its potential or there is a change in strategic direction.
- *Multiple successors*. When the owner has several next-generation managers (family members or not) who are equally capable and interested in running the business, spinning off one or more parts can provide independent pieces of the business for each of them to lead.

Instead of selling, or divestiture, you may want to consider a spin-off, a recapitalization, or a joint venture as an alternative to satisfying liquidity or other goals, without giving up control of the whole company.

## What about Going Public?

The main reason for going public is to raise capital. But even a thriving business that can do all its financing internally may want to sell stock. Microsoft went public in 1986 to provide stock options with which to motivate its employees, and you can't argue with the results. Some family-owned companies go public to provide liquidity for estate planning. Another motivation for offering shares is that it keeps a company on its toes. Once in public view, corporate assets are exposed to buyout offers. It's harder for them to remain mismanaged for a long time.

Any private company with a decent earnings history and a plausible business story—high technology or low—will find investors very receptive to an offering of shares. The money is tempting. But you have to weigh the benefits of having new capital and new partners in the form of stockholders with the negatives:[1]

- Once your company is public, it is accountable to a different kind of stakeholder. Pension and mutual fund managers try to tell you how to run your business. You will spend a lot of time romancing security analysts and then trying to meet earnings expectations every three months.

- Publicly-held companies must bare their souls. There is no doubt that Microsoft's very liquid stock and the options that go with it have been a great magnet for talent. But is there any doubt that public knowledge of the company's fat profit margins has made it a much more tempting target for the government's trust-busters?

- If the share price were to escalate, that could leave your heirs with a much higher estate-tax bill. So what if Wall Street is so eager to get into your industry that it will buy some of your shares for twice what they're worth? You may be better off holding on to all of them and leaving them on your estate tax return at a low value.

- Private companies don't have to play by the same rules as public ones. Try convincing the board of directors of a public company to make your daughter or son-in-law the next chief executive. Many private companies are run by second-generation (or later) members of the founding family. Sometimes that's good for the company, sometimes not—but at least the founder gets to give the kids a chance.

- Private company executives don't stay awake at night worrying about a hostile takeover. Once in a blue moon an outsider may launch a tender offer, hoping to snatch shares from a dissident family member. But most private companies are takeover-proof. Share prices in the private company are usually more stable since there is no public market for the shares. Employees therefore watch the bottom line rather than the stock ticker.

- Private companies don't have to worry about a management coup. Andrew Corp of Chicago went public in 1981 to raise capital to meet MCI and Sprint's demands for its telecommunications equipment. Worried that a corporate raider might attempt a takeover, the board changed the company's bylaws to eliminate cumulative voting for board members by shareholders. The change in the voting structure, however, also meant that family members could be voted off the board—which is precisely what happened a few years later.

## Buyers of Different Stripes

There are four types of buyer: consolidators, financial buyers, strategic buyers, and management. Each has different goals and objectives for buying a private company. The type of buyer you negotiate with will determine the types of strategies and deal structures you and they will pursue.

**Consolidators.** This type of buyer is already active in the industry in which the company operates—they are strong industry leaders busy buying weaker rivals into a public or to-be-public entity. Often the seller will already know who the strategic buyers and consolidators are in his/her industry.

CSM is a Netherlands consolidator of bakery ingredients distributors. Through its U.S.-based BakeMark Ingredients subsidiary, it has acquired 45 distribution centers in the United States. Because BakeMark is such a large distributor in its industry, it can negotiate with manufacturers for best pricing, and can centralize purchasing and other administrative functions to reduce expenses. By eliminating unnecessary costs and by using technology on a broad scale, BakeMark can better meet its customers' demands for lower costs and higher service.

One of the criteria BakeMark applies to a potential acquisition is the ability of the new company to fit within the BakeMark culture. Joe Castor oversees BakeMark's acquisition program and describes a good acquisition for BakeMark as one where the employees already have some accountability. "Generally we meet with the employees and discuss our culture. We want to focus on what they already do well and then we want to add a few things. We want to move from the old to the new. We want individuals to be accountable. We want them to figure it out. Often we're buying companies where the owner has been a patriarch. We introduce a high level of accountability. Generally, in the patriarch model, there is little accountability. Everybody comes to the patriarch for the decisions and for the thinking. We don't tell them how to think—we want them to build a plan and think for themselves, implement the plan, and be accountable for it."

CSM pays 100 percent cash for its acquisitions—no stock. As a European public company, CSM is highly taxed on dividend distributions to its shareholders. Therefore rather than using its cash flow for dividends, it uses its cash flow to buy more companies, which in turn creates greater value for its shareholders.

Another successful consolidator has been EMCOR, which started out as a large electrical contractor and then began combining mechanical and electrical operations through acquisitions as part of their strategy of morphing into a facilities service company. EMCOR's stock has appreciated steadily since going public in 1995 while it has grown to over 90 offices, 20,000 employees, and $3 billion in sales. However, as industries become consolidated and there are fewer sellers, strategic buyers such as EMCOR may become more cautious about paying high prices. Jeff Levy, president of EMCOR, noted in an interview, "We are seeing consolidators pay a lot of money for these businesses. They can't let them alone to do their thing. Buyers have to look for value from integration. This is not a forgiving market. Paying a lot for a company puts a lot of pressure on performance. You have to create an interactive business model and structure. I'm not sure how you integrate all these different companies into one."[2] EMCOR however, has apparently figured out how to bundle services to win a job as well as serve national accounts, since over $1 billion a year of their sales are in projects of under $250,000.

Service Corp. International (SCI) began buying up funeral homes and cemeteries in 1962 and now owns 4,500 of them in 20 countries. SCI vertically integrated by moving into related merchandising areas, including selling insurance to fund prearranged funerals. Throughout the 1990s it successfully created operating efficiencies in what is generally a highly personalized service business and its stock appreciated rapidly. But in 1999 the company experienced earnings problems and its stock dropped by almost 90 percent. A member of SCIs acquisition team used to say that cash is king. For those sellers who took SCI stock as part of their purchase price, they can now fully appreciate those words of wisdom.

**Roll-ups.** This is a type of consolidator, specifically created to consolidate a fragmented industry. Roll-ups have been called "poof" companies because of the way they seem to materialize out of thin air.

A roll-up is created when entrepreneurs set out to create one big company by rolling up dozens of little firms into one large enough to create efficiencies, wield marketing muscle, and create a national brand. These companies also bring in professional management, sometimes to firms where management has been almost an afterthought.

Some industry roll-ups are started and financed by venture capital firms. For example, Golder, Thoma, Cressey, and Rauner (now GTCR), a venture capital firm, has financed more than 45 roll-up companies since 1985. These companies are built from scratch, grow rapidly, and are intended to go public quickly. GTCR takes a front-end approach to industry consolidations by looking for industries that are fragmented. GTCR creates a company specifically to consolidate the industry, and then finds an accomplished executive to go out and start acquiring companies. The venture capital firm can lend credibility, board-of-director level expertise, and help the new company get debt financing to fund its acquisition strategy.

Some of the better-known roll-ups include U.S. Office Products, formed in 1995, which collected more than 140 stationery supply houses and related businesses into a company with annual sales of more than $2 billion. In three years, AutoNation became the world's largest automotive retailer with more than 400 locations. Garbage haulers were the target for Waste Management—now WMX Technologies. Rural Metro bought privately-owned ambulance and emergency medical transportation services and now operates in 450 communities throughout North and South America.

The performance of roll-up artists has been somewhat disappointing, however. Consider, for example, a company called Century Business Systems. Century Business, or now Cybiz, targeted accounting firms and other service providers to businesses in a local community. Cybiz hit a high of $20 per share in 1998. Some sellers took as much as 75 percent of their price in the stock of the company and then watched Cybiz stock fall to $3 per share two years later, because of nonstandard accounting practices. Loewen, a Canadian roll-up alternative to Service Corporation in the funeral and cemetery business, filed for bankruptcy after buying 1,600 funeral homes and cemeteries—often using Loewen stock as currency in the deal. Early sellers to a roll-up sometimes agree to sell their businesses to the roll-up in exchange for stock that has not gone public, often making the mistake of taking all their financial eggs from one basket (the company they control) and putting them into another basket (the roll-up company) over which they have no control.

Veterinary Centers of America, or VCA, offered sellers of pet hospitals a chance to stay on as employees. The pitch was, "here is your chance to cash out, continue work that you like, get rid of duties you don't like, and have the hospital gain strength from being part of a national organization." The typical VCA price for the seller was between 80 and 100 percent of the hospital's annual revenue, paid partly in a note held by the seller and partly in VCA stock. From a high of $33 per share in 1996, the stock fell to $10½ in early 2000. The lesson here is to take cash and then if you want to invest in the roll-up, do so by buying some of their stock.

**Financial buyers.** This group is made up of investors or other entrepreneurs interested in the return they can achieve by buying your business. They are generally interested in cash flow and exit opportunity. Their goals may include increasing cash flow by reducing expenses, increasing sales, and creating economies of scale by acquiring other similar companies, or stripping your company by selling off assets at a profit. Their exit plans may include reselling your company or taking it public at a much higher multiple of earnings than they paid to you.

Financial buyers generally borrow a significant portion (and possibly all) of the purchase price and, accordingly, want to structure the transaction so that the cash flow from your business will cover their debt service. This often means seller financing, which may have to be subordinated to the buyer's bank or institutional financing. Because of these factors, financial buyers may offer lower prices than strategic buyers and prefer to pay the purchase price in cash, subordinated notes, or a combination of the two.

For example, since 1994 nearly 40 percent of all the nation's small newspapers have been sold—many to financial buyers such as Community Newspaper Holdings, formed in 1997 and bankrolled by a pension fund. Two others who buy newspaper companies are Liberty Group Publishing owned by a Los Angeles-leveraged buyout company, and the Journal Register Co., a public company 75 percent of which is owned by a Wall Street investment firm.

Financial buyers make up an enormous segment of the market. Pension funds alone have $3 trillion in assets; somewhere between 7 and 10 percent of that is in alternative investments like buyout funds. In 1997, $25 billion of new money poured into buyout funds in one year from pension plans.

With few exceptions financial buyers value a business by using a multiple of earnings before interest and taxes (after making adjustments for expenses that would not continue for a new owner). They deduct from the price any interest-bearing debt that they will assume. As more buyers have entered the game, the price for sellers has increased from four to six times earnings (in the early to mid-1990s) to a current six to eight times earnings. Alternatively, cash flow multiples are sometimes used.

There are disadvantages to selling to a financial buyer. There are no synergies—such as access to a larger sales force, complementary activities in production, engineering, or any other part of the business; and there are pressures to increase the cash flow because of the added debt. Financial buyers are in business to make deals, so they may overlook some weaknesses. They often leave day-to-day operations unchanged, but they buy with a view to selling, which could disrupt your business life a second time.

One variation on the financial buyer is the acquisition fund. These are professionally managed pools of capital that principally invest in companies that have good management and strong growth opportunities. Their goals are to expand and improve the business and then take it public (or possibly resell it) within a defined period, usually three to five years. Acquisition funds are generally cash buyers, although some use considerable leverage and may require subordinated seller financing. Because of the high rates of return required by most funds, they may offer less competitive prices than strategic buyers.

**Strategic buyers.** This type of buyer creates synergy by matching marketing and distribution channels, and complementing product lines, using existing manufacturing processes, etc. These may be private or public companies, competitors, or friends in the industry.

Strategic buyers are companies interested in growing through acquisitions. Their goals may include extending a product line, eliminating competition, expanding vertically toward the consumer or toward a source of supply, expanding horizontally into new geographic markets, or adding key technology, personnel, or other resources to their existing business. Strategic buyers often offer the best price and may be willing to offer stock, cash, or a combination of the two in payment of the purchase price.

Strategic buyers expect synergies with their other holdings. They can afford to pay a premium, but they may not need to because they know the market. Buyers offering premium prices are in short supply. The best match sometimes comes about if they seek you out after having determined that your business fits their plans. Strategic buyers may diminish your role as CEO, and their goals related to the future of your business may differ from yours.

John Furman, a Phoenix attorney and business consultant who has represented both buyers and sellers, notes: "Strategic buyers know the players, they know the business, they know the industry, and they have people capable of running the company. There's an ease of bringing outsiders in. They may not need the seller to stay on. Their level of due diligence is different because they know what they're looking at. But on the other hand if you sell to a strategic buyer, it's probably less of a risk to take stock in that strategic buyer because they understand the seller's business—they are in the business."

Successful companies in this area include Sysco, the largest food-service distributor in North America with 78 distribution centers, Gannett and Knight-Ridder in the newspaper business, EMCOR in electrical contracting, and the most successful, Cisco Systems, Inc., which has digested over 50 companies between 1994 and 2000 and has become a model in the high-tech sector for its merger and acquisition policies and practices.

Some strategic buyers "talk the talk" but haven't proved they can "walk the walk." For example, some of the large utilities like Pennsylvania Power and Light and FirstEnergy Corporation have acquired large mechanical contracting firms. The utilities want to sell electricity when construction is being planned; acquiring mechanical contractors gives them that opportunity. They are still trying to integrate the newly-acquired entrepreneurial companies into their bureaucratic slower-moving cultures.

At some point, the financial or strategic buyer may become a consolidator in its acquisition practices, but it is important to note the differences between the four groups.

**Management buyouts.** Existing management may also be a potential buyer of your business. Few management teams have the financial resources to pay all cash. Most management acquisitions involve seller financing or support from an acquisition fund or other institutional sources of financing. Because your management team may have the greatest understanding of your business and its future prospects, they may be willing to offer a strong price if seller financing can be provided. In most management-led buyouts, cash flow and the ability to repay institutional or seller financing are the key considerations in establishing the purchase price and other terms of the deal.

Employee stock ownership plans or ESOPs can also be established to serve as a buyer, either in a single transaction or over a period of years. An ESOP is a retirement plan partially funded with stock of the employer. ESOPs obtain their funds either from employer contributions (like other retirement plans) or from a bank loan to the ESOP that is repaid from future employer contributions and dividends on the purchased shares. ESOPs are not generally viable where the aggregate employee compensation is relatively low in comparison to the value of the business.

## Analyzing Potential Buyers

Not all buyers will fit your company's culture. Sometimes the buyer with the highest price is not the one you will be most comfortable selling to.

It is important to do some research, known as *due diligence* on your potential buyers and learn about how they have treated other acquired companies after the deal closed.

Your due diligence on the potential buyer should be focused on the two following areas:

1. *Financial due diligence* determines if the buying company is financially sound, with no hidden skeletons in their closet, or liabilities or lawsuits lurking in the weeds that could impact your company after the sale is completed. Financial due diligence is also about being sure you will get paid at the closing, that you are not wasting your time with the buyer, and that they have the financial strength to perform on promises to pay you if you hold a promissory note for part of the purchase price. If your buyer is a public company there is plenty of information online about the company that will be helpful about its financial condition. But historical financial results don't mean anything about getting paid in the future. Talk to your buyer's banker and find out if funds for your deal are conditional or already committed. Talk to the analysts who cover the company (if they are publicly traded) and ask about their prospects as well as their risks. Have the buyer provide audited financial statements to you if they are a private company.

2. *Operational due diligence* means finding out how your company will be run after the sale is completed. You should check into how successful any previous acquisitions have been. Talk to former owners who sold to your prospective buyer. Find out how well or how poorly the buyer integrated the newly purchased business. How many employees left? Are decisions being made locally or from the home office? Is the former owner still involved? If your company has been a good corporate citizen supporting local charities, find out if the new owner will be willing to send some of their charitable dollars to your community.

Some specific issues to address include:

- *Acquisition history*. Whom have they acquired? How much have they paid? How were the acquisitions financed? What did they do to integrate the new company? Have past acquisitions been successful? If the acquisition was not successful, what happened and what can you as a seller learn from that?

- *Eagerness to carry out new acquisitions.* Are they looking for new businesses? Do they need what your business is offering?

- *Potential synergies that may exist between the companies.* Will cost savings accrue? Can excess capacity be used? Are the customer bases duplicates of each other? Do the products complement each other?

- *Financial condition.* Are they capable of making the acquisition? What is the market for its publicly traded stock?

## Courting Buyers

As in most business transactions, competition, or at least the appearance of competition, can make a difference in maximizing the price you receive for your business.

Try to create a limited auction where you narrow the acceptable buyers to two or three and then enter into parallel negotiations with those two or three parties. You should first identify a small group of likely buyers, be they consolidators, financial buyers, strategic buyers, or management. Then you contact those parties to determine their interest, have them sign a Confidentiality Agreement (see next section) and then forward the selling memo described below to those who want to review it. The potential buyers submit preliminary acquisition proposals or expressions of interest to you or your advisors. You assess each proposal, identify the potential buyer who submits the acquisition proposal that is most attractive, and then begin to negotiate the financial terms of the sale.

There are some situations where this may not be practical. For example, when an acquisition proposal has already been received from a serious buyer, or the owner or board of directors of the business prefers to negotiate with only one or two potential buyers. Before you rush into the deal, keep in mind it may be smart to create competitive bidding, or the appearance of competition, between at least two interested parties. You may have to do some research to get information about comparable transactions that may be helpful in negotiating your deal. For example, you may want to talk to other sellers who have already sold to your potential buyer. You can learn a lot about what went right, and wrong, from those conversations.

Your approach to the acquisition process will depend on whether you are interested in selling all of the stock or other equity in your business or only a majority or minority interest in it. Although sales of the whole company are generally the rule, sales of a partial interest can sometimes be negotiated. For example, at one time Waste Management took a 60 percent interest in a seller's company, allowing the seller or his children to keep 40 percent and grow the company with Waste Management's money. After five to seven years, Waste Management could buy out the remaining 40 percent at the new value. Or, the seller could buy back the 60 percent interest they had sold, based on the new value. Be creative if you want. After all, it's your business, and buyers can be flexible up to a point in getting the deal done.

## Confidentiality Agreement

Also known as a nondisclosure agreement (NDA), this agreement is reciprocal and a pre-condition to further discussions. It should also include a provision to protect the seller (and buyer) from pirating employees whom they meet in the negotiation process. Narrow the buyers down to two or three before releasing information. A sample Confidentiality Agreement is in the Sell Appendix.

## When to Use an Investment Banker or Business Broker

Of course there are pros and cons of using an intermediary versus doing it yourself. You will probably know who the strategic buyers and consolidators are in your industry. If not, call the executive director of your trade association. But, just because you know who the buyers are doesn't mean you should try to sell your business yourself. Use an experienced team to help you negotiate with sophisticated buyers. The fees you may spend are well worth the added value that a savvy group of advisors can bring to the table during this project. If strategic buyers or consolidators are not interested, an investment banker or business broker can help you find a financial buyer. Either way, the advisor team or investment banker will put together the Selling Memorandum described later in this chapter.

Generally if you want to broadly market your company, an investment banker, or the merger and acquisition arm of a large accounting firm, will be the best approach. If the value of your business is $1 million or less, or if the company's EBIT is $250,000 or less, you will probably be better off with a business broker who can advertise your company for you.

Typical fees are based on some amount paid upfront as a retainer, with a contingent fee paid at closing, only if the sale is consummated. The contingent fee is often based on some variation of the Lehman formula which is as follows: 5 percent of the first $1 million, 4 percent of the next $1 million, 3 percent of the next $1 million, 2 percent of the next $1million, and 1 percent beyond $4 million. There are many variations on this formula and you can generally negotiate a lower percentage if the deal size is $5 million or larger.

James Dwyer, Managing Director of MPI Securities, Princeton, New Jersey outlined some of the advantages of using an investment banking firm. They are as follows:

- They are involved with capital markets on a day-to-day basis.
- They can organize and manage a competitive process and bring a certain discipline to the process so the buyers come forth with the best price and terms.
- They are experienced at negotiating.
- They can provide value-added services. For example, they can help the seller decide between a strategic or a financial buyer. One seller had two offers that were similar in price and terms. If the seller wanted to be part of a large organization with resources, then it would be better for them to sell to the strategic buyer. On the other hand, the financial buyer promised the company would continue as a stand alone entity. The buyer decided

to sell to the financial buyer and not lose the identity that the strategic buyer would require.

• The investment banker can think outside the box and sometimes identify potential buyers that the seller hasn't thought of.

Here is one example from Dwyer of providing value-added services: "We were hired by a consulting company that provided health care content and database information. The company thought they would sell as a consulting business. We saw them more as a database content company, which had more value than a consulting business. We repositioned the client's selling memo and marketed it as a health care information business and sold it to a health care information systems business for twice what the seller thought the company was worth as a consulting firm. In addition, the strong earnings of the seller helped the buyer do an Initial Public Offering (IPO). We identified how the additional earnings stream of our client (the seller) would help the buyer do their IPO, which resulted in additional consideration to the seller.

A broker may claim to represent a given buyer, but that can be misleading. Some buyers enter into agreements with dozens of brokers, agreeing to pay them if they initiate deals that are consummated. Be cautious. If you seem interested, you could find people calling your customers and competitors to check out your reputation, and the resulting rumors could hurt your business.

If you receive a misspelled, careless letter from a broker describing many clients, it's probably worthless. "Clients" in the plural signals the broker's intent to look for a buyer if you respond with interest. A broker writing and describing the specific interests of one buyer may merit attention. You could ask for details, saying you are not interested in selling now but might be one day. Even if it is a seller's market, buyers are the aggressors. Buyers and their brokers are relentlessly calling on business owners to lure them into talks. Beware: flattery is part of the pitch.

## Preparing the Selling Memo

The first step in preparing the company for sale is to develop a selling memorandum that provides a prospective buyer with enough information about your company for the buyer to decide whether he or she is interested. A selling memorandum will typically include information about the company's history, the markets in which it operates, the company's competitors, information about the company's products and services, its operations, management, and the company's strengths. Also, the memorandum should include some information about why the owners are considering a sale of the company at this time.

One by-product of completing the selling memorandum is that it provides you, the seller, with the necessary information to begin developing a realistic valuation range for your company.

Deloitte and Touche, LLP, provides the following guidelines about what to include in a selling memorandum:[3]

- *Executive summary*. This should explain in a page or two all the relevant information contained in the memorandum. Also, you can use the summary to send it as a separate document to potential buyers to determine initial interest—if they are interested in seeing the entire document, your attorney can provide them with a confidentiality agreement that must be signed before you release additional information (the complete selling memorandum) to them.

- *Products and services*. This section should describe your products and services, main product lines, why your products/services have a competitive advantage and/or how they are different from the products and services of your competitors. Do you hold exclusive licenses or patents? What technological risks/opportunities exist around your current products and services? If you have sales material describing your products/services, include that.

- *Marketing*. Describe your markets. Are any large customers responsible for a large percentage of your sales? Without identifying your customers, you should provide some general information about your sales, such as, "ten customers are responsible for 80 percent of sales in this product line" or "two outside sales representatives are dedicated to servicing our top three customers."

- *Manufacturing*. This section describes your manufacturing processes, including raw material requirements, and sourcing. If your company has received special certifications, such as ISO

2000, or similar achievements, you should describe these. Production facilities, capacity requirements, constraints, and future needs should also be described. If your company is a member of a buying group or co-operative, you should describe the relationship. Photos of your manufacturing facilities can be helpful. If there are any environmental issues, you should describe those up front. If you have already done an environmental study (for bank financing, etc.), include a synopsis of the report.

- *Management.* Provide an organizational chart, bios of current management, including their positions and experience. Outline who will stay with a new owner and who is expected to retire. Include any compensation changes in the financial projections below.

- *Employees.* Describe your compensation policy, including benefits the company provides. Include a benefits handbook so a new owner can compare benefits between their company and yours. If employees are represented by a union, provide an outline of the union contract.

- *Historical financial statement.* Include three year's financial statements. Audited statements are an advantage here. Most advisors suggest providing restated financial statements, as the company would be run under a new owner. For example, owner's compensation and benefits would be adjusted in a restated statement to reflect the current market compensation for a CEO. Also include an interim statement, including comparison to budgets, etc.

- *Financial projections.* This section represents the owner's estimation about how the company will perform in the future. If expenses will be reduced, or sales will increase from a particular product or service, those should be outlined here in the projections. Five year's of projections should be provided, along with your underlying assumptions. One alternative to providing such detailed information up front is to provide only sales projections and expected changes in margins. This, however, can slow down the process because buyers will determine the value of your company based on their own financial projections for your business.

It is to the seller's advantage to help the prospective buyer reach a favorable conclusion. For example, the seller may have knowledge about why his/her company's margins are better than competitors, which could influence (positively) the valuation a buyer may place on the company.

One alternative to the selling memorandum is a business plan. Financial projections are of primary interest to buyers, and sellers often do not give them the attention they deserve. A business plan has several advantages. It does not signal to employees that the company is for sale. It does not send any messages about how long you may have been talking to buyers. And a good plan reflects well on a company's management—you are describing an enterprise with continuity independent of the owner's instincts. A business plan is a perfect tool to show to prospective buyers without signaling an intense desire to make a deal soon.

## Valuation Basics

Before you pursue a buyer, you should have a reasonable idea of how a third party will value your business. Many owners know the "rules of thumb" common in their industries, and carry that value in their heads. But rules of thumb provide only a rough approximation of value, and can be misleading for a business whose financial parameters do not line up with those of its competitors.

Your historical performance can provide a buyer an indication of the stability of your business and a proven track record. But keep in mind that a sophisticated buyer will not buy your historical value, but your future value, so you have an incentive to devote the necessary resources to developing solid business projections based on reasonable assumptions. Your historical results can be used as a measure of reliability of your future projections.

Perhaps you should hire an appraiser to determine the company's value. The appraiser chosen should have knowledge of and experience valuing other companies in your industry. A business valuation will be based on a set of assumptions about future events, or by assuming that past events will occur in the future in a predictable manner. In other words, the valuation is a starting point, not the endpoint. You probably have some idea of the value of your business, which may have come from several sources such as

- previous business valuations that have been carried out for tax or legal purposes.
- awareness of transactions involving other companies in the same or similar industries.
- public trading multiples for companies in the same or similar business.
- previous offers to purchase the business.
- the owners' own gut feeling.

One resource is Pratt's Stat's, an online database that tracks private business sales transactions in the $1 million to $30 million range. Pratt's Stat's can be found at <www.PrattsStats.com>.

Valuing a business is based on some fundamental concepts.

**A valuation is relevant for only a limited time.** A business valuation typically becomes stale within 90 days. Factors change daily or monthly that affect your business and those factors may also change the opinion of value of your company.

**A valuation is conducted for a specific purpose.** Different professional appraisal standards apply to different purposes, primarily as a result of the development of statutory, regulatory, and common law requirements governing business valuation. The appraiser must match appropriate valuation methods to the intended purpose of the appraisal, and is required to state the purpose of the appraisal in the valuation report. Don't plan on using the valuation done when you gifted 2 percent of your stock to your daughter, to tell you the value you should expect for a sale of the business on the open market.

**Value is a function of future expectations.** Prospective buyers of a business, strategic or otherwise, are primarily interested in the business' future. While historic results are a guide to both the seller and the buyer, it is the expectation about the business' future results that determine the price or value. A business' value is a function of what a purchaser expects that business to generate in earnings or cash flows. As a result, negotiation often focuses on the seller's budgets and forecasts.

**Value relates to the market demand for a business.** The number of legitimate buyers in the marketplace at any particular time directly impacts the seller's price. The market demand for a business is an important factor in establishing the seller's negotiating position. Typically, more buyers increase your opportunity to maximize the price received.

Although various valuation methodologies exist, and some are particularly applicable to a given industry, ultimately the value of a business depends on what a potential buyer is willing and able to pay. Behind this simple statement is the reality that two different buyers may view the value of a particular business quite differently. The value of a business, then, must be considered not in a vacuum but as the value of the business to a particular acquirer. The key question is not what your business is worth, but what it is worth to a specific buyer.

In theory, the current value of a business should approximate the present discounted value of the future benefits that will accrue from it. Under this approach, the future benefits of the business (e.g., earnings, cash flow, or dividends) are projected over a period of years (Figure 8.1) and, often with use of an estimated terminal value at the end of the projection period, discounted back to a present value using a discount or capitalization rate that reflects the buyer's desired rate of return (which will normally reflect both the buyer's cost of capital and its risk/reward premium).

Unfortunately, the problem with this approach is that it depends on the accuracy of the projections (and, in turn, the underlying assumptions). One of the most commonly controversial variables is the discount rate (see Figure 8.2), which the parties involved in negotiating the deal may or may not easily agree upon. Therefore, while many buyers use some form of discounted value (generally discounted cash flow) analysis in valuing a business, these buyers may also use other valuation methodologies that utilize historical financial information. Indeed, experienced buyers often calculate, compare, and contrast several different valuation methodologies.

## FIGURE 8.1—VALUE ESTIMATE USING DISCOUNTED FUTURE CASH FLOW

**Foursale Manufacturing, Inc.**
**Value Estimate Using Discounted Future Cash Flow**
Assume an appropriate discount rate = 29.0%
Assume growth rate = 8.0%

| (000's omitted) | Actual Last Year | Projected Year 1 | Projected Year 2 | Year 3 | Terminal Value |
|---|---|---|---|---|---|
| % increase in sales: | | 7.50% | 8.00% | 8.00% | |
| **Sales:** | 12,400 | 13,300 | 14,400 | 15,600 | |
| Less cost of sales      65.0% | 8,060 | 8,600 | 9,400 | 10,100 | |
| Gross profit | 4,340 | 4,700 | 5,000 | 5,500 | |
| **Expenses:** | | | | | |
| Selling and marketing | 2,480 | 2,700 | 2,900 | 3,100 | |
| General and administrative | 1,240 | 1,270 | 1,300 | 1,330 | |
| Operating income | 620 | 730 | 800 | 1,070 | |
| Other income (expense) | 4 | 4 | 4 | 4 | |
| Income taxes | (250) | (290) | (320) | (430) | |
| Net income | 374 | 444 | 484 | 644 | |
| Adjustment for noncash income and expense items | 30 | 30 | 31 | 31 | |
| Adjustment for nonincome cash inflows and outlays | — | — | — | — | |
| **Cash flow:** | 404 | 474 | 515 | 675 | 3,210 |

**Net present value of after-tax cash flows plus terminal value @ 29.0%**                    <u>**$2,200,000**</u>

**FIGURE 8.2—RANGE OF VALUE ESTIMATES USING THREE DIFFERENT DISCOUNT RATES**

**Range of Value Estimates for Foursale Manufacturing, Inc.
Using Three Different Discount Rates**

| Discount Rate | Value Estimate |
|---|---|
| 20.0% | $3,900,000 |
| 24.0% | $2,900,000 |
| 29.0% | $2,200,000 |

Valuation methodologies using historical data can generally be grouped into three categories. These methodologies may be used alone or in combination to reach a valuation decision. In addition, historical valuation approaches may consider such factors as comparable transaction data and price/earnings (P/E) multiples of public companies in your industry, adjusted where appropriate, to reflect the illiquidity of privately traded securities and the existence of a control or minority position. See Figure 8.3.

**FIGURE 8.3—VALUE ESTIMATES USING MULTIPLES OF HISTORICAL RESULTS**

Using the historical data for Foursale Manufacturing, Inc. presented in Figure 8.1 in the column marked "Actual Last Year," here are some examples of value estimates using multiples of historical results:

| | | |
|---|---|---|
| Multiple of earnings: | 4 times pretax income | $ 2,496,000 |
| Multiple of earnings: | 4 times EBDIT (earnings before depreciation, interest, and taxes) | $ 2,616,000 |
| Multiple of cash flow: | 6 times cash flow | $ 2,426,400 |
| Multiple of gross revenues: | 1 times gross | $ 12,400,000 |

**Multiple of earning power or cash flow.** In the multiple of earnings approach, an agreed upon measure of the company's earnings power is multiplied by a P/E multiple that is typical for the industry. The income stream may come either before or after items such as interest, depreciation, owners' compensation, and taxes. You may use the latest year's income, a straight or weighted average of income from prior years, a trend line value, a normalized or adjusted income stream, or a forecast of the coming years. The key is that the income stream being capitalized must be clearly defined and the multiple chosen must be appropriate for the particular income stream, the applicable industry, and the liquidity of the market (i.e., public or private) involved. In this regard, it is important to note that P/E multiples in publicly traded companies are often much higher than P/E multiples in privately held companies.

Example: P/E ratio for public companies in your industry    10:1
P/E ratio adjusted for your company    5:1
Your company's annual projected earnings
for next three years    $250,000
Business value indication    $1,250,000

**Multiple of gross revenues.** In some businesses, capitalization of gross revenues is a commonly applied approach to valuation. It is perhaps most often applied to service businesses, such as professional practices and advertising firms. Where used, it is essentially a shortcut to a multiple of earnings approach, involving an implicit assumption that a particular revenue level should be able to generate a specific level of net income with a given level of risk and, therefore, provide a particular value. In some industries, valuation multiples are also applied to other volumes, such as beds in nursing homes and subscribers to a cable or cellular system. The key factors in applying these valuation methodologies are determining the multiple that is appropriate for the industry, making any necessary adjustment for a public or private company, and assessing whether other adjustments may be necessary to reflect special circumstances (e.g., outstanding debt) or risks the business being acquired faces. Industry multiples are generally determined by evaluating historical transactions and public company data, adjusted where necessary in private company deals.

**Multiple of net assets or book value.** In this approach, the business is valued by applying an appropriate multiple to the company's net assets or book value. This method requires a careful analysis of the business' assets and liabilities. You may need to adjust value to reflect the excess of fair market value of depreciable assets over (or under) book value, or to discount nonperforming or under-performing assets. The appropriate net asset or book multiple is generally influenced by historical transactions or public company data, adjusted in private company transactions to reflect differences such as a limited market or the absence of management depth. Asset valuation approaches are often less precise than other valuation methods and may be more helpful in confirming a valuation range than in determining a specific value.

Regardless of the valuation method you employ, most buyers have constraints on how much they can afford to pay in a given acquisition. These constraints may include such factors as a minimum required rate of return, a maximum acceptable dilution (or a minimum acceptable accretion) in post-closing earnings or book value, or a level of cash flow necessary to support acquisition or other financing. Understanding these constraints can be helpful in maximizing the price you receive. If the price ceiling that the buyer can afford to pay exceeds the fair value placed on the business by appropriate valuation methods, you may be able to negotiate a price above fair value and below the buyer's ceiling. On the other hand, if the buyer's price ceiling is below the calculated fair value of the business, no amount of negotiation may be effective in getting the buyer to go beyond its price ceiling.

## Valuation Summary

There are five steps involved in valuing a business, regardless of the method you use:

1. Review history of business and industry, including transactions and comparable company valuations (public and private).

2. Based on historical and projected financial information, establish an estimate of the free cash flows that the business will be able to produce in the future.

3. Estimate the risk that the business will not produce those cash flows as compared to a risk-free rate of return.

4. Apply estimated risk rate to cash flows either through a discounted cash flow or a capitalized earnings model to calculate a value.

5. Adjust the value for circumstances that are specific to the business, such as excess or insufficient capital and liabilities, to arrive at a range of estimated values.

## Increasing Your Value to a Buyer

**Cash flow is the most important factor.** Every owner wants a premium for his business, but the purchase prices for private companies usually do not mimic publicly-traded firms. While public firms commonly sell for high multiples of net income, the universal measurement for closely held companies is earnings before interest and taxes (EBIT). There can be a significant difference between the two. Public companies often sell for more than private companies for many reasons, not the least of which are the availability of a ready market, ready financing, and ready egos.

Private companies usually sell for six to eight times EBIT. Higher multiples of EBIT are possible for unusually well run and well-positioned companies. Buyers will pay for identifiable, verifiable, and consistent EBIT. Buyers will pay a premium for companies that can display EBIT that is consistently higher than competitors in the same industry. Therefore, the most fundamental method for adding value to a company is to clean up the income statement towards the purpose of maximizing EBIT. Having done this, you then augment that value by producing at least three years of certified audited financial statements that verify these cash flows.

**Asset quality can influence the cash offer from the buyer.** One difficulty for most owners in selling their companies is their perception of return on investment (ROI). If a company's book value is $3.5 million and the owner is taking home all the company's earnings at $1 million per year in a sub-S corporation, from the owner's point of view the company has an ROI of 28.6 percent. If a potential buyer of this firm offers $6 million (a 6 x EBIT multiple) the owner should be happy. However, if the owner realizes that post-sale he or she only has net $4.8 million after taxes to invest for a 10 percent return, it may feel like a 50 percent pay cut.

Another view (which might be closer to the truth) is that this owner may have been stripping equity out of the company for years. If earnings had been reinvested at a more aggressive rate, the company's assets, book value, revenues, and EBIT would all have been significantly higher. So would the potential purchase price. It's the owner's company of course, but as a seller, it shouldn't be a surprise if others do not see the same value the owner does. Also, keep in mind that this owner also has the money that has been pulled out of the company, and may already have diversified into other investments.

Some advisors believe there is a direct relationship between the cash in a purchase offer and a company's asset value (in an asset sale), or book value (in a stock sale). In theory, the cash you receive in an asset sale, after paying off business liabilities, should about equal the cash you receive in a stock sale (aside from tax considerations). Buyers tend to want to pay $1 in cash for $1 in hard assets. In our example above, that fictitious buyer probably will only offer $3.5 million of the purchase price in cash at closing. The rest would be in the form of seller paper, a consulting fee, or an earn-out. The seller is bound to become even more frustrated.

If you want to beef up the cash at closing in the sale of your company, beef up its assets. Reinvest earnings into assets that directly relate to producing cash flow. Sell or divest assets that are unrelated to your cash flows, such as raw land, redundant warehousing capacity, or headquarters art collections. Reinvest cash proceeds into expanded production capacity, marketing infrastructure, or research and development facilities. If you have a purchase price in mind for your company, your gross assets should equal at least 80 percent of that figure if you want to receive a significant portion of the purchase price in cash at the closing.

**Avoid surprises.** Buyers and bankers hate surprises. It may surprise you to learn that the more information you disclose, the better it is for you, the seller. Public market reporting requirements develop a certain sense of security that private markets often lack. Uncertainty in the mind of a buyer in a private deal results in hold-back escrow accounts and less cash at the closing. Don't expect buyers to solve your problems. Don't count on buyers to not see them either.

Environmental concerns loom ever larger in nearly every transaction today. If there is any area that deserves full and complete scrutiny prior to any sale, it is in environmental and pollution issues. Don't assume that a Phase I, or even a Phase II report is sufficient. Document whatever you do. Also remember that the pain threshold on environmental issues for the buyer is often far higher than it is for the buyer's finance source. Finance sources today do not want to hold title to any EPA problem, especially as a result of a default.

**Get audited financial statements.** Because audited financial statements reduce uncertainty and risk on the part of buyers, having your statements audited can actually impact the purchase price and terms you can command. As Colin Gabriel wrote in *Inc.* magazine's November 1, 1998 issue, "Audited numbers strengthen your hand in the negotiations and allow you to demand better terms and to switch suitors more readily—and threatening to do so is one of your strongest weapons."

Audits can be expensive. Colin estimates they can cost about $25,000 for a manufacturing business with sales of $10 million. However, he points out that some owners have their financial statements reviewed by outside accountants instead. "Buyers know the difference, but at least the review provides a professional presentation," he says.

**Address off-balance sheet and nonoperating assets.** There may be significant assets of the business that do not appear on its balance sheet. Off-balance sheet assets can include intellectual property, licenses or proprietary techniques, patents in process, research and development innovations, undervalued assets, unique operational processes, proprietary product channeling, or just plain good people. If you don't tell the buyer about these off-balance sheet assets, who will?

Are there other assets in the business (such as land) that are not contributing to earning power? Your proceeds will probably be higher, and you will improve your overall financial ratios, if you sell those assets before talking to prospective buyers. Alternatively, consider selling the operating assets and then negotiating a lease with the buyer for the use of the real estate.

Who owns the warehouses, land, and buildings? If your company does, consider buying them yourself or moving them to another corporation. The price for the business might not change much without the real estate, and you will have kept a significant asset.

**Focus on the strengths of your business.** Eliminating weak product lines should increase your overall profit margins and improve your return on assets. Buyers don't want diversified businesses; they want resources concentrated in your strongest activity. Also, buyers like to see data showing gross profit (and return on assets) by activity or product line, so having access to relevant information quickly will be a measure of your competence.

**Management depth and employee teamwork adds value.** A business that is excessively dependent on the owner is risky for a prospective buyer. Appointing a second-in-command and department managers enhances a company's value by alleviating that risk. Just as important as disclosing all financial facts relating to a business, is disclosing the synergism that makes that company work. When one client introduced a gain-sharing plan, they taught their employees to be aware of the costs and profits of each job. Through gain sharing, employees participated in a monthly bonus pool. The synergism of employees working together translated into real bottom-line results.

# Eradicating Value Reducers

The central difference in the valuation of private and public companies is the assessment of the risks associated with both the investment and the business. There are two types of risks: *ownership risks* and *business risks*. The higher the risks perceived by the buyer, the more the buyer will want to hedge the purchase with contingent, non-guaranteed payments. Therefore you will need to think through ownership and business risks for a buyer and be prepared to address these issues.

**Lack of diversification.** Because your capital has been invested in a single enterprise, the risks associated with that industry and market are not easily diversified away. While the focus may be attractive to a buyer, it may also cause some concern. Be prepared to explain why your focus might be to the buyer's advantage.

**Limited access to capital.** As a private business, there may be limited access to the capital required to maintain the business in down times, and to expand the business in good times. Therefore a buyer may need to factor in an infusion of additional capital in their projections to make the deal work. Be prepared to explain why an infusion of additional capital in your company, if necessary, would be a good investment for the buyer.

**Size.** Most private companies are smaller than public companies so there may be a disadvantage in the marketplace (for example lack of distribution or other economies of scale).

A small company may be better assimilated with a larger one by moving its operations closer to other operations of the buyer. Be prepared to explain why the buyer should/should not relocate the business.

**Liquidity and marketability.** The liquidity of your investment is limited because there is no market for shares of a private business, and your ability to withdraw your investment depends on a limited number of potential buyers. Be prepared to explain why, once you have gotten your money out of your company, you will/will not still stay on to help the new owner.

**Management depth.** Often the owner of the business and a few key employees have been and may continue to be the central factor to its success. Will the key people who are not sharing in the economic benefits of the sale be willing to stay on for some period of time to protect the buyer's investment? Will existing management be able to run the company and increase its value to the new owners? How integral to the business is the current ownership? Can the goodwill associated with current owners be transferred to another owner or management team? The more the business relies on a particular owner or management team, the more risk there is associated with its future from a buyer's perspective.

**Past practices versus future goals.** The business may not have been operated with similar goals, or practices as your buyer. A private company may not have been operated with the goals of shareholder value, earnings per share, or even to maximize cash flow. At times, the private business is driven by more personal or family goals, such as the employment of family members or community status. Changes that occur when the company is under new ownership can be extreme. Will you be able to adapt to changes imposed by a new owner?

**Availability of information.** A private company usually does not adhere to the same reporting standards that a public company does, nor will it necessarily produce all the information that a potential buyer wants to make an informed decision. Do you have the technology and systems that a larger company would expect to be able to analyze data about how your company operates?

Internal and external factors can also be risks to a potential buyer. Internal factors can affect both the intrinsic value and the business' market price. If issues such as the following are addressed consistently as part of an ongoing internal planning process, the value of the business will be kept in focus and enable better value optimizing decisions.

**Strength of product or market.** A company strong in either a particular region or in a particular product line, will generally offer greater value to a strategic buyer than will a company perhaps equally successful but, without a specific advantage for the buyer. And while a business may operate in many product lines or regions, its knowledge of its strengths and successes, and its ability to identify and promote them will have a great impact on its potential value. For example, an Arizona business that is strong across the Southwest, due to its distribution system developed over many years, will realize a higher value if its owner can communicate this strategic strength clearly to potential buyers.

**Quality of asset base.** Quality of the asset base refers to both the age and the value of the assets used to produce a business' income. If assets are nearing the end of their useful life, the value ascribed to a company by a buyer will be reduced in the knowledge that additional investment will be required to maintain the earnings as projected. On the other side, a buyer who can use excess capacity of the seller can benefit over and above the business' standalone value. You should be aware of how your asset base will affect the business' value and take a long-term view, so that the impact of investment decisions will produce the most beneficial impact on price and value.

Have you postponed needed capital improvements? A buyer will factor those new expenses in to their projections. Generally, making needed capital improvements is a worthwhile investment for the seller, as buyers will appreciate having newer, better, faster equipment, production lines, or rolling stock, and knowing they don't have to go through the downtime and cost of implementing needed upgrades.

## Other Factors That Can Influence Value to a Buyer

**Streamlining.** Often, a central reason that two businesses are combined is the cost savings realizable upon combination—economies of scale. Administrative costs are often duplicated, sales teams may overlap, and one company may have the capacity to produce the other's products. By enabling the buyer to reduce the overlap and streamline these areas of duplication you add value to the acquisition by increasing post-acquisition free cash flows for the combined businesses and, therefore, allow a purchaser to pay more for a business than would be indicated by its intrinsic value.

**Strategic value.** A business may have strategic value to one or more of its competitors. Market share, product line compatibility, research and development capabilities, or regional strengths may be of strategic value to another company.

**Number of motivated buyers.** If only one buyer can gain strategic or synergistic value from an acquisition, there will be no need to pay more than a marginal amount above the intrinsic value that another buyer would be willing to pay. If there is only one buyer at a particular time, the price may be dependent on the negotiating skills of the buyer and the seller, and the motivation of the seller to sell. An experienced negotiator will play multiple buyers against each other to obtain a maximum price for a seller.

**Competition between buyers.** This intangible factor depends on the potential buyers' perceptions of each other. Maximum value will usually be obtained in a situation of high-level competition between buyers, where the need to purchase a business is raised from the academic to the emotional. The effect of this component, being somewhat emotionally based, is difficult to estimate.

It is important for potential sellers to maintain close scrutiny over trends and developments in their particular industry, regionally, domestically, and internationally. Opportunities to sell your company at the most advantageous price may be temporary. The ability to respond to market factors is a function of preparation, awareness, and the ability to act on opportunities when they arise. Similarly, owners and managers must keep valuation issues in mind when making operating plans and decisions so that when an industry consolidation begins or when a special-interest purchaser presents himself or herself, the business is well positioned to realize maximum value.

"Companies that look to be acquired instead of first focusing on building and growing a sound business, in my opinion, will generally not succeed," says John Chambers, CEO of Cisco Systems. "Companies that are formed that look to be acquired often operate a little softer because they are not laser-beam focusing on the most important aspect of any business: customers." Acquisition, he says, is a by-product of a good idea executed soundly in a business plan.

"I firmly believe in the old adage that companies are bought, not sold," says Tom Burkardt, co-founder and president of the former Castle Networks, who took the company from a start-up to a $315 million acquisition by Siemens AG in 17 months. "You do your business plan and you constantly run your business as if you're going toward an IPO. And if you are successful, companies will come and want to acquire you."

## Ready, Get Set, Go!

Once you have decided to move forward you need to develop a game plan and timeline for what happens next. Here is an eight-step plan that Russ Robb, a Boston-based investment banker with O'Connor Wright Wyman, Inc., recommends:[4]

1. *Make a firm decision about selling the business.* If there are several owners, is everyone in agreement about selling the company? Or, are some owners not sure they want to sell? If so, be cautious about starting a process when all owners are not in agreement on the goal.

2. *Decide up front who is in charge of the sale.* There should be one point person who handles all communications with investment bankers and/or attorneys.

3. *Clean up the balance sheet.* Audited financial statements will generally produce a higher price and less onerous reps and warranties, which implies that audited statements are worth the extra cost. If the prospective buyer uncovers uncollectible receivables or outdated inventory during the due diligence phase, then the buyer will be more skeptical about other aspects of the financial statements. Ideally, you should have statements audited for three to five years before trying to sell the company. If you are concerned about the cost of a complete audit, at least have an audit of key assets such as account receivables or inventory.

4. *Partner with professionals.* The last place to cut corners financially in the sale of a business is on transaction advisors. Make sure the ones you hire are top flight—experience counts for a lot with attorneys, accountants, and investment bankers.

5. *Communicate with your bank.* Bankers hate surprises. Let your bank know what your intentions are. The bank may want to keep the banking relationship and may be a source of financing for the buyer.

6. *Target companies that perceive your company to be the most valuable.* Identify companies where there will be synergy and where the buyer's corporate culture (and ethics) are a fit with yours.

7. *Openly recognize off-balance sheet items.* For example, analyze real estate owned outside the business and leased back, or other entities controlled by you that provide services to your operating business, to determine if they will be included in the business being sold. If so, the financial statements should be adjusted to reflect the increase in earnings, or assets represented by those off-balance sheet items. Other items may be liabilities and should be disclosed such as prepayments or customer deposits, work-in-progress billing, contract obligations with set pricing over the next few years, or lease obligations with escalation clauses.

8. *Set time frames and milestones as target dates.* Here's one example of how to keep the process from dragging:

- 4th week: complete the selling memorandum, and compile a list of target buyers
- 8th week: contact all potential buyers
- 10th week: deadline for letters of interest from interested parties (including confidentiality agreements)
- 12th week: narrow potential buyers down to three or four most probable to probable buyers; receive required information
- 14th week: begin serious negotiations with probable buyers
- 18th week: begin structuring letter of intent with chosen buyer
- 20th week: begin working on final documents; buyer begins on-site due diligence
- 22nd week: trial closing
- 24th week: final closing

This is an ambitious timeline—completion of sale from beginning to end: six months. This could easily take longer if there are delays, which is common. For example, one common obstacle is the buyer's need for an environmental study related to business real estate.

In the next chapter we will look at some of the provisions you may want to include in the legal agreements with a buyer.

# 9

# Negotiating and Structuring the Deal

T he buyer you choose may not be the one with the highest price. He or she should have the best overall deal, though, which could include important other terms: legal, tax, management, and emotional. Getting the best possible deal will require some savvy negotiation skills. This chapter will help you navigate your way through the process. But first, consider the following prenegotiation housekeeping steps.

## Prenegotiation Work

**Create a negotiation team.** As mentioned in Chapter 8, you should put a good team together to help you avoid some of the emotional traps that sellers often fall into. Here are two scenarios a professional team can help you avoid.

1. A corporate attorney who represented a consolidator tells this story. "We used to put a check in the middle of the table made out to the seller and let him look at it during the negotiations. Can you imagine how distracting it is for the seller to keep staring at a check for millions of

dollars payable to him? This guy was already on his way to Florida [in his mind]—the negotiations didn't last long."

2. One buyer used a team to call on sellers consisting of a "good 'ol boy" from Texas who could charm anybody and a CPA who's job was to examine the seller's financial information. In practice, they acted like a good cop and bad cop. The Texas charmer would promise the seller whatever he wanted—including marrying his daughter. The CPA would then come in, shake his head, and say, "No, we really can't...." Sellers loved the Texas charmer and were so caught up in his story of how he and his company were going to take care of everybody and everything, that the sellers often didn't seem to notice as the CPA slowly started taking dollars off the table.

**Narrow the list of potential buyers.** Let's assume you have narrowed your list of suitors to the two that you are willing to sell to. They have both sent letters of interest and they have met with you and your advisors. You have done your due diligence on them and know they can both perform financially. Now you are ready to enter into serious negotiations with each. Both of them will want you to sign a letter of intent before they will invest serious time and resources into your deal. And both of them at that stage are trying to convince you that each one is the preferred company for you to trust with your "baby."

How will you decide? While the dollars and terms of each potential deal may be comparable, the ultimate decision is usually based on which company is the better fit for you, your employees, and the business you have nurtured over the past years.

Jack Blaeser, CEO of Concord Communications, says, "If you plan to stay, if you care about the employees that you've hired, it's really important for small companies to do their homework and evaluate: is this a buyer I want to give my children to? Does the buyer deal with people the way you do? If not, you'll have money but the people you brought in and trusted and treated like family may be working in an environment that's not very pleasant."

A large part of the value of your company, from the buyer's perspective, may be from intangible assets such as the productivity, training, and safety record of your work force, the effectiveness of your management team, your company culture, your brand, reputation in the industry, and relationship with customers and vendors. Therefore, preserving those intangible assets means the fit between the two companies is important.

**Put incentives in place.** Many times, according to Jim Geary, founder and president of SHYM Technology in Needham, Massachusetts, the only people committed to the success of an acquisition are the ones receiving direct economic benefit—the owners and major shareholders. When that happens, employees from the acquired company and the purchaser may not be committed to making the new company work.

"If the people are engaged, and are in a situation where they see both the economic as well as the job benefit, then they're going to be committed," says Geary. "Those people are the blood and soul of the company. Those are the people who have to be integrated, to be committed to success. If they're not participating in that large increase in equity, then many times they're just going to disintegrate immediately."[1]

## Basic Negotiating Principles

- *Let others on your negotiation team do the haggling.* Some clients have used their attorney and my consulting firm to keep the process moving. Others try to do the negotiating themselves. Some turn it over to the investment bankers to put the deal together and are involved only at key times in the process, such as deciding on the two or three best buyers and later decisions about specific negotiating points.

- *Stay involved.* You, the seller, are an important part of the negotiation process. You should be present and part of the process, but let your people do your negotiating. In other words, you are there to represent what the buyer is buying. Trust your team of advisors to set the pace. Be cautious about agreeing or disagreeing too quickly on any issue. Build relationships with the buyers; leave negotiating to your advisors.

- *Don't expect to resolve every issue in one session.* Over the days and or weeks that the negotiations occur, there will be time to come back to tough unresolved issues. When your team and the buyer are stuck on an issue, note it, table it, and move on to issues that can be resolved. At the end of that session, agree with the buyer about where you disagree and schedule another time to address those issues. That way you can cover important ground at each meeting, you can learn to agree with one another on certain issues, and you can build relationship currency for later meetings. Relationship currency is the "chips" that can be used during negotiation to ask or give in on a specific issue.

Before each meeting adjourns, agree on what has been agreed upon and agree on the open issues that need to be resolved. Keep in mind that the buyer wants the deal to work as much as you do. Sometimes a committed buyer will need to spend a few days with his own people trying to sweeten the deal for your benefit. You may not know the limits of the buyer's authority but rest assured there is generally someone else who can always agree to improve the offer if the buyer successfully argues for it. Pressuring the buyer when the buyer has already said "no" once may not improve your position. Forcefully making your points (and your demands) is one thing. Alienating the buyer doesn't help you win your position. Save that issue for your next meeting. Sometimes, distance and time (a few days) makes the buyer's heart grow fonder.

- *Use objective standards to argue your position.* For example, demographic studies can support your projections for sales increases, or a survey of commercial rents in the neighborhood can support why the lease you are negotiating with the buyer should be at a higher rate. Safety records and production information may help you argue why your company deserves a higher price.

- *Don't get carried away by your emotions.* You will experience some heated emotions during parts of the process. You may begin to second-guess whether you should still sell your company. If the offer is fair and the buyer is someone you respect and whom you believe will be good for your company and its people, then stay focused on following through. If, on the other hand, you realize that it isn't the right fit, then walk away. You may not be ready, and there may be a better buyer tomorrow.

One client had a very generous offer from a well-respected public company to do a tax-free exchange of his company's stock for $28 million of the public company's stock (with no restrictions). Agreement in principle was reached and the meeting adjourned while the buyer's lawyers prepared the closing documents for the next morning. At dinner, the buyer disclosed to the seller more details about how the public company intended to run the seller's company. It became alarmingly clear that the public company was going to dismantle the seller's company and retain only the marketing components. Plants would be closed, and loyal long-time employees would be laid off. The plants were in smaller communities where good jobs were not so easy to find. The seller spent a sleepless night. The next morning he had decided to walk away from the $28 million—with no regrets.

## Creating Negotiating Power

You and your team should focus on trying to help the buyer better understand any hidden value in your business, so the buyer can pay the price you both agree is fair. Fisher and Ertel, in *Getting Ready to Negotiate*,[2] suggest you pay attention to the following:

- *Help the buyer see your point of view.* You cannot assume that the buyer will intuitively appreciate the intangible aspects of your business. You should therefore point them out and demonstrate why your product, process, or service is superior (if it is) and why your company should be paid a premium. But producing a superior product or having a great customer base won't mean much if the value doesn't show up in pretax earnings.

  One advantage of selling to strategic buyers is that they may provide cross-selling opportunities for the buyer's own products or services. Your homework and due diligence on the buyer can pay off here if you can demonstrate to the buyer how your marketing and sales people can sell the buyer's products to your customers. One Pennsylvania-based buyer had never been able to penetrate into the southeastern part of the United States with its products. Acquiring a Southern distributor with a successful sales organization gave the buyer immediate penetration into a new market along with loyal, existing customers. The new buyer was smart enough to work hard at retaining the entire sales organization of the seller.

- *Understand the buyer's interests.* If you learn the financial targets the buyers need to meet, perhaps you can help them figure out how to meet their numbers. One client learned the buyer's requirement for post-deal pretax cash flow. Working with the buyer to increase amounts allocated to tax-deductible covenants, such as noncompete and consulting agreements, and lower the amount allocated to the purchase price, helped the buyer explain to his board that the deal met their financial objectives. The buyer reciprocated by "grossing up" the covenants so that the seller received the same monies on an after-tax, present value basis.

Some sellers believe that new profits the buyer creates, from increasing sales or reducing expenses, should somehow be capitalized and paid to the seller as additional consideration. Unless you have already built that in to your own pro forma, don't count on buyers paying you extra for value they create. It's okay to factor sales increases into your pro forma that you are anticipating, or lower expenses that you have already planned. One experienced buyer commented, "The sellers always want to get paid for what we can do. We tell them if they can [increase the value] they should—then we'll pay you for it. So, why don't you wait a year or two, create your own improvements, then come back to us and we'll pay you more."

Try to put yourself in the buyer's shoes. If the buyer invested the money you want them to pay you for your company, then show them how they can get the return they need to justify the purchase price. Each buyer has a set of required financial targets. One buyer's own cost of capital was 15 percent, so that was the minimum return he expected from an acquisition. One of the seller's challenges in that scenario was to obtain a higher price for herself while helping the buyer realize a better than 15 percent return on the deal. Through some creative structuring, the seller and buyer worked together to create a win-win: the seller got her price and the buyer could show a better than 15 percent return to his boss.

- *Use external standards of legitimacy to resolve differences.* Roger Fisher, in *Getting Ready to Negotiate*, advises that, "we will almost always face the harsh reality of interests that conflict." Rather than trying to resolve differences by willpower, Fisher notes, "It is usually more persuasive to convince the other side that a given result would be fair rather than trying to convince by stubbornness." If both sides are open to new ideas, based on a standard of fairness, then what is fair can be measured by external information. In other words, the position you are taking is asking the buyer to do what is legitimate and what is the right thing to do. Therefore, be prepared with external data, precedents, or other objective information to support your position.

If you expect the buyer to take care of your employees be very, very specific about what that means. And get it in writing. You cannot expect to get top dollar for your business and simultaneously restrict the new owner's ability to make changes in your company. If you don't want any changes to occur, then you are not ready to sell. On the other hand, if you want to limit the changes the buyer can make, then expect to make some concessions or price reallocations to your employees for every restriction you create.

For example, one client who had always given generous bonuses to key managers negotiated an earn-out based on conservative assumptions about future profits after the sale. But the profits didn't materialize as expected because the key managers who made the profits happen didn't participate in the earn-out and weren't entitled to bonuses from the new owners. The client restructured the earn-out so the key managers could participate. The expected profits began to materialize as originally projected.

---

**EXAMPLE OF HOW ONE SELLER CONTINUED THEIR COMMITMENTS TO EMPLOYEES, SUPPLIERS, AND COMMUNITY AFTER THE SALE**

As part of the $326 million deal to buy Ben & Jerry's ice cream company, the European firm Unilever contractually agreed to

- make no personnel changes for two years.
- continue contracts with suppliers that provided natural products.
- undergo an audit of its worldwide operations' environmental impact, supervised by Ben & Jerry's co-founder Ben Cohen.
- make a one-time $5 million gift to the Ben & Jerry Foundation, which supports causes ranging from battered women in Vermont to farm workers in Florida.
- donate 7.5 percent of Ben & Jerry's pre-tax income or $1.1 million, whichever is greater, to the foundation for the next ten years.
- donate $5 million to a fund to help minority businesses and others.

---

# Differentiating between Value and Price

What about the huge premiums over recent trading prices (those share prices already inflated) large public companies are paying to buy other large public companies? How does that affect a seller of a private company?

Financial details of the private business deal rarely get reported in the media and therefore the pricing and value information regarding private transactions comes from word-of-mouth speculation. "I heard that Company X pays more than Company Y." "I heard that they got $10 million." This type of information has little practical value. Without details behind the transaction you cannot assess what it really indicates. How much more does Company X pay? Was the $10 million in cash or stock? Was it guaranteed or is it dependent on performance? Business owners have little available solid information regarding what their business may be worth on the open market.

Similarly, management of larger public companies have equally little information about what should be paid for a private business that they are looking to acquire. While aware of public market multiples, they also intuitively know that these multiples may not apply— they are too high—to a private business. They may not fully understand the differences between the public and the private markets.

Value and price represent two different sets of assumptions. Having the correct one in mind can be helpful during the negotiation process. No one wants to overpay for something they are buying. But we often are willing to pay more for something we perceive to be of high value.

| C O N S I D E R | Price is negotiated; value is perceived. If the seller can help the buyer perceive greater value, price will increase. |
|---|---|

In theory, everyone knows what public companies are worth. If we pick up the paper or go on the Internet, we can get the latest trading price for a business' common stock and determine what the market believes it to be worth. In practice, however, it is not that clear cut. Mergers and acquisitions of public companies regularly occur where huge premiums over market prices are paid because the acquirer believes the business is undervalued, or because it is not being operated effectively. So, there is plenty of disagreement as to the value of public companies. When trying to determine the value of private companies, the issues of risk often offset the perceptions of value.

## Letter of Intent

Acquisition professionals have different views about whether to use a letter of intent (LOI). LOIs can be helpful in outlining the anticipated terms of a deal, and some buyers and sellers refuse to allow due diligence to proceed without having one signed. On the other hand, because letters of intent may or may not be binding in whole or in part, they can be extremely dangerous to inexperienced sellers who may not understand which provisions are or are not binding. When signed hastily, they can also ruin your subsequent negotiating position, even when they purport to be nonbinding. Because of these risks, you should never sign any LOI (even one that appears to be nonbinding) without having your attorney review it.

The buyer will want you to sign a nonbinding LOI to indicate your intent to go forward. However, once you have signed the LOI a lot of your negotiating power and leverage dries up. Although the buyer will argue that the agreement is not binding, it prevents you from negotiating with other buyers. The LOI is a form of lock-up provision that takes you and your company off the market for 90 days or so. Watch out for binding agreements to agree, which create a lien on the seller's company. Once the LOI is signed, the courtship is over. So, before you sign a LOI, you should make sure it covers as many critical deal points as possible. Use negotiations about the LOI to work out most details of your deal.

Instead of agreeing to the LOI as presented, use the opportunity to begin serious negotiation over substantive issues of the deal. The LOI becomes a more complex document (and takes longer), but it also helps you iron out 90 percent of the issues. After the more complex LOI is signed, the buyer can immediately begin due diligence and the final contract will be more easily drafted because you and your buyer will already have addressed most of the big issues.

In some business sales, the parties may work out the preliminary terms of the deal on a nonbinding terms sheet and then use that document to prepare a LOI or a definitive agreement. In other situations, the parties may go straight to a LOI or a definitive agreement.

The following issues should be resolved *before* a LOI is signed:

- Representations and indemnities that the seller will be required to make concerning the company's financial and business conditions.

- Price to be paid, assets to be acquired, and liabilities to be assumed. Do real estate and other nonbusiness assets come with the deal? If the buyer will require you to sign a noncompete agreement, you will likely be able to negotiate some compensation for that.

- Method of payment—cash, notes, stock of the buyer, or a combination.
- If the buyer is willing to pay cash, that's great, but you still have to work out the schedule of those payments, and whether they are contingent upon the future performance of the business or will be set regardless of what happens. Factor in the portion of the purchase price, if any, that will be made up of *earnout*, the purchase price being dependent on future performance of the business. Obviously, the more cash you get upfront, the less risk for you. If the buyer will be paying over time, make sure you require collateral security for those installment payments. If there is an earnout, negotiate your deal as if you will never see a penny of it.
- If the buyer is offering you stock in the buyer's company as part of the sales price, be careful to address the following:

  - Is the stock registered or not? If the stock is not registered, as a new stockholder you will be subject to Rule 144 of the Securities Act of 1933, which requires you to hold the stock for at least a year before selling it. (Deloitte & Touche LLP advises asking for registration rights to circumvent the holding period requirement and/or *demand* or *piggyback* rights so the stock can be registered and sold.) If the buyer's shares are being used as part of the purchase price, will those shares be registered, and if so, when?

  - Does the stock have any restrictions? Can you sell the stock immediately or will you be required to hold it for two or more years?

  - If the buyer is a public company, what is the typical trading volume? If the stock is thinly traded, then you may have difficulty selling a large block of your shares on the open market without affecting the price at the time you sell.

  - Is there a guaranteed floor? Public companies can experience volatility in their stock price. Will the buyer guarantee that regardless of how low the price falls, the company will guarantee you a minimum value for the shares?

  - How much stock will you take?

- If the buyer is a private company, and you take part of the purchase price in a promissory note, insist that you are provided audited financial information from the buyer as long as your note is outstanding. If important financial ratios of the buyer deteriorate, while your note is outstanding, your note should have triggering provisions tied to their financial ratios to make sure you get paid. Would your buyer be willing to post a letter of credit as security for the Promissory Note? Also, you should have a payoff requirement in the event your buyer should later sell to someone else after your deal is closed.

- Specify any purchase price adjustments resulting from possible changes in book value between signing and closing. Who keeps the receivables? Generally sellers keep receivables older than 60 to 90 days.

- Tax planning and deal structure. If you will be creating and funding a charitable trust or supporting organization with your stock, with the anticipation that your buyer would purchase those shares from the charitable entity, be sure those charitable entities are in place and funded *prior* to any written documents of any kind with your prospective buyer.

- The size of any hold-back from the purchase price to secure the representations. For example, if the agreement specifies a certain level of cash for ongoing operations will be retained by the buyer, they may credit you with receivables due you at the closing. And they may want to hold-back a portion of the cash due you in case the receivables are not collected as anticipated. Therefore any amounts due you, retained by the buyer, should be put in an interest-bearing account and paid as soon as their risk related to the representations diminishes.

- Any conditions to the buyer's obligations (such as financing, board approval, etc.).

- Employment terms, if any, of selling executives, including family members.

- Nature and duration of noncompetition agreements.

- Continuity of management. At some point you will need to inform your key executives and the rest of your employees about a pending sale. The buyer may want to talk with key management and want to negotiate employment agreements with your top executives. The timing may be awkward since your deal will not be finalized at that time and you will not want to do anything to jeopardize your pending deal. Furthermore, key employees may be reluctant to enter into employment contracts since they may not know much about the buyer. Working on employment contracts for the buyer may be jumping the gun, but is something that the new owner will typically want to discuss, since the realization of the projected earnings is contingent on your having the management in place to realize those projections. If you already have employment contracts or non-compete agreements with your management group, check the documents regarding your ability to assign them to someone else.

## Comparing Different Offers You May Receive

In the following example, the client had already signed up with a broker before we became involved. The broker had initially provided some estimates of the value of the business and was able to bring three buyers to the table with offers that were close to, and in one case, exceeded the broker's estimate of value. We were engaged to help with the negotiations and after several months of negotiating, the client chose to sell to Buyer C (see Figure 9.1). The Letter of Intent that became a definitive agreement is contained in the Sell Appendix. In addition to the terms described below, Buyer C also offered an earnout to the sellers in the form of stock options for exceeding budgeted pro formas. The potential value of the earnout may be significant for these sellers. But even if the earnout doesn't occur as anticipated, the sellers were satisfied with the basic terms of the deal.

## The Essence of a Typical Contract

Whether or not a LOI is used, a definitive contract will need to be prepared to document the final terms of the deal. The contents of a definitive

## FIGURE 9.1—COMPARING OFFERS FROM THREE BUYERS

|  | Broker's Estimate | Buyer A | Buyer B | Buyer C |
|---|---|---|---|---|
| Cash received from buyer | $3,600,000 | $3,265,000 | $3,400,000 | $3,000,000 |
| Note held by seller | — | — | — | — |
| Deferred payment (2 years) | — | — | — | 1,400,000 |
| Gross sale price of stock | 3,600,000 | 3,265,000 | 3,400,000 | 4,400,000 |
| **Add** |  |  |  |  |
| Corporate cash retained (1) | 429,459 | 429,459 | 429,459 | 429,459 |
| Accounts receivable retained (2) | 323,677 | 323,677 | 323,677 | 323,677 |
| Shareholder receivables retained (3) | — | — | — | — |
| Corporate debt assumed | — | — | — | — |
|  | 753,136 | 753,136 | 753,136 | 753,136 |
| **Less** |  |  |  |  |
| Corporate debt satisfied (4) | (598,973) | (598,973) | (598,973) | (598,973) |
| Notes payable to shareholders (5) | (88,856) | (88,856) | (88,856) | (88,856) |
| Working capital requirement | — | — | — | — |
| Corporate leases bought out (6) | — | — | — | — |
|  | (687,829) | (687,829) | (687,829) | (687,829) |
| **Net sale price of stock** | **3,665,307** | **3,330,307** | **3,465,307** | **4,465,307** |

### Taxable Gain Calculation

|  | Broker's Estimate | Buyer A | Buyer B | Buyer C |
|---|---|---|---|---|
| Net sale price of stock | 3,665,307 | 3,330,307 | 3,465,307 | 4,465,307 |
| Basis of corporate stock (7) | 402,000 | 402,000 | 402,000 | 402,000 |
| Broker's attorney fees | 200,000 | 200,000 | 200,000 | 200,000 |
| Estimated other closing costs | 25,628 | 20,343 | 25,618 | 23,618 |
| Total basis & expenses of sale | 628,628 | 622,343 | 627,618 | 625,618 |
| **Total taxable gain on sale** | **3,036,679** | **2,707,964** | **2,837,689** | **3,839,689** |

**FIGURE 9.1—CONTINUED**

## Calculation of Income Taxes

| | Broker's Estimate | Buyer A | Buyer B | Buyer C |
|---|---|---|---|---|
| Net sale price of stock | 3,665,307 | 3,330,307 | 3,465,307 | 4,465,307 |
| (Less owner financing) | — | — | — | — |
| (Less deferred payment) | — | — | — | (1,400,000) |
| Received in year of sale | 3,665,307 | 3,330,307 | 3,465,307 | 3,065,307 |
| Gain as percentage of sale price | 82.8% | 81.3% | 81.9% | 86.0% |
| Capital gain in year of sale | **3,036,679** | **2,707,964** | **2,837,689** | **3,839,689** |
| Federal capital gain tax 20% (yr of sale) | 607,335 | 541,592 | 567,537 | 487,937 |
| Federal capital gain tax (deferred payment) | | | | 280,000 |
| Total federal capital gains tax | 607,335 | 541,592 | 567,537 | 767,937 |

acquisition contract will vary depending upon such factors as the structure of the transaction for tax and accounting purposes and the type of consideration being issued. The provisions you and your advisors hammered out with the buyer for the LOI should be included in the contract. According to Charles Claeys, a partner at the law firm of Peabody & Brown in Boston, most final contracts will include:

- Description of the transaction and the consideration being issued.

- *Representations* and *warranties* by the selling shareholders or other owners of the business being sold and by the acquirer. Representations and warranties are statements of past and existing facts; warranties are promises that existing or future facts are or will be true. These representations and warranties provide the buyer with information essential to the decision to implement the transaction. Typical representations and warranties relate to financial statements, accounts receivable, taxes, employee benefits, and intellectual property. For example, a representation or warranty relative to financial statements may provide assurances to the buyer regarding the quality and accuracy of the statements. The seller provides these representations in good faith and the buyer relies on those statements. Occasionally, undiscovered liabilities can and do arise. If it is discovered after the closing that the seller has breached one or more of the representations or warranties, the buyer can sue the seller. Reviewing sample representations and warranties in advance of the deal documents is often helpful.

- Description of the conditions that must be satisfied for the closing to occur.

- Provisions governing the operation of the business being acquired between the date of the agreement and the closing.

- General covenants relating to such matters as closing procedures, termination, expenses, and indemnification. Most acquisition agreements will also include extensive schedules that support or list any exceptions to the representations and warranties. In most transactions, representations and warranties by the seller are considerably more extensive than those by the buyer. Buyer representations and warranties are usually very short in cash deals and somewhat more extensive when the buyer is issuing stock or notes in the transaction. The content of the seller's representations and warranties and any related indemnification provisions and whether they survive the closing (and, if so, for how long) are among the most critical parts of any acquisition agreement for the seller.

Although contracts in larger transactions are usually signed well in advance of the closing, in many smaller transactions the definitive agreement is signed at the closing. The timing of when the agreement is signed will significantly affect its content.

## Buyer's Due Diligence

After the contract has been signed, due diligence begins. A due diligence phase is included in virtually every business sale transaction. In this period, the buyer and its advisors are given an opportunity to evaluate the business, legal, and financial condition and future prospects of the business being acquired, generally through a series of on-site and off-site inspections and document reviews. Due diligence allows the buyer to verify the accuracy of the data provided by the seller prior to closing. The buyer will want to review copies of corporate minutes, buy-sell agreements, voting trusts, stock transfer ledgers, government filings, permits, licensing, and any information relating to financing: loan agreements, leases, guarantees. It also includes employment disclosures (i.e., employment agreements, compensation histories, and benefit plan information). The due diligence team will also want to review commitments to capital expenditures; deeds; insurance policies; franchise or license agreements; joint venture agreements; partnerships that involve the selling company, marketing, or distribution agreements, etc. Information relating to pending or threatened litigation, consent decrees, judgments, IRS audits, or environmental matters will all be disclosed during this phase.

The timing of the due diligence period varies. When a letter of intent is used, the due diligence is often conducted between the signing of the letter of intent and the definitive agreement. When the parties go straight to a definitive contract, the principal due diligence is generally conducted before that document is signed, but some definitive agreements provide for due diligence after the definitive agreement is signed, with corresponding termination rights if the results are not satisfactory. Regardless of when the due diligence is conducted, the buyer and seller should always sign a Confidentiality Agreement before exchanging due diligence information (see Sell Appendix).

At this point, the deal has usually become public (at least to key executives) because it is very difficult for the buyer to conduct the due diligence phase in secrecy. If the information supplied does not match the buyer's representations, then this is when the deal either becomes smaller (the buyer may want to hold back certain payments until performance is proven) or falls apart.

# Closing

After the principal due diligence is completed, the parties will generally work together to satisfy any conditions to the closing. These conditions may include such factors as regulatory, lender, or landlord approvals; financing; and continued accuracy at the closing of the parties' respective representations and warranties.

Any conditions to closing—usually discovered during the due diligence phase—must be satisfied before the seller gets his or her money. For example, a licensor or franchisor may have to be a party to the transaction. You will need to research any franchise, licensing, and distributor agreements you hold to determine if there are restrictions on transferring ownership to a third party.

In the closing preparation process, the parties focus on the specific documents that must be delivered at the closing. These documents generally include evidence of corporate status, legal opinions, instruments of conveyance, certifications by company officers, the stock certificates and notes being issued by the buyer, and the shares or assets being delivered by the seller at the closing.

The purchase price is paid and any ancillary documents such as the selling executive's employment and noncompetition agreements are executed.

# Common Seller Mistakes and Antidotes

Buyers are generally experienced at buying companies, while sellers may only go through the experience of selling a company once. Sellers often make common mistakes in selling their businesses, such as

- *Emotionally selling the company before the deal is done.* Being too eager to close the deal you run the risk of missing some negotiation opportunities to improve the deal in favor of the seller.

  *Antidote.* If you are too eager you can leave dollars, or unresolved issues, on the table, and regret it later. Use your advisor team to do your negotiating. Keep your perspective. If the deal falls apart it may be because it wasn't the right deal. While negotiations are going on, stay focused on running your business.

Buyers can get spooked if projections are being missed before the deal closes.

- *Taking too much stock (as part of the sale proceeds) in the buyer's company.* Remember you are selling your company, not investing most of your assets in somebody else's company.

  *Antidote.* As attractive as the buyer's stock may look, you need to keep asking yourself: "If I sold for all cash would I then turn around and invest 50, 60, or 70 percent of the proceeds in only one stock?"

- *Not analyzing after-the-deal issues.* These issues generally relate to how the new owner will integrate day-to-day operations and the new reporting relationships. They may include your key employees losing motivation or starting to quit after the new owner takes over, or you becoming frustrated about the terms of a consulting agreement that you negotiated.

  *Antidote.* The general lesson is to understand the culture of the new owner. Is it a bureaucratic structure or are decisions pushed down to the local level? What is the level of authority of the person who will be supervising your operations?

- *Seller's remorse.* Many sellers do not anticipate the emotional impact after they sell the business. Some may react to changes the new owner makes; others have not planned meaningful activities to fill their time.

  *Antidote.* If you don't think you will like the changes a new owner will make, leave town for a few weeks after the deal closes and get some emotional distance between you and your former business. Make sure you find stimulating and fun activities, which could include being more active in your industry association, consulting in the field, travel, and hobbies.

## Doing the Right Thing

"The thing that differentiates us is that we have taken acquisitions and built a business process around it," says Mike Volpi, senior vice president of business development, who heads up acquisitions at Cisco

Systems. "Most companies tend to view the process of buying a company as a one-time event; you just go out and buy a company, something happens, and magically, boom, you have a new company on the back end. We took that process aside and said, if you're going to do this on a repeatable and scalable basis, you can't simply throw out some cash, buy a company, and expect it to work. The classic pitfall of acquisitions is that people do them as a one-time event. Organizations, especially larger companies, are not built around one-time events. They don't deal with a single shock well."

Instead, he says, Cisco has built a business process, much as it would a manufacturing process, with a dedicated team for buying and integrating companies on a regular basis. "By building a process around it we've been able to establish a best practice," he says.

## Not All Deals Are Happy Marriages

What's a good sale? One advisor answered this way: "For the seller, it's realizing that what the buyer said is true, that he gets his stock options, that the parent company grows, that the stock increases in value, that the corporate staff leaves him alone and doesn't try to radically change the seller's company.

"But it's often a slippery slope. The novelty of the buyer doing his first deal is that everybody pays attention, but by the time the buyer has bought 20 or 100 or 160 companies, it becomes a mechanical process. There's no real courtship—the corporate staff is telling the seller what he has to do instead of trying to build a relationship. They are saying 'here's how we do it' and there's no flexibility and they're trying to change things at the seller's company, even though it was a successful company that they're buying—they go in and try to change it to the way they think it ought to be. And oftentimes, the changes that get imposed on the seller are without senior management of the buyer really knowing what those changes are."

What makes a good purchase? "From the standpoint of the buyer, that the company looks like it did in due diligence, the owner still has an entrepreneurial attitude, the owner still runs it like it was still her's, and the corporation continues to make money for the buyer."

In one survey of Fortune 1,000 service and manufacturing companies by Braxton Associates, the surveyed companies had achieved less than a 30 percent success rate in their mergers and acquisitions.[3] Yet the same companies also predicted their merger activities wouldn't slow down but would remain the same or increase. Acquisition failures were in two broad categories: logic failures ("it looked like a good idea but wasn't") and process failures ("it was a good idea that just didn't work"). Logic failures identified by the Braxton survey included the following responses from the acquiring company:

- We overestimated market potential.
- We had poor information about the acquired company.
- The environment changed.
- We acquired a company in an industry too far removed from our own.
- We purchased the wrong company.
- The hoped-for product was never developed.

Process failures are due to poor execution, including integration, after the acquisition was completed.

An interview with Richard Morris, who sold his fourth-generation auto-parts manufacturing company Fel-Pro to Federal-Mogul, gives an example of what might be described as a process failure:

> [They] said all the right things about how people were important...and that [they] wanted to learn from our culture. After Federal-Mogul took over, I realized practically from day one that what [they] said and what Federal-Mogul was going to do were two different things.[4]

Selling your company should be more than just a transaction. It should be a partnering of intent. That intent should be in the combined commitment to continue the process of adding value to the company. Only through this commitment can the seller, the buyer, and ultimately all the people who benefit from the company, come away from the deal feeling that they gained from the transaction.

# Managing
# Taxes and Risk

Tax ramifications of a potential sale should be considered before any documents, including letters of intent, are signed. Surprises in the income tax arena are rarely pleasant ones, so consult with your CPA, attorney, or other tax advisors early on. They can help you understand the impact that tax treatment will have on your deal, advise you on tax-favored strategies, and inform you about state, local, and foreign tax implications.

This chapter is intended to give you an overview of the federal tax implications of different types of sales, and help you appreciate how the tax impact to the buyer can affect the amount your buyer is willing to pay. Generally, we will look at the tax aspects of a sale of a C corporation, and later discuss some of the tax issues on the sale of an S corporation, partnership, or limited liability company.

## Sell Company Stock
## or Sell Company Assets?

Let's assume for simplicity that you own 100 percent of the stock in your company. You can offer to sell the stock to a prospective buyer, with the result that the buyer would own the company's stock, you no longer would own any part of the company, and you would receive the sale proceeds directly. Or you can offer to sell the assets owned by your company, with the result that the buyer would own all the assets of the company (and whatever liabilities would move along with the assets), you would continue to own the stock of your company, and your company would receive the sale proceeds.

A stock sale causes no change in the legal entity; generally, the corporation with its assets, liabilities, and equity, its tax attributes and its history, remains intact but with different ownership. Your asset has changed, however, you have exchanged the stock you owned for other assets: cash, or stock in the buyer company, or debt, or some combination of these. You personally recognize a gain on the sale of your stock: the excess of the amount you receive for the sale over your tax basis in the stock sold, which generally is the amount you paid for your stock. You personally pay income tax on that gain, typically at capital gains rates.

An asset sale involves the exchange of the assets owned by the company for cash, stock, debt, or a combination. Assets sold may include tangible assets such as inventory, receivables, equipment, land, and buildings, and intangible assets such as customer lists, licenses, and distribution channels. Company liabilities often will also be transferred, particularly if the debt is secured by the assets. Your asset remains the same: stock in your company. The company receives the proceeds of the sale and pays income taxes (at ordinary income rates for corporations) on the gain. You then can choose whether to have the company retain and invest the proceeds, or to liquidate the company, or to have the company distribute the net-of-tax proceeds to you. Liquidation of the company would be taxable to you, and the distribution of net proceeds would be taxable to you, typically at capital gains rates.

Comparison of a stock sale in Figure 10.1, to an asset sale can illustrate the effects of the difference in tax treatment. For the stock sale, the seller simply sells all of the stock for cash. For the asset sale, the corporation sells all its assets, liquidates, and distributes the after-tax proceeds of the sale to its shareholder, who is taxed on that distribution.

Use the following assumptions for Figure 10.1 in comparing a stock sale to an asset sale.

- The purchaser is willing to pay $5,000,000.
- The corporation's tax basis in its assets is $1,500,000.
- There are no corporate liabilities.
- The Federal corporate tax rate is 35 percent (exclusive of state taxes).
- The shareholders' tax basis in their stock is $1,000,000.
- The shareholders' personal capital gains tax rate is 20 percent.

The obvious advantage of the stock sale over the asset sale is nearly a million dollars in after-tax proceeds. Another possible advantage is that all liabilities related to the company and its operations transfer to the buyer, which is not true with an asset sale. Clearly, a stock sale is

### FIGURE 10.1—COMPARISON OF A STOCK SALE TO AN ASSET SALE

**Sale of Assets**

*Tax on corporate gain:*

| | |
|---|---|
| Proceeds from sale of assets(a) | $5,000,000 |
| Net assets | 1,500,000 |
| Corporate gain | 3,500,000 |
| Tax rate | 35% |
| Tax on corporate gain (b) | $1,225,000 |
| Net available to distribute to shareholders (a − b = c) | $3,775,000 |

*Tax on shareholders' gain:*

| | |
|---|---|
| Liquidation distribution to shareholders (c, as above) | $3,775,000 |
| Shareholders' tax basis | 1,000,000 |
| Shareholders' gain on distribution | 2,775,000 |
| Tax rate | 20% |
| Tax on shareholders' gain (d) | 555,000 |
| Net proceeds (c − d) | $3,220,000 |

**Sale of Stock**

*Tax on shareholders' gain:*

| | |
|---|---|
| Proceeds from sale of stock(e) | $5,000,000 |
| Shareholders' tax basis | 1,000,000 |
| Shareholders' gain on sale | 4,000,000 |
| Tax rate | 20% |
| Tax on shareholders' gain (f) | 800,000 |
| Net proceeds (e − f) | $4,200,000 |

preferable to the seller. Since the buyer is paying the same dollars in either case, it would seem at a glance that the buyer would be indifferent to the form of the transaction, so most sales would be stock sales.

However, the form of the transaction has a significant impact on the buyer, both tax-wise and legally, which affects the buyer's preference and the amount the buyer is willing to pay. In an asset purchase, the buyer's tax basis in the assets purchased is the amount paid, or $5 million. In a stock purchase, however, the assets retain the same tax basis that they had before the sale, or $1 million. If the assets have short useful lives (e.g., inventory or equipment), or if the buyer intends to sell some of the assets in the near future, the low tax basis may result in significantly higher income taxes for the buyer in the short term. Therefore, the buyer generally would prefer to purchase assets.

The gap between the preferences of the seller and the buyer presents an opportunity for negotiation. Say that your presale analysis indicated that, in order to maintain your lifestyle, you need to net $4 million after-tax on the sale. You think that you must make a stock sale based on the calculations above, but an attractive prospective buyer is interested only in an asset purchase. You can rework the calculations to arrive at the amount the buyer would have to pay on an asset or stock sale to provide you the $4 million you need. Then you would be in a position to enter into sale negotiations knowing that it would cost the buyer $6.5 million to acquire the business assets, while you could accept only $4,750,000 to sell the stock.

## Capital Gain versus Ordinary Income

The gain on a stock sale, where all of the stock of a privately-owned corporation is sold by an individual (or a family group or a small group of owners) will be taxed at capital gains rates, except in unusual circumstances, which is favorable to the seller.

The gain on an asset sale, where all of the operating assets of the business are sold by a privately-owned corporation, is more complicated. Most business assets, such as inventory, will generate ordinary income. Gains on sales of real property and intangible assets like goodwill qualify as capital gains. Gains from depreciable assets such as machinery and equipment are treated as part ordinary income—to the extent of depreciation deductions taken—and part capital gain—for appreciation in value over its original cost. But since the sale takes place at the corporate level, the distinction between capital gains and ordinary income is insignificant because of the 35 percent corporate capital gains rate. As discussed above, when the net proceeds are distributed from the company to the shareholders, those distributions qualify for capital gains treatment.

The capital gains versus ordinary income distinction is meaningful for businesses that operate in the form of a partnership or S corporation, where the gains pass through to the owners for income tax purposes. Capital gains pass through and enjoy favorable capital gains rates, and other gains pass through and are taxed as ordinary income.

## S Corporation, Limited Liability Company (LLC), or a Partnership

The complexities of tax treatment of these types of businesses are beyond the scope of this book, but an overview of the taxation should be helpful. Assume for these discussions that each entity is owned by two individuals, and that all of the ownership interests are sold, or that all of the business assets owned by the company are sold. As with any significant transaction undertaken by a business, tax advisors should be consulted early on and be involved in the process, to assist the owners in understanding the tax implications of the transaction.

The sale of S corporation stock qualifies for capital gain treatment. An asset sale by an S corporation is like an asset sale by a C corporation, but generally all capital gains and ordinary income would *not* be taxed at the corporation level, but would pass through to the shareholders and be taxed to them personally at the applicable rates. If the S corporation was a C corporation for any of the ten years preceding the sale, gains from appreciation before the election to be taxed as an S corporation would be taxed at the corporate level, at the maximum corporate rates.

When the business is an LLC, the sale of the members' interests generates capital gain. An LLC whose members have elected to be taxed as a partnership, treats gain from an asset sale the same way as discussed below for a partnership.

The sale of partnership interests qualifies as capital gain. An asset sale by the partnership causes the calculation of capital and ordinary gains at the partnership level, but no taxation at the partnership level. The gains pass through to the partners, retaining their classification as capital or ordinary, and are taxed to the individuals at the applicable rates.

## Cash, Stock, Debt—What Should I Accept as Payment?

The saying goes that, "cash is cash, and only cash is cash." An all cash deal is fully taxable, but carries the lowest risk, since the seller can make a clean break by taking the cash and walking away from the business. Clearly the safest route is to ask for cash, regardless of the form of the sale.

It is not unusual for the buyer to ask the seller to carry some debt on the transaction; for example, to offer 50 percent in cash and 50 percent in the form of a note payable by the buyer to the seller over a period of years.

Figure 10.2 compares the potential benefits of carrying back debt to possible pitfalls.

The alternative for the buyer is to obtain financing through a bank or other financial institution, and pay the seller in cash. A buyer who is unable to obtain financing may not be a viable candidate.

A seller who considers carrying debt on a business sale should consider building performance and liquidity covenants, similar to what a bank might require, into the loan agreement, and carefully monitoring those covenants. And the larger the amount of cash paid up front, the lower the risk the seller bears on the debt.

A 1999 tax law changed the tax treatment of payments received by a seller who accepts debt as part of the consideration for an asset sale. In the past, deferred principal payments were taxed under the installment sale rules, where the seller could elect to defer tax on the loan principal, rather than recognizing the entire gain for income tax purposes in the year of the sale. The seller would pay tax on the payments

## FIGURE 10.2—BENEFITS AND PITFALLS OF CARRYING DEBTS

**Potential Benefits of Carrying Debt**

- A favorable interest rate might be negotiated.

- Income taxes on part of the gain may be deferred; deferred portion of principal payments on a stock sale is taxed when received.

- Might allow buyer to make a purchase that otherwise could not be consummated.

**Potential Pitfalls of Carrying Debt**

- Interest rate might be lower return than seller could earn otherwise.

- Collection of deferred payments depends on the business success of the purchaser.

- Worst case is that the buyer defaults on payments and seller is forced to take back the damaged business and rebuild it.

as they were received, matching the taxation to the actual receipt of the proceeds. The new provision requires accrual method businesses, which include most businesses other than service providers, that are sold under an asset-sale transaction, to recognize the entire gain in the year of the sale. This provision will make sellers less likely to be willing to carry back debt on an asset sale, unless the buyer is willing to increase the price to make up for the accelerated taxation.

In robust economic times, stories abound of business owners who trade their company stock for stock of the purchaser and make a fortune on the appreciation in value of the buyer's stock. As with most things, the potential for huge rewards carries corresponding risk. There are also many stories of stock-for-stock trades where the seller was hurt. At the time of the transaction, the seller thought he had good reason to believe that the buyer's stock was a sound investment, but time revealed too-aggressive expansion plans by the buyer, or other risky business practices that caused the value of the buyer's stock to plummet. The business seller should exercise great caution in considering the value of the buyer's stock in a stock-for-stock trade or in a part-stock deal, and perhaps discount the value of the buyer's stock to account for that risk, in negotiating the sale price.

Does a tax-free transaction sound too good to be true? A seller in the right position can seek an opportunity for a tax-free reorganization (although tax-deferred is a more accurate term). If the seller has investments outside the business and does not need cash proceeds, a tax-deferred stock-for-stock trade can be an attractive option. The advantage is that no taxes are incurred at the time of the deal, and for as long as the seller holds the stock of the acquirer. The disadvantage is that the rules to qualify are complex and riddled with traps for the unwary. Both the owner who is giving up his business and the acquiring company must follow carefully the specific rules.

The most straightforward version of a stock-for-stock trade is where the sellers trade all of their stock in their company for stock in the acquiring company. Essentially, the sellers trade their active ownership in their business for passive ownership in the acquirer, with the expectation that the dividends paid to them by the acquirer will be a sufficient replacement for the financial benefits of active ownership, and that on the eventual sale of the acquiring company's stock, they will realize a greater gain than they would have by selling for cash and investing the proceeds.

Two essential conditions of a tax-deferred stock-for-stock reorganization are

1. the sellers must receive solely *voting* stock of the acquirer in exchange for their stock.
2. immediately after the transaction, the acquirer must own at least 80 percent of *each class of stock* of the sellers' company.

In addition, requirements are imposed for continuity of ownership and continuity of business operation, which means that the sellers must continue to hold their stock in the acquirer, and that the acquirer continues the business activities of the sellers' company.

Other types of tax-deferred reorganizations include an assets-for-stock trade, where substantially all of the operating assets of the sellers' company are exchanged for voting stock of the acquirer, and then the acquirer's stock is distributed to the seller.

If the seller is considering accepting stock of the buyer, whether as part of the sale proceeds or as a stock-for-stock trade, and the buyer is a public company, federal securities laws may come into play. The seller should be aware of the potential impact of those laws before going forward. Public companies are required to disclose to the Securities and Exchange Commission (SEC), the significant terms of the acquisition, and in some cases the historical financial statements of the seller company. These records are available to the public (and on the Internet), which can be uncomfortable for sellers of private companies who are accustomed to keeping financial information private. You should be prepared to hear the high points of your deal discussed over your golf game or lunch at the club.

Another issue in accepting stock from a public company is whether you will receive registered or unregistered (sometimes called *restricted* or *lettered*) stock from the buyer. Registered stock would be issued pursuant to a registration statement filed under the Securities Act of 1933 and applicable state securities laws. Unregistered stock would be issued pursuant to an exemption from the registration requirements. Subject to some restrictions, noted below, registered stock can be freely traded and resold in the public securities markets. Unregistered stock is not permitted to be resold in the public markets for a specified period (generally two to three years after issuance). In the interim, unregistered stock may be resold only in certain limited private transactions, which, if available at all, may involve a discount from the public market price. Even registered shares may be subject to volume limitations on resale.

If the buyer offers you unregistered stock, you may be able to negotiate *demand* or *piggyback* registration rights that will allow you to require that the buyer register the shares for resale at some future time. Demand rights, which are generally viewed as more valuable, give you the right (sometimes to be exercised with others) to demand that the buyer register the shares even if the buyer is not planning to file a registration statement for other purposes. Piggyback rights give you the right to make the buyer add your shares to a registration statement that the buyer independently decides to file covering other shares. Registration rights agreements are complex documents that require solid legal advice.

## Other Negotiating Items

Beyond the price and terms the seller and buyer can agree on lie several options that can sweeten the deal for the buyer. Most sellers actively involved in the business are aware that they can request, and the buyer may require, a consulting agreement. The consulting agreement provides the buyer continuing access to the experience and expertise of the selling business owner, and often can provide a bridge that eases the transition for employees, vendors, and customers of the selling business. The buyer may be willing to pay for an effective executive to stay on as a full-time employee of the business, or for a consulting agreement for a specified period of time, on a full-time or part-time basis. The payments for the consulting agreement should be over and above the sale proceeds, and should be a reasonable amount for the services provided. Unlike the sale proceeds, the consulting payments are tax-deductible to the buyer, and might provide an attractive option to paying a higher price to purchase the business.

Sometimes it is advantageous to both the seller and purchaser to allocate a reasonable portion of the total price to a covenant-not-to-compete. The proceeds designated to the noncompete covenant commonly are paid directly to the active shareholders of the corporation, over a specified period of time. Although the noncompete payments are taxed as ordinary income, they do avoid the corporate-level tax in the case of an asset sale. The purchaser generally can amortize the noncompete payments over 15 years, regardless of the time period covered by the covenant.

The seller also should look for intangible assets that are not reflected on his company's books and appraisal report but have value to the buyer, such as customer lists, specialized technology, or favorable leases. Payments for these items can add to the sale price, or a portion of the price can be assigned to them. Purchased intangibles can be amortized by the buyer over 15 years with a resulting tax deduction to the buyer.

## Buyer's Accounting Method Can Matter to the Seller

Through 1999, the buyer's financial accounting treatment of a transaction could impact the price that buyers would pay for your business. Buyers had two options, to account for the purchase of a company as either a *pooling of interests* or as a *purchase*. A pooling of interests does not apply in cases where the sellers are divesting themselves of the business, because it occurs when two companies combine in a joint undertaking, creating one company from the two, with stockholders of each company maintaining ownership in the combined entity. Essentially any transaction that fails to meet the requirements for a pooling of interests is accounted for as a purchase, including an asset purchase or a stock purchase.

Purchase accounting requires that the price be allocated among the assets purchased according to their fair market value, with any excess of the purchase price over the values of those assets recorded as goodwill. The increased recorded value of the assets is depreciated, and the goodwill is amortized, over future years, creating higher expenses and therefore lower reported profits than under pooling accounting for the buyer. This acts against paying a premium to buy the seller's business.

If you are willing to sell your business through a business combination where you accept the buyer's stock in exchange for your stock, and you maintain ownership after the combination, you should consider structuring the deal so that it can qualify for a pooling of interests treatment and accordingly, a higher price from the buyer. You should also do so soon. New accounting rules have been proposed by the Financial Accounting Standards Board (FASB) that could be implemented in the year 2001, which would require the buyer to use the purchase method of accounting. If the change is passed, there may be a flurry of acquisition activity at the end of 2000, as buyers rush to complete deals that can be structured as a pooling of interests.

## Liquidity and Risk Planning When You Take the Buyer's Stock

In certain situations, usually a tax-free reorganization, there are financial instruments that enable a seller who receives a buyer's public stock to limit the volatility risk of the stock being acquired. It will be important to clarify during your negotiations that the planning steps described below will not violate any of the conditions of the buyer or accelerate any taxes that are deferred.

A *collar* is a combination of options intended to protect the downside risk of the seller (also called the option holder). This transaction occurs post-closing and provides the seller a way to limit the risk of holding the buyer's stock and, depending on how the collar is structured, also to receive some cash while continuing to defer taxation. When a seller exchanges stock with a buyer, there are several opportunities to be considered.

## Go Naked

The riskiest opportunity is to hold the stock of the buyer and do nothing. You can sell the new shares and pay the gain (subject to any restrictions imposed by the buyer), or keep the stock and defer the gain. If you keep the stock and defer the gain, you are also at risk on any fluctuation in the price of the shares you received. If the shares go up as you hope, then the appreciation in stock value may be an unexpected bonus over and above the price you negotiated for the sale of your business. If however, the price goes down, you may lose a significant amount of the value that you negotiated for.

## Be Perfectly Hedged

This means evaluating alternatives that get you out of an awkward position. For example, here are two ways to be perfectly hedged:

1. *Short the stock.* This involves selling shares you don't own today, in expectation that the price may drop (tomorrow) so you plan to purchase those shares at a lower price after the drop. For example, say you sell shares you don't own at $40 and tomorrow the stock goes to $35. You buy the $35 shares and deliver them to the person who paid you $40. You have a $5 profit per share. Meanwhile, the shares you received from the buyer (at $40 per share) when you sold your company have also dropped to $35 per share. But if you sell short the same number of shares that you received on the sale, the $5 per share profit from the short sale perfectly hedges you since you still have $40 of total value: $35 in share price and $5 in cash from the short sale. The hedge also works if you short the stock, and the shares appreciate instead of dropping in value.

2. *Contribute the stock to a Charitable Remainder Unitrust (CRUT).* If your company is a C corporation, you may want to consider creating a CRUT before any letters of intent or agreements of any kind are signed. A CRUT is a nontaxable entity (an irrevocable trust). By conveying some of your shares to a CRUT before a deal is negotiated, the trustee of the CRUT can exchange shares with the buyer at the same time that you do (i.e., at the closing) with no tax consequences. The buyer's shares now in the CRUT can then be sold on the open market immediately, also with no tax consequences. See the section below about CRUTs, CRATs, and CLUTs. This hedge gives the seller an opportunity (through the charitable trust) to immediately dispose of some of the buyer's shares and diversify assets without taxation.

## Be Somewhere in the Middle

This would involve the seller working with his or her attorney to sell a prepaid forward contract (called a collar), which reduces the downside risk of owning the buyer's stock by requiring the seller to give up some of the upside potential. For example, say you took stock in Newco when you sold your business. At the closing, the stock of Newco was trading at $30 a share and you want to protect yourself from Newco's stock falling below a certain price, say, $25 per share. You might structure a collar at $25 *and* at $35 a share. That means you would limit your downside risk so you would never receive less than $25 a share and simultaneously you would limit your upside potential to never be greater than $35 per share. The more downside risk you keep, the more upside potential you also get to keep. When the collar is sold to an investment banker or a third party, in some circumstances you can get cash for Newco's stock without paying the gain until the option is exercised. So if a collar is structured for three to five years, you may be able to get your cash immediately while deferring the gain, and the taxation, until the collar's term ends.

There are two general types of collars. They are as follows:

1. *Zero cost collars.* They are not free, but involve simultaneously selling a call option and buying a put option. A call option gives

someone the right to call the stock away from you at a specified price and for a specified time period. A put option is the opposite: it gives you the right to require someone to purchase your shares at a specified price and for a specified time. For example, assume a stock is trading at $20 per share, and you sell a six month call option at $30 per share. If the stock goes to $33 a share, or higher (within the six months), the person you sold the call to would buy your shares at $30 per share. If you also sold a six month put option on the stock at $15 per share, and the stock price fell to $10 per share (within the six months), you could require the person to whom you sold the put, to pay you $15 per share, regardless of how far the stock price dropped.

The premium you get for selling the call option generally pays for the price of the put. You wouldn't necessarily see any money from the zero-cost transaction; you'd put your securities in your account as collateral for these options. What you have accomplished, though, is to limit your downside risk if the company you sold your business to goes under or the stock price drops precipitously. If either of those events happened, you would have limited your downside to the put price that you sold your stock for. Meanwhile, an investment banker will usually let you borrow 75 to 80 percent of the value of the securities you have in your account. With a zero-cost collar you have limited your risk, and if you need liquidity you can borrow 75 to 80 percent of the value of the securities in the account. There are a number of items to be negotiated with an investment banker, including who retains the dividends on the public stock. Another issue is the duration of the collar, which may be six months, two years, or longer.

2. *Income producing collar.* This type of collar is structured to provide the seller additional income. For example, say Newco's stock is trading at $30 a share. The upside in this example might be limited to $33 a share, while the floor, or downside risk, may still be $25 a share. Since the upside is less than in the Zero-Cost Collar, there is a pricing difference reflected in greater income to the seller. The investment banker may give you more income

than when you sold the put on the stock. You're taxed as if you wrote a call, but the tax treatment is not determined until the call expires. Since the tax issues are quite complex, it is important to seek advice from your CPA and attorney. Often the tax issues are misunderstood by those who are selling the products.

<table>
<tr><td>C O N S I D E R</td><td>The collar represents an opportunity to realize two objectives: sell your business via a tax-free reorganization with a public company for their stock, while separately creating an opportunity for tax-deferred liquidity and diversification. Therefore, it helps the buyer do a stock deal while simultaneously providing a method to address the seller's risk regarding the stock received from the public company.</td></tr>
</table>

## Charitable Remainder Unitrust (CRUT) and Annuity Trust (CRAT)

Charitable remainder trusts are deferred-giving devices that are often implemented prior to the sale of a business. They were legislated into being in 1969 by Congress. They are split-interest trusts whereby one (or more) individuals have an income interest and a charity has a remainder interest. A donor transfers assets to a charitable trust and retains an income interest in the assets transferred for a period of time (not to exceed 20 years) or for life. The assets in the trust are invested and the income realized is paid out to the donor, who has the income interest. At the death of the donor, or the end of the trust term, whatever is remaining goes to the remainderman, which is one or more public charities as designated by the donor.

Since the donor retains an interest in the property transferred to the trust (the income interest), your charitable deduction for income tax purposes is based on the value of the gift to the charity reduced by the present value of the income interest retained by you. It provides a method to defer the capital gain taxes you would incur if you sold the shares yourself. Since the principal amount in the trust isn't reduced by taxes, those assets reinvested by the trustee can produce a greater income benefit to you.

A charitable remainder unitrust (CRUT) and charitable remainder annuity trust (CRAT) differ in some important ways. The unitrust or CRUT pays out a fixed percentage of the initial fair market value of the trust's assets each year to the income beneficiary. Therefore, the unitrust amount may fluctuate each year if the underlying assets change in value.

In the Taxpayer Relief Act of 1997, Congress modified the payout requirements so that any charitable trust created now, must pay out at least five percent, but no more than 50 percent, of the value of the assets (valued annually if a CRUT and at initial contribution if a CRAT). The amounts due must be paid within a reasonable time after the end of the applicable calendar year. The 1997 legislation was intended to eliminate short-term trusts (e.g., two years), which paid out a high percentage (80 percent), and challenge the ones that had been created as abusive. The 1997 legislation also required that the present value of the remainder interest passing to charity must be at least 10 percent of the initial value going into the trust. Comparable rules were also implemented for CRATs.

There are several different ways a CRUT can be structured. For example, if you put an asset into the trust that has no current income (such as C corporation stock that pays no dividends), but someday might (when the stock is sold and the proceeds reinvested in income-producing securities), the CRUT can be structured to make up income to the donor for the years when the trust paid out less than was originally defined. This is called a Net Income Makeup CRUT or NIM-CRUT. Another alternative created in the 1997 Tax Act was the FLIP CRUT, structured so that when a triggering event occurs (e.g. a specific date or event such as the sale of the closely-held business' shares), the income flips from a unitrust to a fixed percentage with no makeup of previous distributions.

The charitable remainder annuity trust or CRAT pays a fixed amount each year to the income beneficiary; the amount is established when the trust is created. The amount paid out each year does not change after the trust is created.

For example, if a CRUTs assets were invested in a portfolio of equities that were appreciating, the payout each year might increase as the value of the assets grew. The CRAT, on the other hand, pays out a fixed amount to the income beneficiary regardless of the appreciation (or depreciation) in the value of the assets in the trust.

Income distributed from a charitable trust is taxed to the recipient under a tier system depending on whether it is ordinary income, capital gain, tax-exempt income, or nontaxable return of principal. Your tax advisor should be consulted prior to creating a charitable trust.

One planning idea is to create a private foundation, or a supporting organization or donor-advised fund with your local community foundation, and have that entity as the remainderman of the charitable trust. When coordinated with a charitable remainder trust, the family foundation would be funded when the income interest is terminated.

## Charitable Lead Trust (CLT)

The charitable lead trust is the opposite of a charitable remainder trust. With a CLT, the income from the trust is paid to charity for a fixed period, and at the end of the term, the remainder is paid to your beneficiaries—your spouse, children, or grandchildren.

If the annual income paid to the charity is a percentage of the trust's assets, and the amount fluctuates depending on investment performance, it's called a charitable lead unitrust (CLUT). If the income is a fixed amount (the same dollar amount paid each year) it is called a charitable lead annuity trust (CLAT). Since the charity receives the income from the trust each year, the income tax deduction is based on the present value of the income paid to charity. The amount transferred may be excluded from the grantor's estate (depending on how the trust is structured). These are called super charitable lead trusts. There may be a gift tax due when a trust is created during lifetime. The gift tax is based on a number of factors including the term of the trust and the payout to the charity; the gift tax liability may be partly offset by the income tax benefit and by the use of available unified credit, which will reach $1 million by 2006.

Three components influence the charitable lead trust: (1) the amount paid to charity, (2) the length of time the trust is established, and (3) the prevailing IRS discount rate at the time the trust is established. The discount rate is the percentage by which the government determines money will grow over time, based on the mid-term government bond rate. The rate fluctuates monthly. The combination of the three variables determines the value of the gift to the beneficiaries, and therefore, the amount of the taxable transfer.

For example, on a trust established for 15 years, with a 6 percent payout rate, the donor would pay tax on $0.45 of each dollar given to his or her children, assuming that the portfolio has an annual total return of at least the charitable payout. Assuming a 55 percent gift tax rate, that means the gift tax would be about $0.25 for each dollar transferred. Plus, any growth or appreciation in trust assets would also go untaxed. You can pass more to your family than if the asset were passed directly during lifetime or at death.

The chart below demonstrates the portion of a dollar subject to gift tax when placed in a charitable lead trust.

| Income | Term of Trust | | |
|---|---|---|---|
| Percent earned | 10 years | 15 years | 20 years |
| 5% | 0.65 | 0.54 | 0.47 |
| 6% | 0.58 | 0.45 | 0.36 |
| 7% | 0.51 | 0.36 | 0.26 |
| 8% | 0.44 | 0.27 | 0.15 |
| 9% | 0.37 | 0.18 | 0.05 |
| 10% | 0.30 | 0.09 | 0.00 |

Several IRS letter rulings in 1998, and one Tax Court ruling permitting private foundations to be the recipient of the income from a charitable lead trust. A 1999 ruling permitted a lead trust to hold S corporation stock. One planning idea is to fund the lead trust with closely-held stock (an income tax deduction is received when the stock goes into the trust), name the family foundation as recipient of distributions from the trust for its term, and when the trust terminates, its assets pass to the donor's beneficiaries without further taxation or being includible in the donor's estate. If the business is sold (a stock sale) there is no income tax liability relating to the shares in the lead trust (it is a tax-exempt entity). The lead trust can serve as an effective way to fund your family's philanthropic interests while magnifying the transfer of wealth between generations, since there is no erosion of value from taxation.

Managing taxes and managing risk are complex subjects. You'll need competent advisors to help you, but the time spent and efforts made can yield great results.

In the next chapter, we will explore ways to manage the newly liquid assets.

# After You've Decided to Keep or Sell

# Beyond the Sale—
## Investing the Proceeds

F or business owners who have sold their company, there are new challenges. The most important is learning to manage newly liquid assets for retirement and for the next generation. In other words, it's time to become a smart investor.

## How to Become a Smart Investor

Mark Feldman, CPA, who manages the Private Client Services Group for Arthur Andersen in the western U.S. and is vice chair of the firm's registered investment advisory practice, notes that it is important to understand the purpose of liquidity and to develop an understanding of what you want your investable dollars to do for you. Feldman notes that the process of becoming educated and successful in this area typically involves the following steps.

### Set Goals

According to Feldman, "A client's goals change significantly within 24 months of having the cash from the sale of his or her business. Most business owners have no idea what it's like being cash rich. They cannot envision what will come their way—solicited or unsolicited. It's critical to integrate financial affairs, because proper investment advice can not be given until goals have been established." A by-product of setting goals is that you prioritize and reconcile different objectives such as your customary cash flow needs, special purchases or investments, your charitable objectives, your plans for transferring wealth to your children, and your estate planning.

For example, let's say you have $20 million after tax from the sale of your business and you've determined you need $10 million to live on for the rest of your and your spouse's life. In that case, volatile investments with potentially high returns are not required. You have to ask, "Do I need a high-return investment? Can I realize a targeted return with less risk?" Without first setting goals, you may automatically target high returns (with higher risk) and invest in financial instruments you don't need.

There are two issues you need to address in this first step:

1. Determine how much of the sales proceeds you will need to live comfortably. In the example above, you've realized you need $10 million or one-half of the sales proceeds. You should have come to this decision only after sophisticated financial modeling and testing a variety of assumptions. It's important to know what your basic annual financial requirements are. For one client the amount is $50,000 per month, one-half of which is given to charity. For another it's even higher, to support his purchase of goods. In business, you based decisions on rational, objective information such as fixed and variable costs. Now you have to apply the same analysis to your personal lifestyle (including the acquisition of toys). Feldman notes, "Few will tell you how much is enough, but many will give you ideas for spending it."

2. Identify how you plan to spend your time. It's not uncommon for owners to experience some depression after they sell their business. You no longer have the rush or the day-to-day successes of the business. So you have to find new areas that send you a surge of adrenaline and provide new ways to be and feel successful. Some people spend their time and their activities in the following areas:

- *Starting a new company.* This is a natural for the entrepreneur. You can choose a company they either know a little or a lot about.
- *Chasing deals.* In the right circles and depending on the publicity of your own deal, investment opportunities will find you.
- *Allocating time to family.* This isn't as simple as it sounds.
- *Philanthropy.* This can involve giving of your time and your money, to organizations that you find meaningful.

For example, after one client sold his business, his two adult children, who were stockholders, decided to allocate their time to investments differently. The son takes an active role in doing due diligence on prospective investments. He helps structure the deals. His sister makes her investment decisions based on a limited amount of time she's willing to invest. As a family you can become very active in managing your assets, or you can choose to be passive and structure your investments in a way that limits the amount of time you will need to spend in this area. Feldman points out that for many there is a low correlation between highly active involvement and returns.

Let's say you choose to allocate your time to philanthropy. If you've determined that your extra $10 million can benefit charities, then you should organize your time, activities, and (importantly) your investment strategy around that.

You'll need to ask yourself, "how much is enough for children, grandchildren, and other heirs?" This question may be balanced against your interest in philanthropy. As we will see in the next chapter, you can find many opportunities to creatively structure philanthropic activities, if you find that of interest. In some cases, the amount you've already carved out for your own needs for the rest of you and your family's life may consume all of the proceeds from the sale. In the event there are additional funds, will you designate those for your children? Charity? To buy a new company? What do you do with the other $10 million?

The right investment strategy for you depends on which "buckets" you choose.

| Personal Needs | Estate Entities | Charitable Entities |
|---|---|---|
| The investment strategy here may be lower risk, with a time horizon for investments equal to life expectancy. You should choose investments based on how successfully they meet personal cash flow needs. No hedge funds here. Lower risk investments include marketable securities such as international and domestic equities, and fixed income securities that produce income. | You may create Generation-Skipping Trusts for future generations or Family Limited Partnerships to hold investment assets. The time horizon here may be 30 to 40 years or longer. In many cases the time horizon here could be perpetuity. You may not need cash flow from this area; instead choose investments based on their potential to appreciate. Hedge funds, real estate, or alternative investments may belong here because of their potential for high appreciation. | If you set up a private foundation or used a charitable trust to tax plan the sale of the business, the investment time horizon may be perpetuity. Cash flow from investments may be needed for grant-making. Hedge funds may not be appropriate here. Fiduciary standards may dictate the investments chosen. A balance between income producing investments and equities (for appreciation) may be the right mix. |

## Create Your Plan

During step two, it is important to structure the big picture, which includes the following:

- *Family mission.* This is generally a written document that outlines the family constitution and includes a description of the family's values and traditions. The mission becomes the game plan for the family—and can help future generations connect across time about what the family stands for. Ideally, all family members contribute to this project.

- *Family and individual goals.* The family should also work together to articulate their individual and joint goals and create plans to realize those goals. Some of the family's newly liquid wealth can then be targeted to support family goals. For example, one family created a family bank with part of its proceeds from the sale, to finance entrepreneurial activities for other family members.

- *Education about areas of interest.* You can achieve this, both formally and informally, by reading, talking with others, attending classes and workshops, and becoming knowledgeable about hobbies you never had time to pursue before, or about the new job of managing your wealth.

- *Communication with family members and advisors.* This is especially important during this step so that everyone is knowledgeable about personal and investment goals.

If you skip step two, you're investing your time, money, and energy without a purpose. It's not uncommon for someone's investment screen to be too broad. Investors without a purpose tend to accept many types of investments. Or, as Lewis Carroll wrote in *Alice in Wonderland*, "Any path looks good if you don't know where you're going."

In business you wouldn't buy a machine unless you knew what it's for. You can apply that same principal here. You don't buy an investment unless you know what it's for. First you develop the plan, then you can acquire appropriate investments. It is far easier to analyze investments against a plan rather than vice versa.

## Develop Your Asset Allocation Models

Your asset allocation models for each of your "buckets" should balance expected returns with their risks and volatility. According to Feldman, volatility is the downside risk you're willing to accept.

Here is an example of volatility. Let's say you get cash from the sale of the business and invest it immediately in the stock market. The market goes down 10 percent the next week. With your first investment experience, you've lost 10 percent of the amount that it took 30 or so years to build. If you hadn't understood or been willing to accept the possibility that a loss might occur, then it is likely that your future attitude about investing will be influenced by that one experience.

How would you feel if 10 percent of your assets evaporated in a short period? Although it's unlikely that a downward turn would be sustained, how would you react? Would you be able to remind yourself that you are a long-term investor, that the market is bound to bounce back, that you haven't actually lost money unless you sold at a loss? Or would one bad experience influence future decisions (i.e., don't invest in equities)?

If you could remain objective and emotionally detached, that means you can tolerate the risk to pursue higher returns. If you would react negatively, then you should structure your investments to avoid volatility and, of course, target a lower return for your investments. Or, you might decide that a certain degree of volatility is acceptable in one of your buckets—say, the Generation Skipping Trust for grandchildren—but not acceptable in the bucket holding your personal investments.

Asset allocation modeling quantifies risks and probable returns from different investment classes and then helps you decide how to allocate investment funds across the classes according to the goals you have established.

Risk is not necessarily bad. All investments involve some degree of risk, and to allow your assets to grow, you must accept some risks. In fact, the more growth you want, the more risk you must assume. The point at which your dislike of risk outweighs your desire for asset growth is your risk tolerance. In other words, your risk tolerance is your answer to the question, "What's the maximum drawdown in my portfolio that I am comfortable with?"

Your risk tolerance will depend on many factors, including your time frame, your goals, and your natural tendency towards conservatism. A private foundation obligated to disburse annual or quarterly grants will probably be a more conservative, risk-averse investor. If you are investing for a newborn grandchild's college tuition, you may feel comfortable with a more aggressive, somewhat riskier investment plan.

It's vital to define your risk tolerance. Once you have identified your risk parameters, you can eliminate investment products and managers that are deemed too risky.

## Allocate Funds to Investment Classes

Now it's time to choose the appropriate investment vehicles to use. At this point, you will know enough about what gets allocated to look at other investment vehicles, such as hedge funds, private equity deals, emerging markets, etc., if they are appropriate. Because you have specified dollar amounts for each asset class, you can now choose the vehicles based on the dollars being allocated. For example, you can't put $100,000 into a hedge fund (which typically requires a minimum investment of $1 million), but you could put $100,000 into a pool that invests in hedge funds. You may not want to put $10,000 into one individual bond, but you could use $10,000 to buy a mutual fund of corporate or tax-exempt bonds to gain diversification, and lower risk, for your $10,000. The dollar amounts in each asset class will dictate the vehicles that are available.

## Select Investment Vehicles

At this point, according to Feldman, most people mistakenly think the next step is to pick money managers. However, there is one more set of questions to consider before choosing investment managers. They are as follows:

- How many dollars are you committing to a particular bucket and will the funding occur over time or all at once?

- What is the overall tax impact of funding the different buckets and what is the tax impact on the buckets of the investments being acquired? There may be a gift tax liability with the trusts you fund, and an income tax benefit with charitable entities you set up. If you plan properly, you may be able to use the income tax benefit (from the charitable gift) to fund the gift tax due on trusts you create. If trusts are Grantor Trusts, investment income or gains realized by the trusts will be taxed to you, if you are the grantor. Your decision should also take into account your need for steady income—or, in certain cases, your desire to avoid taxable income or incurring taxable capital gains. For example, if you expect your investments to distribute regular cash payments, you should seek money managers who specialize in balanced or fixed-income products. If you are tax-sensitive, you may wish to use managers who, for example, offer municipal bond-based products, or who can work with your CPA to coordinate your portfolio.

- Determine if you will be a passive or an active investor. For example, active investors in real estate would buy property and manage it by themselves. Passive investors in real estate might buy publicly traded Real Estate Investment Trusts (REITs), which are similar to a mutual fund that holds real estate properties.

- Are you trying to beat or match a benchmark? One common benchmark is the S&P 500 index, which is a composite of the 500 largest publicly-traded stocks. If your goal is to equal the benchmark, then you can acquire an index fund that will accomplish this inexpensively. If your goal is to beat the benchmark, then you need to have realistic expectations about what is possible, before choosing investment managers to help you.

## Select Investment Managers

Now it's time to select those who can help you accomplish your goals. If you want performance-related data on a regular basis, it may impact whom you select. For example, brokers may not provide performance data, such as benchmarking. Trying to beat a benchmark is not easy and requires higher risk and usually, higher fees.

Most people try to beat benchmarks instead of matching them. In *The Independent Fiduciary*, Russell Olson, retired head of investments at Eastman Kodak, comments, "When we find a manager we think is about the world's best in his asset class, how much excess return above his benchmark, net of fees, might be expected long term in the years ahead? Depending on the asset class, I would be well pleased with 3 percentage points per year net of fees." Olson goes on to note that he once studied the performance of all 63 common stock mutual funds that had been in existence over the prior 30 years. The results for the 30-year interval were that 35 funds under-performed the S&P 500, 4 equaled the S&P 500, and 24 out-performed the S&P 500. Of those that out-performed the S&P, 12 did so by less than 1 point per year, 9 by about 2 points per year, and only 2 exceeded the S&P by more than 4 points per year. Therefore, if you want to beat benchmarks, then you should have a realistic target of 1 to 3 percent in excess of the benchmark each year as a realistic goal.

Feldman adds, "If benchmarks get you there [regarding your goals], then it may be smarter to just buy the benchmark."[1] This works very well for asset classes like large U.S. equities, but may be more difficult for hedge funds.

Finally, it's best to sort through this with someone who has no ax to grind and who will look at both the cost and tax efficiencies of the various investment choices.

It's very common to hire out-of-state managers. After all, most investors prefer to evaluate managers based on performance, not physical location. However, you may prefer to work with a manager whom you can meet and visit. Or, you may want a manager who will stay in extra close contact with you about developments in your portfolio. If you are such an investor, you will obviously want to look closely at managers located in your city or region. Less obviously, you should find out whether a prospective manager is adding clients at an unusually high rate. A young, fast-growing manager must devote more time and attention to administering the daily affairs of a developing business. This can sometimes divert resources away from securities research and portfolio management.

How many money managers should you hire? One or several? How should you choose? To make this decision, you must consider several factors, including whether you should use a professional consultant to help you in your search.

Many investors turn to professional consultants for the same reason they hire a money manager: it takes time, effort, and research to draw up a short list of suitable manager candidates. However, some investors feel more comfortable seeking the assistance of an experienced consultant. A consultant is a full-time professional with broad knowledge of the investment management industry and access to information. If you are an investor seeking to place funds with a money manager, a consultant may be able to provide valuable assistance.

## Due Diligence

Before hiring a money manager, you should first establish that the manager is responsible and reliable. You should apply the same process that the buyer of your business applied to you before finalizing the deal, to prospective managers. Your due diligence on the manager, and his or her organization, should include the questions in Figure 11.1 provided by Northern Trust Bank.

---

**FIGURE 11.1—ISSUES TO CONSIDER WHEN SELECTING YOUR INVESTMENT MANAGER**

provided by Northern Trust Bank

**The Company**

- How many years have they been in business? How large is the organization?
- What are the convenience factors, (i.e., ease of contact with my portfolio manager)? Do I have control over the account? Can I move funds? Is the account easy to open and close?
- What is the stock and bond portfolio management style?
- Who designs my portfolio?
- Are assets diversified? How is the diversification determined?
- How extensive is the organization's insurance coverage?
- How is investment research obtained? Credit analysis?

**The Manager**

- Educational background?
- Years as an investment manager with the organization?
- How many accounts per manager?
- Method of compensation?
- Would you enjoy working with the manager?

**Performance**

- Most recent annual performance? Last three years? Last five years?
- Is performance consistent? If not, why?
- What level of risk was undertaken in the bond and stock selections to achieve the investment performance?

---

**FIGURE 11.1—CONTINUED**

- Is computer modeling utilized for stock selections and if so, do you understand how the modeling is used?
- How much of the performance is based on market timing? What were performance results in an up and down market?
- What types of accounts are used to derive investment results?
- Are fees included in the performance?

**Mechanics**

- How is my portfolio risk controlled day by day?
- Who handles the custody of securities?
- Can my securities be lent, used as firm capital, or firm collateral for trading of the firm's account?
- Who does the trading and how are trades executed?
- How are the tax issues handled?
- What reporting is available? What is the frequency of the reports?

**Fees**

- What fees are charged, in total and how are they calculated?
- What do the fees include?
- What will cause an increase in fees?

---

## Other Resources

- *Smart Questions to Ask Your Financial Advisers*, by Lynn Brenner (Bloomberg Press, 1997).
- *Money Manager Review*, an online resource that tracks and ranks manager performance. <www.ManagerReview.com>.
- *Form ADV*. The Investment Advisors Act of 1940 mandates that all money managers register with government regulatory agencies (see Figure 11.2). As part of the registration process, managers must file various disclosure statements, the most important one being the Form ADV. By law, the manager must provide Part II of this form (or equivalent disclosure) to all prospective clients.

Form ADV provides basic background information on a manager's ownership, financial condition, state registrations, and potential conflicts of interest with fees or commissions, as well as the background of the firm's principals and any disciplinary or legal problems. Investors should keep in mind that the purpose of Form ADV is to place basic information about the manager on the public record. The SEC never passes on the merits or accuracy of the information provided in the ADV.

With an ADV in hand, you have the opportunity to conduct a rudimentary background check. Prior employment of the firm's principals is an obvious area of interest. If legal actions against the firm are discovered, investors should try to obtain copies of the complaints. By checking with state and/or SEC enforcement divisions, the investor may uncover actions taken against a manager for regulatory violations.

- *Quarterly 13F statements.* SEC regulations require investment advisors who manage $100 million or more in equities to file a quarterly 13F statement, listing the equity positions and number of shares held. Investors can compare the manager's publicly reported numbers with the 13F filing of record to get a rough verification of performance.

  You can access 13F statements at the SECs Web site <www.sec.gov/edaux/formlynx.htm>, by searching the Electronic Data Gathering, Analysis, and Retrieval (EDGAR) database.

---

### FIGURE 11.2—INVESTMENT ADVISOR REGISTRATION REQUIREMENTS

| Assets under Management | Registration Requirement |
|---|---|
| $25 million or more in assets | Manager must register with the SEC. |
| Less than $25 million | Manager must register with the appropriate authorities in all states where company business is transacted. |

- *Referrals.* To learn more about a manager's reputation, it's logical to look at the manager's existing clientele. You may wish to ask a prospective manager for referrals, or for a list of active clients. Size up the manager by finding out the number of clients and the total value of assets under management. It's also prudent to ask for the number of new accounts acquired and lost during the past five years. A good manager has little to fear from this question.

- *Risk analysis.* When selecting a manager, it is not enough to assess returns alone. To make an informed choice, you must look at a manager's underlying risk. Risk is the statistical likelihood that your investment will perform unfavorably.

Risk can be mathematically defined and calculated. Usually, risk is measured with standard deviation, or the variability of a series of numbers about their average. For example, a $1 million portfolio with a quarterly standard deviation of 5 percent history has fluctuated $50,000 (5 percent of $1 million) or less per quarter two-thirds of the time. Low standard deviation means low risk. High standard deviation means high risk.

When this risk factor is considered, managers who might have seemed similar can suddenly look very different. Money Manager Review (MMR) provides the following example from two managers.

|  | Manager A | Manager B |
|---|---|---|
| Returns achieved | 20% | 20% |
| Risk assumed | 10% | 5% |

On the basis of returns alone, these managers might seem the same. But once risk is added to the equation, it becomes clear that these managers have not performed equally. All other factors being equal, most investors would rather choose the lower-risk option—Manager B.

Of course, most managers do not achieve identical returns. How do you compare two managers if, say, one manager has posted superior returns, but the other has achieved lower risk?

|                   | Manager A | Manager B |
|-------------------|-----------|-----------|
| Returns achieved  | 25%       | 16%       |
| Risk assumed      | 15%       | 4%        |

To compare these managers, simply divide risk into return. The higher the ratio, the more consistent the performance. The lower the ratio, the more erratic the performance.

|                  | Manager A         | Manager B         |
|------------------|-------------------|-------------------|
| Return/risk ratio | 1.667            | 4                 |
| This ratio is . . . | Low = erratic   | High = consistent |

- *Performance measurement.* To compare and understand a manager's true performance, you must look beyond returns, and even beyond risk-adjusted returns. When choosing managers, evaluate their performance against an index, not against their peers. Feldman points out that "you can't buy their peers, but you can buy the indexes. Peers are subject to whoever builds the model for analysis. Indexes are simple. For example, did the manager beat the Russell 2000? For 20 basis points, you can buy the Russell 2000. So is there justification for paying a manager fees in excess of 20 basis points a year? If their performance can't beat the index, why pay the extra fees?"

MMR, an online database, suggests you ask prospective managers the following four questions:

1. *Is the performance composite, representative, or proforma?* It's reasonable to assume that performance means "real money earned or lost for all clients." It's reasonable—but it's not always correct. Many managers do not report performance on a composite basis—that is, by tallying up profits or losses for each client and aggregating the results. However, some managers may show you representative performance numbers. This means that one, or a few, client portfolios have been singled out and are being presented as a fair representation of an average discretionary account. Other managers may use model or proforma numbers, drawing on backtests or something else other than actual managed portfolio returns to provide a hypothetical historical performance.

As you search for a manager, you should always make sure you know what you're looking at. Require your prospective managers to clarify whether performance numbers are composite, representative, or a pro forma model.

2. *Is the performance audited?* A manager may hire a third party, such as an accounting firm, to check and verify the firm's reported performance figures. This procedure, called an audit, can provide some independent confirmation of performance claims. Ask prospective managers whether their performance figures are audited and if so, by whom. Also carefully examine what is being audited. If the audit is too restrictive in scope it may give a false impression as to the manager's composite performance. You may wish to obtain and review a copy of the audit.

3. *Is the performance reported net or gross of fees?* Naturally, money managers are paid fees for their services. A manager's reported returns may or may not reflect these fees. If performance is reported on a net basis, you are looking at the profits or losses posted after all management fees have been subtracted out. If performance is reported gross of fees, the returns do not include any adjustment for fees paid.

4. *Is the performance AIMR compliant?* In 1991, the Association for Investment Management and Research (AIMR) endorsed a set of Performance Presentation Standards for the investment management industry. These standards provide managers with a standardized format for calculation and presentation of their performance for clients. Investors should check to see whether prospective managers report their performance in compliance with AIMR standards.

## Alternative Investments

For the newly rich, a variety of alternative investments that fall into two primary categories may be worth considering: hedge funds and private equity funds. Many of the new products today are versions of investments that have long been available to institutions and the extremely wealthy. Historically these types of investments required minimums of $10 million or higher, making them out of reach of all but the wealthiest investors. Some of the newer products today carry minimums as low as $250,000, making them more affordable, as well as giving the investor an opportunity for greater diversification by being able to invest in more than one company's offering.

### Hedge Funds

Hedge funds offer a broad range of strategies ranging from high to low risk. The universe of hedge-fund strategies includes global, emerging markets, arbitrage, and short selling. As a result of these diverse strategies, the returns vary tremendously. Hedge funds specializing in global markets had a median 10-year annualized return of 19.5 percent through 1999, net of fees, compared with -0.2 percent for short selling funds. In most cases, the attraction of the hedge fund is that it does not move in line with the stock market, so they offer an attractive means of diversification.

MAR/Hedge, a unit of Managed Account Reports Inc., estimates there are 3,000 hedge funds worldwide, managed by 2,000 different firms. Assets in hedge funds have increased from $50 billion in 1990, to more than $400 billion in 1998, according to a *New York Times* article.[2]

### Private Equity Funds

This category includes venture capital and leveraged buyout funds as well as mezzanine funds, which invest in the debt of established companies. Here the attraction is investing in private companies and getting in on the ground floor of the next new thing (for venture capital funds) or play investment banker (in the case of leveraged buyout or mezzanine funds).

## Creating a Family Office

Some families with significant liquid assets have decided the best way to manage family assets and coordinate different family activity is through a family office. A family office typically has at least one full-time individual (and sometimes more) who's sole job is to integrate and coordinate family investments, philanthropy, estate and income tax planning, cash management and bill paying, investment manager due diligence, selection and monitoring, and even the family's travel planning or career counseling for young family members. Family office managers often are CPAs or attorneys who may have been long-time family advisors and have been recruited now to work exclusively for the family. Besides having technical skills they also must be problem solvers, skilled negotiators, and consensus builders.

The most obvious advantage of the family office is its ability to focus exclusively on the needs of one client. In addition to managing assets, the family office also manages relationships. Some institutions provide seminars and educational programs for family offices and their managers including Northern Trust, Harris Trust, Bessemer Trust, Pitcairn Trust, and others. The Family Office Exchange in Chicago, Illinois, as well as Arthur Andersen (offices worldwide), can assist families in structuring a family office and recruiting qualified individuals to staff it.

# 12

# What Do I Do with My Time Now?

Immediately after the sale, most business owners are busy interviewing money managers about what to do with their newly liquid wealth and satisfying a consulting agreement that was hammered out during the negotiations. In the back of their minds, a small, sometimes trembling voice is wondering what they will do with their time after the consulting agreement ends in two to three years. During the adrenaline rush of hammering out the deal, it doesn't occur to most sellers that they soon will be facing what feels like the void known as the rest of their lives, which could be 20, 30, or more years.

For most sellers, there are many options to explore. In this chapter we'll consider three main areas that sellers are likely to find as engaging as their former business: hobbies and new ventures; strategic philanthropy; and wealth preservation, education, and transfer. But first, let's explore some of the likely emotions sellers often experience and must work through before they will be able to move fully into the future.

## After-Sale Emotions

Some sellers feel no remorse and move easily into their new phase of life, whether they start a new company, retire, or spend their time on their investments. For others, the emotions can run the gamut from joy to grief. As one client observed a few years after the sale, "I had a four-year consulting agreement, but my involvement declined over the four-year period. As long as I was busy with them [the new owners] I didn't notice it as much, but when they began to use me less I did begin to experience sadness." Five years after the sale, this client looked back and noted positives and negatives.

Some of the positives were as follows:

- "I dropped off all the concerns and worries and anxieties—the normal things of being in business. Today if you have less than 500 employees it's tough to meet all of the regulatory requirements that range from maintaining fiduciary and ERISA standards for retirement plans to being compliant with hiring practices and sexual discrimination laws."

- "I liquefied myself. It was a chance to have some money and also transfer some money to my children who were minority shareholders. I thought it was better to do it while alive."

Some of the negatives:

- "I miss the people. Some of them I'm glad I don't have to see anymore, but I do miss some of the vendors, employees, and customers."

- "I may not have been realistic about how I'd be used by the new owners. Initially for the first six months I was very busy. Then I wasn't as busy as much. At first, they called me to work on a project about once a month, then once every two months, then once every three months, then they stopped calling. I've also lost touch with some of the key people at the buyer's company. The people changed. They got promoted, or fired or transferred, and the company got extremely big. The guy I was closest to became vice president of an international division and I lost touch with him. Also, the bureaucracy got in the way. Whenever I had an idea, it always got bogged down in legal problems. The legal department had to approve everything. You just couldn't get the action you got when you own your own business. So consulting wasn't that satisfying after all. I could have been more valuable but I didn't get used."

- "I haven't learned to structure my day the way I structured it when I had my own business. On Monday, I used to know I had a product acquisition committee meeting, and on Tuesday a financial committee meeting and there were conventions and trade shows I would schedule. My life was planned out. Now, I don't have that schedule. There is a certain amount of meandering. All of the running around I do is somewhat disconcerting."

One client replaced his entrepreneurial activities with nonprofit involvement, but found that even those had some limitations. "It was difficult going from being a benevolent monarch to collective decision making, working through committees, and with an executive director who is not your employee. I had to get used to decision making taking a long time, working within a stringent budget and working through fiduciary issues. It's not as fulfilling as I thought it would be."

However, another client found significant benefits in working in the nonprofit sector. This individual discovered entrepreneurial philanthropy—"you get in, you do the job, and you get out." Some projects that have worked well for her have been as follows:

- *Turnaround expert.* "We worked to save the temple when it looked like it would go under. We restructured the board, got a new Rabbi, and paid off debt. It was a turnaround situation. We built a pre-school in six months and it's running well."

- *Start-up.* "We established an Israel Center. We recruited a full-time citizen representative from Israel to work in our community. We started from scratch, but now he makes presentations at public and private schools, and he sits on panels at universities, etc. He's built awareness in the community about Israel and its issues."

- *Conference manager.* Running a conference that involved strategic planning and creating new initiatives for the community.

Many who claim they have retired are busier than ever—traveling, boating, golfing, learning (yes, some go back to school), volunteering, and, in general, staying active in managing their affairs. Of course, some are bored and regret selling or letting go. But even these folks usually realize they did the right thing for their company and their families.

## Hobbies or New Ventures

Some entrepreneurs have started new companies. One client sold his medical-claims processing software company and then started a new business that buys airplanes and sells shared interests in these executive jets to other business owners. Another sold his software business and then started a venture capital fund that invests in closely-held companies. Carl Ball had taken time as a business owner to volunteer weekly in the Chicago public schools. After he turned the business over to his children and was no longer involved, he focused his interest in education on starting and running three charter schools in Arizona.

One client balances his time between charitable activities, involvement with family, taking courses at the local college, and keeping up a weekly poker game that has been going on for 25 years.

How you spend your time is a function of how well prepared you are for a transition, whether you keep the business and let go, or sell it, and find new outlets for your experience and energy. The more prepared you are for change, the more likely that the change will be experienced as a successful next step in your life.

## Strategic Philanthropy

In 1989, Peter Karoff started a not-for-profit organization called The Philanthropic Initiative in Boston, Massachusetts. The purpose of the organization was to help new and experienced philanthropists make their charitable giving more effective by becoming more focused. Karoff's work led to the concept of *strategic philanthropy*. Strategic philanthropy is about making a difference, about focusing resources, articulating one's passion, and applying accountabilities to charitable activities. Many business owners who have sold their companies and become more involved with charitable activities use their business experience and apply investment principals and due diligence to their own philanthropy. For example, like financial investors, these new philanthropists conduct due diligence on the organizations that apply for grants. They review management of the programs to be funded. They review proposals, visit sites, check references, and use external resources and information to benchmark progress.

The phenomenal growth in the creation of private foundations and charitable trusts, and in the growth of assets in community foundations from new supporting organizations and donor-advised funds, provides ample evidence of wealth being shared all over the United States. As families seek to make a difference in their communities, they are also using charitable vehicles to create permanent legacies for their family values. A recent study by the Boston College Social Welfare Research Institute estimates that between 1998 and 2052, the low-range estimate of wealth transfer will be $41 *trillion,* and may be double or triple that amount.[1] This is four times greater than the $10 *trillion* projected in a 1990 study by researchers at Cornell University. The low-range estimate was based on a 2 percent growth of wealth, and produced the following estate distribution dynamic (see Figure 12.1).

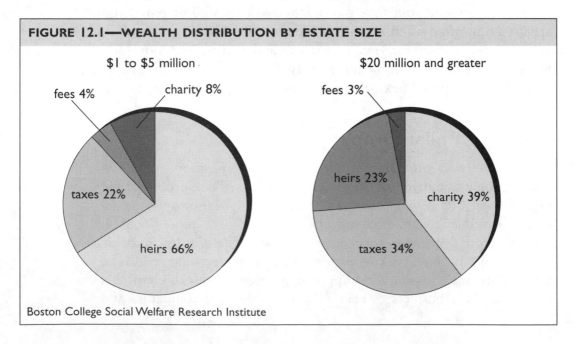

**FIGURE 12.1—WEALTH DISTRIBUTION BY ESTATE SIZE**

$1 to $5 million

fees 4%
charity 8%
taxes 22%
heirs 66%

$20 million and greater

fees 3%
heirs 23%
charity 39%
taxes 34%

Boston College Social Welfare Research Institute

Havens and Schervish, who authored the study, predict over $15 trillion of this money will find its way to charitable organizations over the 55-year period—from lifetime as well as testamentary gifts. A *golden age of philanthropy* may be dawning. As individual's financial resources and the self-perception of financial security increases, there are emotional incentives to devote one's wealth to charity. As Karoff has found with his work in strategic philanthropy, a values-based approach to planning can increase individual and financial commitments.

---

**EXAMPLE OF NONTRADITIONAL STRATEGIC PHILANTHROPIC ROLES**

Strategic philanthropy provides opportunities to focus your charitable activity. The following are some examples of nontraditional strategic philanthropic roles.

- *Capacity builder* for an organization, or neighborhood.
- *Innovator/incubator* of new ideas, programs, or organizations.
- *Disseminator* of effective models and best practices.
- *Change agent* of cultural, social, or legal structures and expectations; addressing underlying causes and systems.
- *Community builder* who seeks to develop human, social, or physical capital of an area.
- *Critic or advocate* of public or social policies.
- *Venture capitalist* supporting social entrepreneurs who are starting or building capacity of organizations or new approaches.
- *Developer of leaders* in organizations, schools, or communities.

©The Philanthropic Initiative, Inc., 2000. Used by permission of The Philanthropic Initiative, Boston, Massachusetts.

---

There are an unlimited number of ways for you to be creative and proactive in your philanthropy. The Philanthropic Initiative provided the following examples of what others have done.

## Issue a Request for Proposals (RFP)

The RFP process can be a very effective way to serve as a catalyst, by soliciting proposals that respond directly to the donor's goals and interests.

RFPs are particularly appropriate when a funder seeks to stimulate innovation, encourage collaboration, increase attention on an issue, or simply find the best organizations to do the job.

Example: *After-School/Mentoring Initiative.* In the fall of 1998, the trustees of this Boston-based family foundation decided to focus on after-school and mentoring programs for children and youth in under-served Boston neighborhoods. After conducting research on best practices and needs of Boston area youth, the family implemented an RFP process that resulted in multiyear grants of $1.6 million to 14 youth-development programs.

## Develop a Special Awards Program

An awards program can be an effective approach for drawing attention to an issue, or for uncovering and supporting talent or leadership.

Example: *Boston Neighborhood Fellows Program.* One family funds the Boston Neighborhood Fellows Program, which honors unsung neighborhood heroes and heroines of Boston. Modeled after the MacArthur genius awards, this program provides three years of no-strings attached financial support, as well as visibility to tireless but unrecognized neighborhood leaders who have been nominated by neighborhood spotters.

## Convening Conferences and Other Forms of Technical Assistance and Support

Funders interested in exposing organizations to interesting ideas/models/best practices and sparking innovative thinking in a specific field may hold a conference or establish a regular convening mechanism for people in the field to network and learn from each other.

Example: *AOL Foundation Interactive Education Initiative (IEI).* Through an RFP process, the AOL Foundation identified 54 teams of educators and others around the country with innovative ideas for using the online medium to enhance teaching and learning for K through 12 students. After awarding the grants, the

Foundation sponsored a national conference attended by representatives of all 54 grantees. Conference participants received training on evaluation approaches, online networking, and community outreach strategies. They forged strong and lasting relationships with one another. Following the conference, the Foundation launched an online network to enable grantees to continue the dialogue around challenges, effective strategies, and common interests.

## Create or Seed a New Organization

When a knowledgeable funder identifies a critical need that is not being filled by the current organizational infrastructure, she or he may decide to help create a new organization to fill that gap. The decision to form a new organization (versus strengthen or expand an existing one) may be particularly appealing when there are political/bureaucratic barriers in existing organizations and/or when a funder identifies emerging leaders with innovative ideas.

Example: *Center for Collaborative Education-Metro Boston.* The family foundation associated with Stop & Shop Grocery chain was interested in promoting major school reform in Boston during the early '90s. After visiting with identified innovators in the area, they decided to seed a new organization called the Center for Collaborative Education, which provided committed schools support and technical assistance in implementing whole school reform.

## Join or Build a Collaborative to Leverage Dollars and Learning

Joining or forming a collaborative funding group allows the funder to aggregate resources, draw on varying expertise and experience, learn from each other and outside experts, as well as draw public attention to an issue.

Example: *The Remmer Family Foundation.* Through participation in the Ms. Foundation's Healthy Girls/Healthy Women funding collaborative, this family foundation sought to increase its knowledge about best practices, meet and learn from other funders, and support a national initiative that would test new models and draw attention to girls' issues.

## Use a Portfolio of Approaches to Focus on an Issue

Foundations that become deeply involved in a particular area may use a variety of approaches intended to augment and act in synergy with each other.

Example: *The Melville Charitable Trust*. This family foundation is committed to addressing the root causes of homelessness in Connecticut. It has also addressed areas directly tied to homelessness, such as education, employment, mental illness, and substance abuse. The Trust takes a multi-faceted approach to its work, supports research, funds nonprofit practitioners, supports statewide coalitions; and provides extensive technical assistance to grantees. The foundation makes program-related investments in the form of low or no-interest loans to build critically needed affordable housing throughout the state.

## Fund a Comprehensive Array of Strategies Targeting an Underserved Neighborhood or Region

Some foundations choose to focus on very poor, underserved geographic neighborhoods or regions and address the complex of inter-related factors that contribute to the area's poverty. Such an approach is particularly appropriate when the funder is willing to work with community leaders over an extended period of time.

Example: An anonymous family foundation chose to focus on the poorest neighborhood in their hometown of Jackson, Mississippi. They seeded the formation of a community development corporation, funded after-school programs, and worked with the local school system to provide enrichment opportunities for kids and families.

# Wealth Preservation, Education, and Transfer

One final piece of this plan is to reconsider and possibly restructure your wealth transfer and estate planning documents in a way that protects wealth from unnecessary estate taxation, provides guidance to family members in the future, and preserves important family values. In Chapter 11, we discussed "how much would be enough" for future generations. Most business owners prefer to transfer excess assets (after satisfying their own needs for a comfortable standard of living and an amount to charitable trusts or a family foundation) to children or grandchildren if they can be assured that the money will be used responsibly. A common goal is for parents to see their assets preserved for future generations in a way that helps them become productive members of society. One of the important side benefits of wealth transfer is to create a family legacy and pass on family values.

The two most common vehicles are the Family Limited Partnership and the Generation Skipping Transfer Trust.

## *Family Limited Partnership (FLP)*

A FLP typically has two classes of partners: general and limited. General partners make day-to-day decisions for the partnership and control the assets of the partnership. Limited partners have no voice in management of the partnership, and may have restricted rights to partnership assets due to state laws and the terms of the partnership agreement. Typically the limited partners are entitled only to receive distributions when the general partners declare them. Because of these restricted rights, the value of a limited partner's interest is often discounted (from a pro rata value of the partnership's assets) when appraised for transfer purposes such as gifting partnership interests to family members. Limited partners are passive investors, with limited liability (limited only to their invested capital) while general partners are responsible for the partnership.

While there are a number of tax-oriented reasons to use a FLP as part of one's planning, Stacy Eastland, a noted Houston attorney with Baker & Botts LLP, has outlined several other advantages of holding family assets in a FLP:[2]

- The general partner (usually the donor) can reinvest partnership cash flow rather than making distributions to partners. When descendents are limited partners, they do not have access to partnership assets unless distributed to them by the general partner.

- It provides a way to consolidate and manage assets for family members. For example, a FLP can hold privately held stock of a C corporation (S corporation stock cannot be owned in a partnership under current law). Pooling assets can mean lower operating costs, and can increase diversification (other investments can be acquired in the partnership name). By keeping assets in the partnership, limited partners have some protection against creditors. Creditors would only have rights to distributions, not to any underlying assets of the partnership.

- General partner succession, outlined in the agreement, provides for continuity of the partnership.

- Since the partnership is a "pass-through" entity for income tax purposes, gains and losses are passed through to the general and limited partners according to their ownership of the partnership's capital. In some states, partnerships are not subject to franchise taxes and/or an intangibles tax.

- FLP interests can be effectively combined with other planning techniques. For example, FLP interests can be frozen by limited partners selling their partnership interests to a GST Trust in exchange for a promissory note. Properly structured, the sale of the partnership interests would *not* trigger income or capital gain taxes at the time of sale. As assets in the partnership appreciate, the GST Trust owns the limited partner units and all future appreciation on those interests.

- Charitable planning can also be coordinated with FLPs. One planning opportunity is to transfer FLP interests to a charitable lead trust with a GST Trust as the remainderman of the Charitable Lead Trust. Properly structured, the gift of partnership assets to the charitable lead trust may be partially income tax-deductible and the later transfer to the GST Trust may not be subject to gift tax. (A remainderman is a contingent beneficiary who receives assets after a specified period of time. As described in Chapter 10, a Charitable Lead Trust is a split-interest trust with the charity receiving income for a period of years and then after a specified time, the assets pass to the remainderman.) In this case a charity would receive income from the partnership (as distributed by the general partner) for say, ten years. At the end of ten years, the partnership interests would be transferred from the charitable trust to a Generation-Skipping Trust (GST). In one case, a private foundation was permitted to be the income beneficiary of the charitable lead trust, which provided a way to initially build assets in a family foundation and later distribute those assets to grandchildren.

By taking advantage of current valuation discounts applicable to partnership units, extraordinary wealth in the form of partnership units can be transferred without gift tax to tax-protected family trusts.

These vehicles act as protective devices for family wealth to consolidate management and family voice, and to shield assets from divorce, creditors, or just to keep spendthrift beneficiaries from spending everything.

## Generation-Skipping Transfer Trust (GST)

A GST can be designed to be the repository of family wealth for several generations, and can be designed so that future family members do not pay estate taxes on the assets that are held for them in the trust. Without the erosion of estate taxes, family wealth can grow more efficiently. While the tax benefits of GSTs are extremely attractive—avoiding the 55 percent estate tax for future generations—often nontax issues cause clients to pause. Some common responses are, "We know our kids but we don't know what our wealth will do to or for our grandchildren or later generations"; or "We want our wealth to go to our children"; or "We're not sure that leaving wealth for future generations is such a good idea." Creatively planning for wealth transfer from a multigenerational perspective can be very rewarding when nontax issues, such as those described below, are included.

First of all, some basics. If the 55 percent estate tax is levied on each generation, without growth, an initial $1 million (owned by parents) will only be worth $202,000 when it reaches grandchildren (third generation). The same $1 million inside a Generation-Skipping Trust conceivably still will be worth $1 million (again assuming no growth) when it reaches grandchildren. Who wouldn't want to avoid an 80 percent reduction in family asset value over three generations?

GSTs are irrevocable. They can protect assets from divorce (or bankruptcy) for the next generation because they can be made spouse- and creditor-proof. In addition to shielding wealth from estate taxes (because they can be made estate tax-proof), they can be structured with flexible provisions regarding investments and distribution of income. They can last as long as the grantor wishes—two, three, or more generations (even longer in some states), usually splitting into separate trusts for the various family lines that evolve.

Furthermore, through the use of special trustees with specific pow- ers, children (and grandchildren) can have access to some or all of the trust's principal during their lifetimes, if the grantors create that option when the trust is drafted. Committees of beneficiaries can choose suc- cessor trustees, can vote family business stock, and can select invest- ment advisors to manage assets.

### Before You Generation Skip, Consider These

GST Trusts can buy assets from the grantor (for a promissory note with interest), thereby creating an estate freeze. The appreciation on those purchased assets can remain in trust for the benefit of future generations without estate taxation. Properly structured, up to perhaps $20 million of current asset value can be transferred to a GST without taxation. When used in conjunction with a FLP, that amount can double. A GST Trust can be the remainder beneficiary of a charitable lead trust (described in Chapter 10). And, if the GST Trust owns survivorship insurance on the grantors, assets in the trust can be leveraged or multi- plied to an even larger number while remaining nontaxable. For the individual interested in creating a legacy, the GST Trust is the way to go.

Each individual has a $1 million generation-skipping exclusion ($2 million per couple).

This is the amount that can be transferred to grandchildren (or later generations) without incurring a generation-skipping tax. Amounts beyond that are subject to a generation-skipping transfer tax (at 55 percent) when distributions are made to grandchildren or lower generation beneficiaries, in addition to an estate or gift tax (up to 55 percent) at the donor's level.

Many families mistakenly believe that, for only a $2 million benefit, the complexity of creating a GST isn't worth the aggravation. What they and their advisors are missing is the extraordinary opportunity to leverage the transfer of wealth from generation to generation by incorporating other planning techniques and making the GST the "basket" to hold family assets in the future.

Our experience has been that when the nontax issues also can be successfully addressed, clients become excited about the possibilities of preserving their assets for future generations. And the beginning of that process is to involve adult children in early discussions about whether generation-skipping should be considered as a family wealth-transfer strategy.

Here are some issues you should address before setting up a GST Trust.

**Single pot trust or family lines trust.** Let's say Mom and Dad have three adult married children and nine grandchildren. They want to explore a GST Trust but aren't sure where to start. One of the first questions is to determine whether the trust established by Mom and Dad will continue as one trust (for all nine grandchildren) or, at Mom and Dad's death (or sometime sooner) the trust can divide into three separate trusts, one for each family line. A single-pot trust would keep the assets consolidated in one entity, and the trustee could use the assets to support a grandchild with special needs even if it wasn't proportional to what the other grandchildren received. With a family-lines trust, each of the three children would be assured of their children receiving their proportional (one-third) amount.

**How long should the trust last?** The short version of a GST Trust is one that skips the next-generation children for estate tax purposes, although the trustees could distribute trust income to the next generation and also allow principal to be used for their benefit. The next generation has the use and enjoyment of trust assets without technically owning those assets. At the death of the children, the trust assets would be distributed to grandchildren, usually when the grandchildren are at least 25-years-old or older. The trust would typically include some form of sprinkling provision so that the grandchildren receive some percentage of trust assets after the death of their parents and after they reach age 25 or 30, another percentage at age 35, and a final distribution at age 40, or later. A longer version can last for 100 to 120 years, or about four generations. Every GST, when created, must comply with state law. Until recently, each state had some kind of rule about how long trusts could last in that state (called a rule against perpetuities). Generally, the state law will base the trust's life on the youngest living grandchild's life expectancy plus 21 years. So, with a two-year-old grandchild who lives for 85 years, the trust could last 83 + 21 years, or 104 years. If that isn't long enough, there is a longer version. Seven states have abolished their rule against perpetuities (Arizona, South Dakota, Delaware, Alaska, Wisconsin, Illinois, and Idaho), which means that if you create a trust in those states, the trust's life can continue forever. If you want to carefully consider a trust lasting for 100+ years, you must keep in mind that the assets in the trust will never be subject to estate tax erosion, as long as the assets stay in the trust.

**Who should we name as trustees?** Children can act as co-trustees (along with an independent trustee), but cannot make decisions about distributions to themselves unless distributions are limited to health, education, and support needs. Children can, however, have the power to remove and replace the independent trustee, can select investment managers, and can vote family business stock held by the trust. Many families incorporate a successor trustee selection process, which involves a family council or a committee representing family lines selecting successor trustees to serve. Some use Trust Protectors to choose successors and remove and replace trustees. Since the trust may last for several generations, representation of family members in the future is generally important in achieving family goals.

**Should descendants be given limited or general powers?** The next generation (e.g., children of the grantors) can have certain rights, or powers—known as limited powers—to receive benefits from the trust.

As long as the powers remain limited in scope, the assets in the trust will not be taxed in the children's estate when they die.

In other words, restricting the next generation's powers keeps the trust's assets shielded from estate inclusion. Some of those limited powers are

- the right to all income from the trust, plus 5 percent (or $5,000, whichever is higher) of the principal each year.

- the right to additional withdrawals based on an ascertainable standard for education, welfare, maintenance, and support (or a more flexible approach based on a comfortable standard if the children are not trustees for themselves).

- the right to appoint assets at death to children, spouses, or charity (but not to themselves or their estates).

Children can be co-trustees (along with an independent trustee) and can be involved in decision making as long as the decision does not violate their limited powers. For example, children (or beneficiaries of the trust) can purchase houses or second homes in the trust for family benefit.

A special, independent trustee can be authorized in the trust document (uncle, aunt, trusted family advisor) to expand the powers granted to the next generation, (e.g., to give the children a general power during their lifetime to invade the trust if so desired).

The use of a special trustee preserves the limited powers of the next generation (and, therefore, the generation-skipping benefits) while providing a mechanism for the children (the skipped generation) to invade the trust. If the trust is a grantor trust, then a special trustee also can turn off the grantor trust status if desirable in the future.

**How can I ensure my wishes and vision will be respected?** Parents can enhance the chance that after their death, their assets will be used according to their values by attaching an informal letter of wishes to the trust document. Addressed to trust beneficiaries, this letter can encourage future generations to maintain family values, stimulate entrepreneurship, and encourage educational and/or artistic endeavors in the next generation. This personal message to future generations can guide trustee actions, articulate an important family message for future generations (better than an impersonal legal document), and create a way for grandchildren and others to feel connected with those who created the trust.

**How can I discourage certain behaviors and encourage other behaviors?** Trust provisions can reward, and discourage, behavior by restricting or increasing distributions to beneficiaries. For example, beneficiaries with a substance abuse problem could find their share of income directed to a treatment center for their benefit instead of to them personally. A grandchild who felt unfairly treated and elected to sue the trustee (or other family members) could find his or her share forfeited.

These trusts have also been called family incentive trusts since the transfer and enjoyment of wealth by future generations can be contingent on descendant's accepting one's core values. For example, some trusts deny payments if beneficiaries don't have prenuptial agreements. Incentive trusts have an on-off faucet for distributions based on beneficiaries' adherence to family philosophies. Some clients see them as a way to encourage future generations to be the best they can. To prevent trustees from becoming arbitrary in their decisions, the trusts usually have objective criteria built in regarding business achievement, academic excellence, or social contribution.

You can encourage certain behaviors by allowing the trustee to make special distributions to beneficiaries with unusual accomplishments. Some clients want special distributions for individuals who attain a graduate degree, go on a sabbatical and do missionary work, or make an unusual contribution to society (arts, music, social work, etc). Similarly, income distributions can be tied to earned income or the trustees can make additional distributions for doing socially important work such as the Peace Corps. The trust also can operate as a family bank to finance or invest in family entrepreneurial endeavors.

Families with significant assets have long been concerned about doing the right thing for the next generation. Creating and funding a GST Trust, with input from next-generation adult children, can be an effective bridge-builder for perpetuating family values. A facilitator may be needed to help work through the issues. This process can be challenging and rewarding by creating a true legacy for future family members in addition to providing a tax-efficient vehicle that preserves family wealth.

# 13

# Concluding Thoughts

A fter all is said and done, the decision to keep or sell your business is based on some combination of financial, emotional, and gut feelings.

Keeping your business may seem like less of a commitment in some ways than selling it. After all, once you sell the business, it's gone. But if you decide to keep the business for now, you'll still have the option to sell later, right? Not necessarily. Market conditions can change faster than the weather forecast in Chicago.

Yet both avenues involve considerable potential risk. Hanging on to the business, even though your commitment to it and passion for it may be waning, could possibly result in diminishing profitability. Yet, after spending however many years building the business with your sweat, equity, and vision, if you sell, you are faced with finding a secure place to invest the proceeds.

Both avenues also present tremendous potential rewards. Keeping a thriving business may be your most profitable and safest investment option. You also may enjoy the many benefits of ownership, including exposure in your industry and community, and building or continuing a legacy that may have been handed down to you and that you may feel emotionally inclined or obligated to pass down to the next generation. Selling can finally bring you the liquidity to pursue travel, hobbies, other investments or other business ventures you were never able to afford before. Plus you have been watching many of your competitors, vendors, and corporate clients cash in by selling their company. There is no longer a stigma attached to selling out. In fact, many owners consider it an emblem of success.

We hope that the assessment exercises in this book have helped lead you to a decision with which you feel confident and comfortable, and that the action plans we have presented will help make the path you've chosen smooth.

As we mentioned in Chapter 1, the decision to keep or sell involves endings and beginnings. We hope your endings feel peaceful and your beginnings spark just the right combination of financial and emotional challenges. Good luck!

# Keep Appendix

## Stockholder's Memo of Understanding

This memo was adopted by one client as the first step in articulating a new owner-investor relationship; one stockholder was active as the company's CEO, two were not active.

1. Stockholders agree to meet on a regular basis and discuss business matters. An agenda will be prepared before each meeting. Meetings will be run in an orderly fashion, and at each meeting reasonable time will be allotted to address and resolve difficult issues.

2. There will be full disclosure of business and financial information to all shareholders. The company's CFO, or Controller, will be available on an as needed basis to answer stockholder questions.

3. Information regarding contemplated transactions will be sent to stockholders in advance. They will have opportunity for comment and questions.

4. Company officers will act in the highest fiduciary manner for all stockholders of the company.

5. A policy will be developed regarding access to corporate perks, including airplane, yacht, vacation homes, and invitations to third party affairs.

6. Corporate officers agree to spend full-time on corporate affairs and agree that no transactions will be acquired for their own account unless having been presented and fully disclosed to all of the stockholders first.

7. An employment and compensation policy will be entered into with family members/corporate officers that describes a fair market compensation structure as well as bonus opportunities based on meeting performance criteria to be mutually established on a regular basis.

8. If any family member has a proposal which he or she would like considered by the Company as a business investment or venture, the family member will prepare, in writing, a reasonably detailed outline of the proposal including the likely economic and financial benefits and risks. The proposal will first be considered by a committee of _____. The committee will give serious consideration to all proposals and will prepare a written recommendation to the Board of Directors. If the committee recommends the Company move forward on the proposal, the Board of Directors will formally consider it at its next meeting.

## Establishing Boundaries

This client created a management company to oversee business operations, stepped out of day-to-day management, and also formed a family council. This memo was drafted to define the separate responsibilities for the newly-created Management Company and the Family Council.

### *Management Company (an S Corporation)*

A management company organized, incorporated, and owned by the Family Voting Trust.

**Primary mission.** Develop short- and long- term goals for operating companies, create and maintain management agreements with operating companies, provide board functions, governance, and oversight of operating companies, responsible to Family Voting Trust.

- Interfaces directly, and through its board, with operating companies.

- Interfaces with Group CEO and CFO.
- Establishes compensation and success sharing policies for senior teams of operating businesses.
- Responsible for corporate governance and long-term strategic planning.
- There are five trustees of the voting trust: four family and one to be selected by these four. Each trustee will pick his or her own successor approved by a majority of the trustees and in the absence of a successor-trustee, then the remaining trustees will pick a successor, with majority approval of the other trustees.
- Provide board functions for operating companies.
- Maintain management contracts with operating companies.
- Inform family council regarding business activities, progress, accomplishments, major decisions, etc.

## Family Council

A family council comprised of 2nd, 3rd, and 4th generation, not a separate legal entity.

**Primary mission.** To live as an unbreakable unit of support, encouragement, and unconditional love which respects and cherishes the uniqueness of each member and challenges each to fully develop his or her God-given gifts. To utilize all these gifts to leave this world in a better condition spiritually, intellectually, physically, and emotionally than the way we found it.

- Acts as a forum for maintaining "family glue."
- Maintains and implements family employment policy describing requirements for family members to be employed in operating companies. Does not hire or fire family members, or influence their employment, other than to encourage family members to gain requisite skills and experience to be considered for employment.
- Develops and oversees family interest in philanthropic activities.
- Arranges meetings for family members to keep different generations informed about family business activities and happenings.
- Responsible for family newsletter.
- Responsible for commemoration of history.
- Responsible for the structure of the Family Council, meetings, minutes, etc.

- Responsible for building and maintaining family teamwork.
- May use space as available in management company's offices for family council activities.
- Elects members to the Family Council, but not to the management company Board. Current officers of the council are: Chair, Chair-Elect, Secretary-Treasurer, Program Chair, Chaplain, Newsletter.
- Maintains committees: Legacy Committee and Program Committee and other committees as necessary.

## Compensation Agreement for a CEO Family Member Who Was Not a Controlling Shareholder

... WHEREAS, the Company wishes to employ Chief Executive Officer as its President and Chief Executive Officer on the terms and conditions set forth herein, . . .

### Definitions

- *Incentive payment* means the portion of the Company's Net Income payable to Chief Executive Officer...
- *Minimum returns* shall mean for the Operative Performance Period, seventy-five percent (75 percent) of the Target Annual Return and Target Net Income for the two (2) years included in such Period.
- *Net income* of the Company shall mean the net operating income of the Company and other family-controlled Entities arising from the ownership or operation of its various Enterprises, before payment of federal or state income taxes, but after allowance for depreciation and amortization for each fiscal year of the Company commencing with the fiscal year beginning _____.
- *Target annual return* shall mean average pre-tax return on equity for all of the Entities of 8 percent.
- *Target net income* shall mean an average Net Income for all of the Entities of $1 million for the Operative Performance Period.

### Terms and Duties

- The Chief Executive Officer shall be the chief executive officer of the Company and shall be responsible for the general and active management of all operations of the Company and all Entities. It shall be his duty to attend to the overall managerial, administrative, and related aspects of the Business of the Company and maintain strict supervision over all of its affairs and interests. He shall keep the Chairman and the Board of Directors fully advised as to the financial affairs and conditions of the Company, and shall manage and operate the Business in accordance with such policies as may be prescribed from time to time by the Chairman and the Board of Directors . . . Chief Executive Officer shall have the duties of leadership and responsibility normally associated with the position of a chief operating executive officer of the Company.

- For as long as he is employed by the Company, Chief Executive Officer agrees (i) to devote all his time, energy, and skill during regular business hours to the performance of the duties of his employment, and (ii) not to engage directly or indirectly in any active work (other then pursuant to this Agreement) for which he receives compensation or remuneration of any kind.

## Compensation and Benefits

- During the initial Term of the Agreement, Chief Executive Officer shall receive a Base Salary of One Hundred Fifty Thousand Dollars ($150,000.00) per year. At least annually, the Board of Directors shall review the Base Salary of the Chief Executive Officer and may make upward adjustments thereof, based on the Chief Executive Officer's performance or an increase in his duties and responsibilities, or both.

   Additionally, subject to the other terms and conditions of this Agreement, Chief Executive Officer may receive annual bonus compensation based on a percentage of the Net Income, ("Incentive Payment") according to the following Schedule.

By way of illustration, if the Company and other Entities, generate, in its fiscal year-ending Net Income of $3,500,000, the incentive payment amount to be paid to Chief Executive Officer shall equal $175,000 (five percent times $3,500,000).

- The Company shall provide Chief Executive Officer with such health and term insurance benefits as are provided to other management employees of the Company.

| NOI Net Operating Income after depreciation/amortization | CEO Base Comp | CEO Incentive Bonus |
|---|---|---|
| $0–1 MM | $150,000 | 0% |
| $1–2 MM | | 3% |
| $2–3 MM | | 4% |
| $3–4 MM | | 5% |
| $4–5 MM | | 5½% |
| $5–6 MM | | 6% |
| $6–7 MM | | 6½% |
| $7 + MM | to be determined | |
| Also subject to minimum pre-tax Return on Equity of 8%. Target ROE is 15%. | | |

- Company shall provide an automobile to Chief Executive Officer every three (3) years, having a value of not more than $40,000, or lease a vehicle for him having an equivalent value.

- Company shall reimburse Chief Executive Officer for all travel, entertainment, promotional, and other related expenses incurred by him in performing his duties hereunder, provided such expenses are reasonable and proper back-up is provided to the Board of Directors, if requested from time to time. Chief Executive Officer shall be issued a Company credit card for such purposes.

- Company shall pay for all reasonable cellular phone charges incurred by Chief Executive Officer in performing his duties hereunder.

- Chief Executive Officer shall be entitled to four (4) weeks paid vacation annually.

- Subject to the specific terms and limitations thereof, Chief Executive Officer shall be entitled to participate in the Company's "cafeteria plan," the Company's 401(k) plan, and deferred compensation plan, on the same basis as the other full-time employees of the Company.

- Upon Chief Executive Officer's termination for any of the reasons stated in Paragraph (a) hereof (other than in the event of a Cause Termination), Chief Executive Officer shall be paid severance compensation in the form of a multiple of his then annual Base Salary plus Incentive Payments, in accordance with the following chart:

| Termination Reason | Base Salary Due | Incentive Payment Due |
|---|---|---|
| Involuntary termination | Five (5) years | One (1) year |
| Nonperformance termination | One (1) year | None payable |
| Voluntary termination | Balance for year of termination | One (1) year |
| Change in control | Three (3) years | One (1) year |
| Catastrophic termination | Three (3) years | One (1) year |
| Cause termination | None payable | None payable |

# Sample Compensation Policy for Executive Top Team Group

The Committee reviews the compensation of Executive Officers on an ongoing basis, developing and implementing plans to serve the following objectives:

- Support, communicate, and drive achievement of the Company's business strategies and goals.
- Attract and retain the highest caliber Executive Officers by providing compensation opportunities comparable to those offered by other firms with whom the Company competes for business and talent.
- Motivate high performance among all employees in an entrepreneurial, incentive-driven culture, free of any sense of entitlement.
- Closely align the interests of Executive Officers and all employees with stockholders' interests.
- Promote and maintain high ethical standards and business practices.
- Reward short-term results achieved and the long-term creation of stockholder value.

. . . as part of its overall compensation philosophy, the Committee has determined that the appropriate total compensation for Executive Officers should be targeted at the 50th percentile with the opportunity to meet or exceed the 75th percentile based on superior performance. Consistent with its desire to support a pay-for-performance environment, the Committee has determined that base salaries should be targeted at the 50th percentile . . .

. . . the Committee utilizes the services of an independent consulting firm with experience in executive compensation matters, as well as historical marketplace survey data. The data provided compares the Company's compensation practices to a group of comparative companies . . .

## Hybrid Model Shareholder's Agreement with Tag-Along Provisions

1. *Limited redemptions*. To provide certain owners of nonvoting shares some liquidity, the Corporation hopes to be in a position in later years to begin redeeming some of their shares. The Corporation will attempt on a best-effort basis, beginning January 1, 1998, to repurchase nonvoting shares from certain Shareholders on an annual program as follows:

   - During the years 1998, 1999, 2000, 2001, 2002, 2003, 2004, and 2005, the Corporation will determine and announce each year the amount of funds that it will make available for the redemption of its nonvoting shares from those Shareholders herein below identified, after considering the financial success of the Corporation and its anticipated operational needs. The funds so allocated for such purpose shall be prorated among the following for the repurchase of a portion of their nonvoting shares: The price that the Corporation will offer and pay for such shares shall be as provided in Section 3 hereof.

   - Commencing in 2006, the Corporation plans to expand the number of Shareholders from whom it will offer to redeem a portion of their nonvoting shares to include all grandchildren of _____ and _____. As in the past, the Corporation will determine and announce annually the availability of funds for the redemption of nonvoting shares and the allocation of such among the selling Shareholders on a pro rata basis. The price which the Corporation will offer and pay shall be as provided in Section 3 hereof.

   - Notwithstanding the foregoing the Corporation may redeem any other or all of its shares of stock, whether voting or nonvoting and regardless of the owner thereof, if its Board of Directors determines that there are hardships or other special circumstances which warrant the repurchase of shares by the Corporation.

2. *Purchase price.* The purchase price of all shares of stock purchased under this Agreement by the Corporation shall be their fair market value as determined by an independent appraiser.

3. *Future resale profits.* Once nonvoting shares have been sold to the Corporation, the selling Shareholder shall be entitled to share in any profits realized by the Corporation if the Corporation, or substantially all of its assets, are sold to, or merged or exchanged with, a third party (unaffiliated with the Corporation) within ten (10) years thereafter. The formula for sharing shall apply only to the number of shares actually sold by a Shareholder to the Corporation. In case the Shareholder retains other nonvoting shares, the formula shall start anew with each sale transaction. To determine the extent of sharing, the following formula shall be applied (without pro ration for a part of a year):

| | | |
|---|---|---|
| Year 1 | 100% | of their pro rata share in the proceeds of a third-party sale in excess of the price they previously received *less* simple (not compounded) interest on the price they received at the prime commercial rate applicable over the period since the sale |
| Year 2 | 90% | |
| Year 3 | 80% | |
| Year 4 | 70% | |
| Year 5 | 60% | |
| Year 6 | 50% | |
| Year 7 | 40% | |
| Year 8 | 30% | |
| Year 9 | 20% | |
| Year 10 | 10% | |
| Year 11 | 0% | |

By way of example in applying the foregoing formula, assume the following: The Corporation purchases from a Shareholder his shares for $10 per share and sells them to a third party three years later for $30 per share. During the three-year period the prime commercial interest rate was unchanged at 5 percent. Such Shareholder would be entitled to receive the following from the Corporation: $30.00 less $10.00 = $20.00 times 80 percent = $16.00 less $1.50 (3 year interest @ 5 percent on $10.00) = $14.50.

## Drafting Put and Call Options into a Shareholder's Agreement

### Put and Call Rights

- If, within thirty (30) days after the end of every two (2) fiscal years beginning _____, any Shareholder desires to sell all or any portion of such Shareholder's Shares, such Shareholder shall have the right to require the Company to purchase such Shares at the price and upon the terms and conditions set forth below (the "Put Right").

- If, within thirty (30) days after the end of every two (2) fiscal years beginning _____, the Company desires to purchase from any Shareholder all or any portion of such Shareholder's Shares, the Company shall have the right to require such Shareholder to sell such Shares to the Company at the price and upon the terms and conditions set forth below (the "Call Right").

**Determination of purchase price.** The purchase price to be paid for the Shares purchased by the Company pursuant to this Article shall be the aggregate Fair Market Value Per Share (as hereinafter defined) of such Shares in effect on the date the Put Right or Call Right is exercised by a Shareholder or the Company, as the case may be. For purposes of this Agreement, "Fair Market Value Per Share" shall mean the amount equal to the Company's fair market value, as determined by an independent, qualified appraisal professional with at least ten (10) years of experience valuing businesses and assets similar to that conducted and owned by the Company.

### Alternative Language with Different Valuation Clauses Applicable to the Put Option and the Call Option

**"Put" period and terms.**
- *Exercise period.* Example, January 1 to March 31, May 1 to July 31 of every odd number year beginning six years from this date.
- *Mechanics.*
  - Shareholder sends a Put Notice during the Exercise Period.
  - If Corporation declines, other Shareholders may exercise and purchase pro rata.
  - If all the Shareholders decline, then the Corporation must purchase.
- *Payment terms.* Twenty percent down, 80 percent Promissory Note.

- *Valuation.* Lack of control and marketability discounts (2) to apply.

## "Call" period and terms.

- *Exercise period.* January 1 to December 31 of every odd-number year beginning 8 years from this date.
- *Mechanics.*
  - Corporation (by vote of its board of directors) may decide to purchase all of a Shareholder's shares in that corporation.
- *Payment terms.* Thirty percent down, 70 percent Promissory Note.
- *Valuation.* Lack of marketability discount (1) to be applied.

# Protecting Nonvoting and Minority Shareholders

## Dividends to Pay Tax Liabilities (S Corporations)

With respect to any taxable period of the Corporation during which it is an S corporation, the Corporation shall declare and pay to the Shareholders annual dividends sufficient for the Shareholders to satisfy their respective income tax liabilities arising by virtue of the allocations of the Corporation's profits and losses.

## Recapitalizations—Provisions for Nonvoting Shareholders to Vote on Major Issues

Providing special occasion voting rights for inactive or nonvoting shareholders can be one method of addressing the dynamic tension between those who operate the company and those who have an equity stake, but no voice. Nonvoting shareholders would be able to vote on the following:

- The sale, exchange, lease, mortgage, pledge, or transfer of [all or substantially all] [50 percent] of the assets of any of the Companies in a single transaction or series of related transactions.
- A change in the capital structure, an increase in the authorized capital stock, or a reclassification of the capital stock of any of the Companies, provided however that the sale or issuance of up to [5 percent] of the shares of capital stock of any Corporation to its key executives shall not constitute a change in capital structure.
- Any material change in the distribution or dividend payments or policies of any of the Corporations.

- The termination, dissolution, or wind-up of any of the Corporations.

- The merger of any Corporation with or into any other corporation or entity.

- Any capital expenditure or expenditures by any Corporation [not in the ordinary course of such Corporation's business] (or any incurrence of other obligations of such nature) in excess of $5,000,000 individually or $ _____ in the aggregate over the course of such Corporation's fiscal year.

- Any assumption, incurrence, guarantee, or refinancing by any Corporation of any indebtedness by any Corporation in excess of $ _____ over the course of such Corporation's fiscal year.

- Any Corporation (1) applying for or consenting to the appointment of a receiver, trustee custodian, or liquidator of such Corporation or of all or a substantial part of the assets of such Corporation, (2) being unable, failing, or admitting in writing such Corporation's inability to pay its debts as they become due, (3) making a general assignment for the benefit of creditors, (4) having an order for relief entered against such Corporation under applicable federal bankruptcy law, or (5) filing a voluntary petition in bankruptcy or a petition or an answer seeking reorganization or an arrangement with creditors or taking advantage of any insolvency law or any answer admitting the material allegations of a petition filed against such Corporation in any bankruptcy, reorganization, or insolvency proceeding.

- The making by any Corporation of a loan to any Shareholder or beneficiary of a trust-Shareholder.

- The execution or amendment of any transaction between the Corporation and any shareholder or beneficiary of a trust-Shareholder or any family member or affiliate of any of them, except in connection with transactions made on an arm's-length basis at the then-prevailing market rates.

- The execution of any agreement or authorization of any action on behalf of any Corporation that is unrelated to its purpose as set forth in its Articles of Incorporation or that otherwise contravenes this Agreement.

# Family Employment Policy

This client created a voting trust to hold all voting shares of the company and then attached the Family Employment Policy to define how trustees of the voting trust would be added in the future.

*This policy defines who may serve as a member of the Family Management Group, which is one of the Voting Co-Trustees of the Family Companies Voting Trust Agreement. This policy services only as a guideline and then current members of the Family Management Group reserve the right to interpret any of its contents.*

**Requirements.** Any nonvoting Stockholder of the Company who desires to become active in the business of the Companies and a member of the Family Management Group shall:

1. Receive a bachelor's or higher degree in area of study related to
   _____.

   - Maintain a "C+" or better grade point average in that area of study.
   - Come before the then current members of the Family Management Group with a resume and a written statement of intent. This statement shall also be verbally presented to the Voting Co-Trustees. A question and answer session shall follow presentation. (The statement of intent must describe how the area of study relates to and benefits the business.)

2. Receive a vote of confidence for employment from a majority of the then current members of the Family Management Group.

   If an applicant passes the vote of confidence, a meeting will be set where the Voting Co-Trustees will provide such applicant with a job description outlining expectations, accountabilities, and evaluations for the particular field of interest. Once the field of interest is established, the applicant will be required to do the following:

   - Work in the defined field of interest as an hourly employee for a period of one (1) year.
   - Float around in a variety of jobs within the desired work area for a period of one (1) year.
   - Serve as a Front Line Supervisor for a period of two (2) years.

- Be evaluated as Front Line Supervisor and explore the possibility of a paid leave of absence to pursue further education.
- Serve as a Regional Manager for a period of two (2) years.

  If the voting co-Trustees feel that applicant has not successfully completed his/her duties at any one stage, they reserve the right to hold the employee back until they feel confident applicant can move to the next step. The voting co-Trustees reserve the right to terminate or change the employment status of an employee at any time and for any reason.

3. Receive the vote of 80 percent of the voting co-Trustees, voting in accordance with their Percentage Interests (as set forth in the Agreement).
4. Any member of the Family Management Group who terminates employment with the Companies shall no longer be a member of the Family Management Group.

## Analyzing Financial Performance
excerpted with permission from Deloitte & Touche LLP

When analyzing financial statements it is easy to be overwhelmed by the volume of data available for analysis. For this reason many analysts use ratio analysis to help with the task. Using ratios is a good way to spot trends and raise issues for further analysis but is never a substitute for thorough analysis. Company performance should not be looked at in a vacuum; rather, it should be compared with similar companies operating in the same industry as there are significant variations in typical performance, as well as differences in what measures are most relevant.

### Return on Equity (ROE)

This is the most commonly used measure of financial performance. Generally this ratio is computed using average common shareholder equity as a basis. We also recommend that you calculate this ratio on an **after-tax** basis. In some situations you may need to calculate this ratio on a **pre-tax** basis, but in those circumstances you should clearly indicate which basis you are using.

$$\text{ROE} = \frac{\text{Net income}}{\text{Average common shareholder's equity}}$$

## Profitability Ratios

Profitability ratios are a good measure of operational parameters. It can help you understand a company's product or service pricing strategy as well as its operating costs.

$$\text{Gross margin} \ = \ \frac{\text{Gross profit}}{\text{Sales}}$$

$$\text{Profit margin} \ = \ \frac{\text{Net income}}{\text{Sales}}$$

## Short-Term Liquidity Measures

Liquidity ratios measure the company's ability to meet its current obligations as they come due. The *quick ratio* eliminates inventory since it is generally the least liquid current asset. You should consider calculating this ratio after stating current investments at market value.

$$\text{Current ratio} \ = \ \frac{\text{Current assets}}{\text{Current liabilities}}$$

$$\frac{\text{Quick ratio}}{\text{or Acid test}} = \frac{\text{Cash} + \text{Cash equivalents} + \text{Marketable investments} + \text{Receivables}}{\text{Current liabilities}}$$

## Activity Ratios

Activity ratios measure how efficiently a company uses its assets.

**Accounts receivable turnover.** This ratio is either expressed as the number of times per year that receivables turn over on average or as the average number of days required to collect accounts. If you are evaluating a business with seasonal characteristics you should compute this ratio over shorter periods of time, such as quarters. Be sure to exclude cash sales from the calculation if material.

$$\frac{200 \times \text{Sales}}{\text{Accounts receivable EOY 200(X-1)} \ + \ \text{Accounts receivable EOY 200X}}$$

To determine days required collecting accounts, divide the above turnover amount by 365 days.

**Inventory turnover.** When comparing inventory turnover between companies, be sure you know which basis was used to value the inventory. If you are evaluating a business with seasonal characteristics, you should compute this ratio over shorter periods of time, such as quarters.

$$\frac{200 \text{ x Cost of goods sold}}{\text{Inventory EOY 200(X-1)} + \text{Inventory EOY 200X}}$$

To determine average days in inventory, divide the above turnover amount by 365 days.

## Financial Leverage Ratios

This ratio measures the long–term solvency of the business and its ability to deal with the opportunities and challenges that may arise in the future.

$$\text{Debt to equity} = \frac{\text{Total liabilities}}{\text{Total equity} - \text{Intangible assets}}$$

# Sell Appendix

## What Should Be in a Selling Memo

### Company History

- Why you are selling the business.
- Date company founded, structure, and any previous change in ownership.
- Changes in name structure and line of business.
- State of incorporation and states in which licensed to do business.
- Growth pattern in sales, profits, physical plant, and employees.
- Any divestments or significant write-offs over the years.

### Employees

- Total number of employees.
- Details of key personnel, such as length of service, job description, compensation, and willingness to stay under new ownership.
- Organization chart.

- Employment contracts.
- Historical employee turnover.
- Company's wage and personnel policies.
- Details on fringe benefits.
- Any special training required of employees.

## Market and Competition

- Growth potential of products.
- Name, size, and market position of competitors.
- Ways company's product differs from competition.
- Company's market niche.
- Sales trends and patterns, such as growth and seasonal.
- Product pricing and history.
- Gross profit margin on products and track changes.
- Any research and development expenditures.

## Sales and Distribution

- Compensation of sales people.
- Details of advertising methods and expenditures.
- Details of sales terms, discounts offered and return policies.
- Information, if applicable, on distributors pay and responsibilities.
- Sales volume of major customers for last few years.
- The years customers have done business with company.
- Credit rating of major customers.
- Historical bad debt experience.
- Review any maintenance agreements on sales.
- Do express or implied warranties exist on sales?
- Review any product liability problems.
- Sales loss or declining sales in certain customers.
- Could company product be made obsolete by any new products?
- Does the company lease any of its products?

## Manufacturing

- Types and availability of materials to be manufactured.
- Length of production cycle.
- Quality control procedures.
- Licenses needed to manufacture.
- Present capacity based on current equipment.
- Lead time for new equipment.
- Safety record in factory.
- Stability of supplier relationships.

## Physical Facilities

- Appraisals.
- Present condition of facilities, including equipment.
- Are facilities adequate for current or projected needs.
- Expansion plans.
- Adequate insurance maintained.
- Details of sprinkler system and burglar alarms.
- Accessibility to required transportation.

## Analyze the Investment Required

Will the business generate enough profit to . . .

- allow a fair salary for the owner or manager.
- pay-off money borrowed to purchase business.
- allow a fair return on the initial investment, in addition to the above.

## Adjustment to Profit

You should also identify items which are now an expense of the company that might not be for a new owner. Referred to as perquisites, called perks (which are a privilege, gain, or value received in addition to regular salary), these items should be added to the pretax income to determine the true profit of the company.

Examples of perks are

- excess salary to the owner (the salary in excess a manager would earn for a comparable job in the same field).

- excess benefits received by the owner, such as: company car, insurance, travel and entertainment, retirement plan, bonus, and any other special payments.

Additional items that should be added to the pretax income would be expenses that are not recurring. Some examples: abnormal legal or bad debt write-off in one year, consulting or computer fees that would not recur.

After adding back some examples of the above items, a true profit can be arrived at for the business.

## Sample Confidentiality Agreement

This Confidentiality Agreement is entered into by and between [Client], and its affiliated companies ("[Client]") and _____ (the "Recipient").

A. *Purpose.* The parties acknowledge and agree that [Client] may find it necessary or desirable to disclose confidential information to the Recipient for the purpose of evaluating and conducting a business relationship between the parties. Therefore, in order to protect the confidentiality of such information and to ensure that it will be used only for the purpose of furthering their mutual business interests the parties have agreed to the terms and conditions of this Confidentiality Agreement (the "Agreement").

B. *Effective date and term.* The effective date of this Agreement is the latest date on which it is executed by both of the parties. This Agreement shall remain in effect for a term of five years from the effective date. The obligations of confidentiality and nondisclosure of the information subject to this Agreement shall continue without expiration with respect to information which is not returned following the written request of [Client] under subparagraph C.4 of this Agreement. Unless such information is released under the exceptions described in paragraph ___ of this Agreement, the limitation on use of the information subject to this Agreement in competition with [Client] shall survive the term of this Agreement without expiration.

C. *Basic agreement as to confidentiality.* The parties agree that all information furnished by [Client] to the Recipient shall remain confidential and shall not be disclosed to any person or entity not a party to this Agreement.

1. *Subject matter of this agreement.* The information which shall be kept confidential and not be disclosed to any other person shall include all information furnished by [Client] to the Recipient, whether furnished before or after the effective date of this Agreement. Such information shall include, but is not limited to, all intellectual property rights (including electronic and computer programs and data processing technology), business and market analysis, financial data and analysis, customer lists and information, marketing plans, and all other analysis, compilations, data, and documents.

2. *Disclosure by [client].* The information described in subparagraph C.1 shall be deemed to have been furnished by [Client] to the Recipient and be governed by this Agreement when it is disclosed or delivered by any shareholder, director, officer, employee, independent contractor, or agent of [Client] to any shareholder, director, officer, employee, independent contractor, or agent of the Recipient. An agent shall include, without limitation, either party's lawyers, accountants, consultants, and financial advisors. Disclosure shall have occurred when it is delivered in any form, whether in electronic form, by written documents or by oral communication. [Client] may, in its sole discretion, decline to furnish any information which may be requested by the Recipient.

3. *Disclosure by the recipient.* The information which is subject to this Agreement may be disclosed only to those shareholders, directors, officers, employees, independent contractors, or agents of the Recipient that need to know the information in order to conduct the business relationship of the parties. Such disclosure shall be made only to those persons having a purpose in knowing the information, who are aware of the existence of this Agreement and who agree to be bound by its terms. [Client] shall be informed of the identity of those persons to whom disclosure has been made. The Recipient agrees to be responsible for any breach of this Agreement by any person to whom it has disclosed the information and shall make all reasonable efforts to safeguard the information from unauthorized disclosure.

4. *Permitted uses.* The Recipient may use the information disclosed to it under this Agreement for any purpose directly related to the mutual

business interests and relationship of the parties. No part of the information subject to this Agreement shall be used, directly or indirectly, in a manner which is in competition with [Client] or which relates to a business opportunity otherwise available to [Client].

5. *Return of information.* Upon the written request of [Client] and for any reason whatsoever, the Recipient agrees to promptly return and deliver to [Client] all documents and information furnished by [Client], whether in written or electronic form, without retaining any copies of such documents or information, either in written or electronic form.

D. *Exceptions.* The obligations imposed on the Recipient shall not apply to any information which (1) is or becomes generally available to the public other than as a result of a disclosure in violation of this Agreement; (2) becomes available on a nonconfidential basis from a source other than [Client]; or (3) was known to the Recipient on a nonconfidential basis prior to disclosure by [Client]. The exceptions described in this paragraph shall not apply to information which is acquired by the Recipient in violation or any other confidentiality or non-disclosure agreement between [Client] and any third party.

E. *Compelled disclosure.* In the event that the Recipient becomes legally compelled (whether by oral questions, interrogatories, requests for information or documents, subpoena, civil investigative demand or other similar process which is ordered by any court or other body having appropriate authority to compel disclosure) to disclose any information subject to this Agreement, the Recipient will provide prompt notice to [Client] and will cooperate with [Client] should [Client] endeavor to seek relief from such disclosure. The Recipient will furnish only that portion of the information that is legally required and will, in making such compelled disclosure, exercise its reasonable best efforts to obtain reliable assurances that the recipient will accord confidential treatment to the information received.

F. *Remedies.* The parties agree that [Client] would not have adequate remedies in damages and that [Client] would be irreparably harmed in the event that any of the provisions of this Agreement were not performed in accordance with its terms. Accordingly, the parties agree that [Client] will be entitled to injunctive relief to prevent a breach of this Agreement and to specifically enforce its terms in addition to any other remedy to which [Client] may be entitled in law or in equity. The prevailing party in any litigation relating to a breach of this Agreement, whether in seeking injunctive relief or otherwise, shall be entitled to payment by the other party of its legal fees and costs, including court costs and other expenses of enforcing, defending, or otherwise protecting its interests under this Agreement.

G. *Governing law.* The validity of this Agreement shall be determined under the laws of any jurisdiction having sufficient connection with the subject matter of this Agreement so as to establish its validity. The interpretation of this Agreement shall be determined under the laws of the State of Oklahoma. The enforcement of this Agreement shall be in the State of Oklahoma or in such other jurisdiction selected by [Client] having sufficient connection with the subject matter of this Agreement so as to permit enforcement.

Agreed to by each of the parties on the date indicated:

Date: _____    [Client]  By:_____

Its:_____

Date: _____    [Recipient] By:_____

Its:_____

## Sample Letter of Intent

This Letter of Intent was hammered out over a four-month period. The closing occurred 45 days later.

Dear _____:

I am pleased to submit our revised proposal for the purchase by _____, of the stock of _____, Inc. The major points of our proposal are as follows:

### Sellers

Owners of all outstanding shares of stock of _____, Inc. (the "Company"). The current shareholders of the Company are _____.

### Buyer

_____, Inc., or an affiliated entity. If Buyer is other than _____, Inc., then all obligations and performance of the Buyer shall be irrevocably, absolutely, and unconditionally guaranteed by _____, Inc.

### Form of Purchase

Stock Purchase.

### Assets Included with Purchase of Stock

_____ business, related equipment, vehicles, inventory, names, and rights to use names. Cash, marketable securities, cash value of life insurance, and Accounts Receivable shall be for the benefit of the Sellers. Additionally, certain assets of a personal nature as set forth on a schedule to be prepared by Seller shall be excluded from the transaction.

### Liabilities to Be Assumed

None.

### Purchase Price

The following consideration shall be paid by the Buyer for the purchase of the shares of stock of the Company (including ten (10) year noncompete agreements from _____, and her spouse):

a. At closing, Buyer shall pay the sum of Three Million Four Hundred Thousand ($3,400,000) Dollars in cash or shares of stock of _____, Inc., as shall be directed by the Sellers in their sole and absolute discretion;

At closing, Buyer shall pay to the Sellers, the sum of One Million Four Hundred Thousand ($1,400,000.00) Dollars to be evidenced by a Promissory Note in said amount, providing for monthly payments in the amount of Eleven Thousand Six Hundred Sixty-Seven ($11,667.00) Dollars each, commencing on the first day of the month following the closing and continuing on the first day of each and every month thereafter until paid in full. Such note shall provide events of default customary in commercial transactions of this nature, upon which the Sellers will be entitled to accelerate the obligation.

## Real Estate

The owner of the real estate located at _____, (the "Premises") shall enter into a lease with the Buyer containing the following basic terms:

a. A base lease term of fifteen (15 years) with two five (5) year options;'

b. Base rent shall be $_____ dollars for the first two (2) years of the base lease term and then shall increase annually based on the cumulative increase in the Consumer Price Index from the commencement date of the base lease term, but in no event shall the base rent in any year decrease from that of the prior year. Base rent during each of the option periods shall similarly be the base rent of the prior year adjusted upward only by any increase in the Consumer Price Index.

c. The lease shall be triple net to Landlord (i.e., Tenant shall pay all real estate taxes, insurance, repairs, maintenance, and capital improvements as if the absolute owner of the Premises.

d. Landlord shall have the right to refinance, mortgage, and pledge the Premises. Tenant shall furnish any requested subordination of lease to a lender of the owner. The owner shall use its best efforts to furnish Tenant with a reasonable nondisturbance agreement.

e. Tenant shall have the option to purchase the Premises at the end of the base lease term or at the end of any option period providing Tenant is then in compliance with the lease terms. The option price shall be the greater of (i) $_____ dollars, being the value of the Premises as set forth in that appraisal conducted by _____, dated _____, or (ii) the Fair Market Value of the Premises, based on the highest and best use thereof, as determined by an MAI appraiser familiar with the area.

## Five-Year Employment and Noncompete Agreements

Buyer shall enter into five (5) year employment agreements with _____. Each agreement shall contain noncompete covenants for a period of five (5) years and shall delegate duties and responsibilities as executives consistent with their current positions. In particular, _____ shall serve as manager of the Company.

Such employment agreement shall provide among other terms, the following:

a. Annual base salary of $_____ dollars, payable bi-weekly.

b. Health, medical, and dental insurance consistent with current coverages.

c. Automobile allowance sufficient to permit the use of an automobile of comparable quality to that being used currently, with a new such vehicle every four (4) years.

d. Allowance for country club or similar club dues in such amounts as reasonably determined to be necessary for business development and consistent with current practices in accordance with the budget developed by the Seller and Buyer.

e. Paid vacation of eight (8) weeks in year one, nine (9) weeks in year two, ten (10) weeks in year three, eleven (11) weeks in year four, and twelve (12) weeks in year five.

f. Provision for disability and life insurance in accordance with customary benefits for executives.

g. Severance provision in the event of "Good Cause" termination by employee.

h. Full health, medical, and dental coverage until employee attains age sixty-five (65), notwithstanding termination of employment.

i. Eligibility for Key Employee Stock Option Plan; and

j. Eligibility for 401(k) or other retirement plan with full vesting credit for service with the Company.

### Incentive Compensation Plan

_____ and other mutually agreeable Key Employees would participate in an Incentive Compensation Plan. Under this plan, they and any other mutually agreeable employees would share a $_____ dollar bonus (allocation to be mutually agreed by Sellers and Buyer prior to close) for achieving Budgeted Operating Income, or EBITDA of _____.

### Operating Plan Assumptions

Sellers and Buyers, prior to closing, will work toward creating a mutually agreeable Operating Plan that will realistically achieve Budgeted Operating Income, or EBITDA of $_____ dollars annually.

### Contingent Consideration

For each year which the Company exceeds Operating Income or EBITDA of at least $_____ dollars during the first five (5) full calendar years succeeding the Closing, Sellers will receive options to purchase _____ shares of nondiluted Common Stock of _____, Inc. provided, however, that the maximum number of options earned shall be fifty thousand (50,000) nondiluted shares. The option price of each share of stock shall be the price per share of the stock as of the close of business on the date of closing (subject to adjustment in the event of any recapitalization or dilution). The options will vest immediately upon satisfaction of each earning contingency. Sellers will have ten (10) years from such date of grant to exercise such options.

### Due Diligence

This proposal is subject to due diligence and Sellers will cooperate with Buyer to allow for further review of the financial and operating components of the Company.

### Inspections

Sellers will cooperate with Buyer to obtain, at Buyer's sole expense, an environmental audit, facility safety inspection and structural inspection of the property and facilities used in connection with the business of the Company.

Sellers will perform the remedial action recommended pursuant to such inspections up to a maximum amount of Twenty Five Thousand ($25,000.00) Dollars. In the event that the cost of such remedial action exceeds Twenty Five

Thousand ($25,000.00) Dollars and Sellers do not elect to pay all such costs, this letter will immediately become null and void.

## Closing Costs

Buyer shall pay all expenses for surveys and title insurance. Buyer will initiate the title work with Commonwealth Land Title Company. Taxes and other proratable expenses will be adjusted based upon the amount accrued through the closing date.

## Anticipated Closing Date: _____

## Offer Expiration Date: _____

By signing this Letter of Intent, Buyer and Sellers acknowledge and agree that the within document is not (except as set forth in the next paragraph) intended as a legally binding document and is only an expression of their desire to attempt to reach a formal agreement as to all matters. In the event that formal agreements are not approved and executed by Sellers and Buyer on or before _____, 2000, this Letter of Intent shall be null and void and of no further force or effect and that the parties hereto will bear their own expenses and will have no claim against the other party hereto in regard to this Letter of Intent, or any negotiations between Sellers and Buyer, other than in regard to any breach of the next paragraph below.

Buyer agrees to keep any information obtained from Sellers confidential and to keep all negotiations between Buyer and Sellers confidential and further specifically agrees to not contact or advise any creditor or anyone with whom Sellers have a business relationship of the matters dealt with herein unless specifically authorized by Sellers in writing to do so. Sellers agree that while this Letter of Intent is in effect, Sellers will not enter into any agreements, commitments, negotiations, discussions, or solicitations regarding the possible sale or other disposition of the Company (whether by sale of stock or assets, merger, consolidation, or otherwise).

If you believe that the foregoing sets forth our understanding in principle and the present intention of the parties is to enter into definitive documentation, and this letter will serve as a declaration of good faith intent to move forward to the contemplated transaction, please so signify by signing in the space provided below and returning an executed copy to the undersigned.

We look forward to successfully concluding this transaction and to a long and mutually rewarding relationship.

# Stock Purchase Agreement

This Agreement is entered into this ____ day of _____, 2000, by and among Sam Spade and Susan Spade (the "Sellers"), Judy Knickerbocker, William Wallace, and Wanda Watson (the "Buyers") and Wonderful Widgets, Inc. (the "Corporation"). Each of the Sellers and the Buyers is a resident of Phoenix, Arizona. The Corporation is organized under the laws of the State of Arizona.

## Recitals

A. *Outstanding stock.* The Corporation has issued and outstanding 25,000 shares of common stock. The Sellers are the owners of 12,751 shares of the issued and outstanding shares of common stock of the Corporation. The stockholders' ownership is as follows:

| Shareholder | Number of Shares | Percentage |
|---|---|---|
| Susan Spade | 6,376 | 25.6 |
| Sam Spade | 6,375 | 25.5 |
| Judy Knickerbocker | 4,083 | 16.3 |
| William Wallace | 4,083 | 16.3 |
| Wanda Watson | 4,083 | 16.3 |

B. *Purpose.* The Sellers desire to sell, and the Buyers desire to purchase, all of the shares of the common stock of the Corporation owned by the Sellers (the "Shares") upon the terms and conditions described in this Agreement.

C. *Basic agreement.* In consideration of the mutual promises made in this Agreement, and in consideration of the representations, warranties and covenants contained in this Agreement, the Sellers, and the Buyers agree as set forth in this Agreement.

## Agreements
### Section 1—Purchase and Sale of Shares; Closing; Payment

1.1 *Purchase and sale of shares.* Subject to the terms and conditions of this Agreement, at the Closing the Sellers shall sell, transfer, convey, assign, and deliver the Shares to the Buyers, and the Buyers shall purchase, acquire, and accept the Shares from the Sellers, as follows:

| Buyer | Number of Shares |
|---|---|
| Judy Knickerbocker | 4,251 |
| William Wallace | 4,250 |
| Wanda Watson | 4,250 |
| Total: | 12,751 |

1.2 *Purchase price.* The Purchase Price for the Shares shall be cash in the aggregate amount of $700,000.00, to be paid at the Closing by the Buyers to the Sellers as follows:

| Seller | Purchase Price |
|---|---|
| Susan Spade | $350,027.45 |
| Sam Spade | $349,972.55 |
| Total: | $700,000.00 |

1.3 *The closing.* The closing of the purchase and sale of the Shares shall take place upon the satisfaction of each of the conditions set forth in Section 3 of this Agreement on such date no later than _____, 2000, and at such time and place as the parties to this Agreement shall mutually agree. At the Closing, the Buyers shall pay for the Shares, and the Sellers shall deliver certificates representing all of the Shares, duly endorsed, free and clear of all Encumbrances, and with evidence of payment of all necessary transfer taxes and fees.

## Section 2
## Representations and Warranties

2.1 *Representations and warranties of the sellers.* Each of the Sellers represents and warrants to the Buyers as follows:

    2.1.1 *Ownership of shares.* Each of the Sellers has full and valid title to the Shares indicated in this Agreement, free and clear of all Encumbrances, and no impediment exists to his or her sale and transfer of the Shares to the Buyers.

    2.1.2 *Authority, validity and binding nature.* Each of the Sellers has full right, power, and authority to enter into this Agreement and to perform his or her obligations under this Agreement. This Agreement has been duly executed and delivered on behalf of each of the Sellers and constitutes his and her legal, valid, and binding obligations enforceable in accordance with its terms, except as limited by applicable bankruptcy, insolvency, reorganization, moratorium, or similar laws affecting the rights of creditors.

2.1.3 *No violation.* The execution and delivery of this Agreement on behalf of each of the Sellers does not, and the consummation of the transactions contemplated by this Agreement will not, conflict with or constitute a violation of or default under any other contract or agreement to which either of the Sellers is a party or by which either is bound, and no consent of or notice to any other person or entity is required in connection with their execution and delivery of this Agreement or the consummation of the transactions contemplated by this Agreement.

2.2 *Representations and warranties of the buyers.* Each of the Buyers represents and warrants to the Sellers as follows:

2.2.1 *Authority, validity and binding nature.* Each of the Buyers has full right, power, and authority to enter into this Agreement and to perform his obligations under this Agreement. This Agreement has been duly executed and delivered by each of the Buyers and constitutes his legal, valid, and binding obligation enforceable in accordance with its terms, except as limited by applicable bankruptcy, insolvency, reorganization, moratorium, or similar laws affecting the rights of creditors.

2.2.2 *Business prospects.* To the best of each Buyer's knowledge and belief, there is no agreement, transaction, or business opportunity foreseeable by him which may in the future materially enhance the value of the Corporation's business operations, prospects, properties, assets, or financial condition.

2.2.3 *Liabilities.* To the best of each Buyer's knowledge and belief, there is no basis for assertion against either of the Sellers as shareholders, officers or directors of the Corporation, of any material claim or liability which is not fully reflected in the financial statements of the Corporation.

2.2.4 *Guarantees.* As of the Closing, neither of the Sellers remains personally liable under, nor is any of their property pledged as security for, any loan guarantee, whether contingent or otherwise, with respect to any loan or other credit arrangement to which the Corporation is a party.

2.3 *Representations and warranties of all parties.* Each of the parties to this Agreement represents and warrants to the other parties as follows:

2.3.1 *Broker's or finder's fees.* All negotiations relating to this Agreement and the transactions contemplated by this Agreement have been conducted without the involvement of any person on behalf of any of the parties in such a manner as to give rise to any claim against such party for any seller's, broker's or finder's fee or similar compensation.

2.3.2 *Full disclosure.* No representation or warranty of any of the parties under this Agreement contains or will contain any untrue statement of a material fact or omits or will omit any material fact necessary to make the statements in this Agreement not misleading.

## Section 3
## Conditions to Closing

3.1 *Conditions to the buyers' obligations.* The Buyers' obligation to purchase the Shares and to consummate the transactions contemplated by this Agreement is subject to the fulfillment of the following conditions at or prior to the Closing:

3.1.1 *Representations and warranties.* The representations and warranties of the Sellers contained in Section 2 of this Agreement shall have been true and correct in all material respects as of the date of this Agreement and shall be true and correct in all material respects as of the Closing.

3.1.2 *Performance.* The Sellers shall have performed and complied with all terms, conditions, and covenants required by this Agreement to be performed or complied with by each of them at or prior to the Closing.

3.1.3 *Delivery of certificates.* The Sellers shall have delivered to the Buyers the certificates representing the Shares in accordance with the provisions of Subsection 1.1 of this Agreement.

3.1.4 *Resignations.* Each of the Sellers shall have submitted their resignations as members of the Corporation's Board of Directors and as officers of the Corporation to be effective on and after the Closing.

3.1.5 *Corporate action.* The Sellers, acting as owners of a majority of the issued and outstanding common stock of the Corporation, as directors and as officers of the Corporation, shall have caused the Corporation to perform all acts necessary to effect the transactions contemplated by this Agreement.

3.2 *Conditions to the sellers' obligations.* The Sellers' obligation to sell the Shares and to consummate the transactions contemplated by this Agreement is subject to the fulfillment of the following conditions at or prior to the Closing:

3.2.1 *Representations and warranties.* The representations and warranties of the Buyers contained in Section 2 of this Agreement shall have been true and correct in all material respects as of the date of this Agreement and shall be true and correct in all material respects as of the Closing.

3.2.2 *Performance.* The Buyers shall have performed and complied with all terms, conditions, and covenants required by this Agreement to be performed or complied with by them at or prior to the Closing.

3.2.3 *Evidence of release of guarantees.* The Sellers shall have received evidence satisfactory to their legal counsel to the effect that each of the Sellers has been released from all obligations and personal liability, contingent or otherwise, under any loan guarantee agreement or other credit transaction in which the Corporation was or is the borrower.

3.2.4 *Corporate action.* The Buyers, acting as owners of a minority of the issued and outstanding common stock of the Corporation, and as directors and as officers of the Corporation, shall have caused the Corporation to perform all acts necessary to effect the transactions contemplated by this Agreement.

3.2.5 *Indemnification.* Each of the Buyers and the Corporation, jointly and severally, shall indemnify and hold the Sellers harmless against expenses, including attorneys' fees, fines, judgments, and amounts paid in settlement, reasonably incurred by each of the Sellers in connection with any action, suit, or proceeding brought against either or both of the Sellers by reason of the fact that they were a shareholder, director, officer, or employee of the Corporation, provided that the Sellers acted in good faith and in a manner reasonably believed to be in or not opposed to the best interests of the Corporation, and, with respect to a criminal proceeding, had no reasonable cause to believe their conduct was unlawful. The Buyers shall cause the Corporation to indemnify and hold the Sellers harmless to the extent permitted by law. This indemnification from each of the Buyers individually and from the Corporation shall continue as to each of the Sellers even though they have ceased to be a shareholder, director, officer, or employee of the Corporation.

## Section 4
## Definitions

In addition to the definitions set forth in the Preamble and Recitals to this Agreement, the following terms shall have the meanings set forth below:

4.1 *Agreement.* The agreement is this Stock Purchase Agreement and all modifications or amendments thereto.

4.2 *Closing.* The closing is the date and time on which the transactions contemplated by this Agreement are consummated, as provided in Subsection 1.3 of this Agreement.

4.3 *Encumbrance.* An encumbrance is any type of security or surety interest created by any pledge or hypothecation of all or any portion of the Shares, or any other transaction involving all or any portion of the Shares, which is intended to secure any type of debt or obligation, whether incurred voluntarily or involuntarily, and in any manner whatsoever.

4.4 *Purchase price.* The purchase price is the price for which the Buyers will purchase the Shares, as provided in Subsection 1.2 of this Agreement.

4.5 *Shares.* The shares are the 12,751 issued and outstanding shares of the Corporation's common stock which are owned by the Sellers and which are the subject of this Agreement.

## Section 5
## Miscellaneous

5.1 *Binding agreement.* This Agreement is binding on and enforceable by and against the parties, their successors, legal representatives, and assigns.

5.2 *Governing law.* This Agreement will be governed by and construed according to the laws of the State of Arizona.

5.3 *Severability.* No part of this Agreement will be affected if any other part of it is held invalid or unenforceable.

5.4 *Notices.* All notices required or permitted to be given under this Agreement must be given in writing, and will be deemed given when personally delivered or, if earlier, when received after mailing by U.S. registered or certified mail, postage prepaid, with return receipt requested. Notice to any of the Stockholders is valid if sent to him at such Stockholder's address as it appears in the Corporation's records.

5.5 *Voting.* Upon the consummation of the purchase and sale of the Shares at the Closing, the Sellers shall cease to have the right to vote the Shares.

5.6 *Specific performance.* The parties agree that the Shares are unique and that failure of any party to perform the obligations under this Agreement will result in irreparable damage to the other parties and that specific performance of these obligations may be obtained by a suit in equity.

5.7 *Waiver.* Any party's failure to insist on compliance or enforcement of any provision of this Agreement shall not affect its validity or enforce-ability or constitute a waiver of future enforcement of that provision or of any other provision of this Agreement.

5.8 *Copies.* More than one (1) copy of this Agreement may be executed, and all parties agree and acknowledge that each executed copy shall be a duplicate original.

5.9 *Gender and number.* Whenever the context of this Agreement requires, the masculine gender includes the feminine and neuter, and the singular number includes the plural and *vice versa*.

Agreed to by each of the undersigned on the date first noted above.

Sellers:                                    Buyers

_____          _____
Susan Spade                         Judy Knickerbocker


_____          _____
Sam Spade                           William Wallace


                                    _____
                                    Wanda Watson

Wonderful Widgets, Inc.

By:_____

Its:_____

# Resources

## Business Valuations

Gary Ringel
Ringel Valuation Services
5150 N. 16th Street, Suite B-250
Phoenix, AZ 85016
602-266-5060
Web site: <www.ringelvs.com>

Bill Cranshaw
Management Planning, Inc.
10 Station Street, Suite 3
Simsbury, CT 06070
860-651-8185
Web site: <www.mpival.com>

Brad Van Horn
Comstock Valuation Advisors
129 W. Wesley Street
Wheaton, IL 60187
630-462-9100
Web site: <www.comstock.com>

## Compensation Consulting

Alec Berkman and Jim McMahon
CFG Business Solutions, LLC
510 S. Grand Avenue, Suite 302
Glendora, CA 91741
626-914-2333
Web site: <www.cfgllc.com>

## Executive Search

Mike Zwell
Zwell International
300 South Wacker Drive,
Suite 650
Chicago, IL 60606
312-663-3737, Ext 111
Web site: <www.competency-suites.com>

## Investment Consulting and Family Offices

Mark Feldman, CPA
Arthur Andersen LLP
501 N. 44th Street, Suite 300
Phoenix, AZ 85008
602-286-1444
e-mail:
Mark.D.Feldman@US.ArthurAndersen.com

## Investment Consulting

Gail Bradley
Northern Trust Bank of Arizona
7001 North Scottsdale Road
Scottsdale, AZ 85253
480-468-2505
Web site: <www.ntrs.com>

## Business Consulting

John B. Furman
8524 N. Golf Drive
Paradise Valley, AZ 85253
602-684-8371
e-mail:
john.furman@worldnet.att.net

## Strategic Planning and Team Building

Craig Cantoni
Capstone Consulting
9922 E. Doubletree Ranch Road
Scottsdale, AZ 85258
480-661-8175
Web site: <www.craigcantoni.com>

## Team Building

Leslie Dashew
Human Side of Enterprise
21839 N. 98th Street
Scottsdale, AZ 85255
480-419-4243
e-mail: LDashew@aol.com

## Investment Banking

Jim Murphy
DeVisscher Olson & Allen LLC
104 Field Point Road
Greenwich, CT 06830
203-629-6500
Web site: <www.devisscher.com>

Jim Dwyer
MPI Securities
101 Poor Farm Road
Princeton, NJ 08540
609-924-4200
Web site: <www.mpival.com>

## Strategic Philanthropy

Peter Karoff
The Philanthropic Initiative, Inc.
77 Franklin Street
Boston, MA 02110
617-338-2590
Web site: <www.tpi.org>

# Endnotes

## Chapter 1

[1] Stan Davis and Christopher Meyer, *Blur: The Speed of Change in the Connected Economy*, 7.

[2] *Mergerstat* Newsletter, Jan. 2000, Kurt Kunert, Ed., Los Angeles, CA.

[3] Noel M. Tichy and Mary Anne Devanna, *The Transformational Leader*, 69.

[4] William Bridges, *Transitions: Making Sense of Life's Changes*, 112.

## Chapter 2

[1] Adam J. Fein, *Consolidation in Wholesale Distribution: Understanding Industry Change*, 17.

[2] American Family Business Survey, 1997, Arthur Andersen/Mass Mutual.

[3] Craig E. Aronoff, Ph.D. and John L. Ward, Ph.D., *Preparing Your Family Business for Strategic Change*, 20.

[4] Ibid.

[5] Ibid, pg 16.

[6] Gail Sheehy, *Understanding Men's Passages*, 21.

[7] Ibid, pg 99.

[8] Francis Fukuyama, *Trust: The Social Virtues and the Creation of Prosperity*, 156.

## Chapter 3

[1] Dyer, W. Gibb, Jr., *Cultural Change in Family Firms*, 130.

[2] Kerry Dolan, "The Age of the $100 Million CEO," *Forbes*, April 3, 2000, 129.

[3] M. Financial Group Private Company Compensation, Benefit, and Wealth Transfer Study. "Reaching for Higher Performance: How Private Companies Can Secure the Future." 1998.

[4] Marshall B. Paisner, *Sustaining the Family Business: An Insider's Guide to Managing across Generations and Ensuring a Legacy of Opportunity*, 47.

[5] Stan Davis and Christopher Meyer, *Blur: The Speed of Change in the Connected Economy*, 188.

[6] Ivan Lansberg, *Succeeding Generations: Realizing the Dream of Families in Business*, 75.

[7] Ibid, pg 79

## Chapter 6

[1] Noel M. Tichy, and Mary Anne Devanna, *The Transformational Leader*, 146.

[2] Abraham Zaleznik, "Managers and Leaders: Are They Different?," *Harvard Business Review*, Vol. 55, No. 5.

[3] McGregor, Douglas, *The Human Side of Enterprise*.

[4] Jay Lorsch and Rakesh Khurana, "Changing Leaders: The Board's Role in CEO Succession," *Harvard Business Review*, May-June 1999, 97–105.

[5] Ivan Lansberg, *Succeeding Generations: Realizing the Dream of Families in Business*, 183.

[6] Dennis T. Jaffe, Cynthia D. Scott, and Glenn R. Tobe, *Rekindling Commitment: How to Revitalize Yourself, Your Work, and Your Organization*, 34.

[7] Ram Charan and Geoffrey Colvin, "Why CEOs Fail," *Fortune*, Vol. 139, No. 12, 21 Jun. 1999, 68–76.

[8] Gibb W. Dyer, Jr., *Cultural Change in Family Firms*, 61.

[9] David A. Heenan and Warren Bennis, *Co-Leaders: The Power of Great Partnerships*, 5.

[10] Ibid.

[11] M Financial Group Private Company Compensation, Benefit and Wealth Transfer Study, "Reaching for Higher Performance: How Private Companies Can Secure the Future," 1998.

[12] Kerry A. Dolan, "The Age of the $100 Million CEO," *Forbes*, April 3, 2000, 129.

[13] Carolyn Geer, "Sharing the Wealth, Capitalist-Style," *Forbes*, December 1, 1997, 158.

## Chapter 7

[1] Dennis T. Jaffe, Cynthia D. Scott, and Glenn R. Tobe, *Rekindling Commitment: How to Revitalize Yourself, Your Work, and Your Organization*, 161.

[2] Arthur Andersen/MassMutual American Family Business Survey 1997.

[3] Dennis T. Jaffe, Cynthia D. Scott, and Glenn R. Tobe, *Rekindling Commitment: How to Revitalize Yourself, Your Work, and Your Organization*, 141.

[4] W. Gibb Dyer, Jr., *Cultural Change in Family Firms*, 130.

## Chapter 8

[1] Kitchen, Steve and Tina Russo McCarthy, "Wall Street? No, thanks!" *Forbes*, December 1, 1997.

[2] Joe Salimando, "Large Contractors Cast A Bigger Shadow," *Electrical Contractor Magazine*, Vol. 65, Number 3, March 2000, 64.

[3] "Selling Your Business, Growth Company Services," Deloitte & Touche LLP, 1999.

[4] Russ Robb, "Key Points on Selling a Company," *Association for Corporate Growth* newsletter, January 1999.

## Chapter 9

[1] Eddy Goldberg, "The Art of Acquisition," *Success Magazine*, Vol. 47, Number 2, June 2000, 64.

[2] Roger Fisher and Danny Ertel, *Getting Ready to Negotiate: The GETTING TO YES™ Workbook*, 72.

[3] "Selling Your Business, Growth Company Services," *Deloitte & Touche LLP*, 1999.

[4] Howard Muson, ed., "The Sale of Fel-Pro," *Family Business*, Winter 2000, 20.

## Chapter 11

[1] Russell Olson, *The Independent Fiduciary*, 110.

[2] Hilary Rosenberg, "Awaiting the New Rich: Alternative Investments," *New York Times*, Sun, February 20, 2000, B-8.

## Chapter 12

[1] John Havens and Paul Schervish, "New Estimates of the Forthcoming Wealth Transfer and the Prospects for a Golden Age of Philanthropy," *Gift Planning Digest*, February, 2000.

[2] Planning Techniques for Large Estates, American Law Institute and American Bar Association, April 26, 2000, New York, New York, Vol II.

# Glossary

**ASA.** An abbreviation for two things: (1) American Society of Appraisers (Herndron, Virginia), and (2) a professional designation awarded by them: Accredited Senior Appraiser. Designations are given by the ASA in specific disciplines—you would want one whose ASA designation is in business valuation.

**accounting estimate.** An approximation of a financial statement element, item, or account. Accounting estimates in historical financial statements measure the effects of past business transactions or events, or the present status of an asset or liability.

**accounting policies.** The principles, bases, conventions, rules, and procedures adopted by management in recording financial transactions and preparing and presenting financial statements.

**accounting system.** The principles, methods, and procedures relating to the recording, classification, and reporting of the financial transactions of an entity. In most contexts, the term is synonymous with financial information system.

**acquisition process.** The basic stages of an acquisition are:
- *strategy*: developing a good strategy for strengthening the competitive capabilities of the existing business.

- *planning*: detailing a well-planned, team-based approach to making an acquisition.
- *execution*: completing the negotiations and closing the deal on favorable terms.

**acquisition team.** The group of people assembled by the buyer to manage the acquisition process. It may include senior management of the buyer and advisors such as lawyers, accountants, and other consultants.

**agency role.** A person or company that has the authority to act on behalf of another (e.g., someone who makes an agreement on behalf of the buyer).

**agreement in principle.** An outline of the understanding between the parties, including the price and the major terms. It is often referred to as a letter of intent. Usually, the agreement is subject to the negotiation of a mutually acceptable definitive agreement.

**agreement of purchase and sale.** See purchase agreement.

**analytical procedures.** The application of comparisons, computations, inquiries, inspections, and observations to analyze and develop expectations about relationships among financial and operating data for comparison to recorded account balances or classes of transactions. Analytical procedures include reasonableness tests, trend analysis, and ratio analysis.

**auction.** An invitation for bids on a business by a specified date. In practice, the date is often extended for three or four top bidders, who then are invited to improve their offers.

**business appraiser.** A professional employed in the provision of business valuation and related services.

**business broker.** One who is involved with businesses or companies in the sale and/or purchase of a typical transaction value (selling price) of less than $1 million.

**business valuation.** The act of determining the value of, or the estimated value of, a business enterprise or an interest therein.

**comfort letter.** A letter provided by independent accountants reporting on the financial condition of a company, usually for an interim period since the last audit.

**competitive advantage.** The strategies, skills, knowledge, resources, or competencies that differentiate a business from its competitors.

**conditions.** Situations subject to third party control, such as bank financing, or a list of actions that must be taken prior to closing.

**confidentiality agreement.** A legal document whereby the Buyer pledges to keep strictly confidential, and return on request, any and all information provided by the Seller.

**contingency.** An existing condition, situation, or set of circumstances involving uncertainty as to possible gain or loss to an entity that will be resolved when one or more future events occur or fail to occur.

**core competencies.** Unique combinations of knowledge, skills, and technologies that the business has developed, either intentionally or unintentionally, that give it a competitive advantage.

**covenant.** A commitment made by the buyer or seller. For example, a commitment by the seller that, subsequent to signing the purchase agreement but prior to closing, they will preserve the assets and continue to operate so that the business and goodwill being acquired will not diminish.

**culture.** The beliefs, habits, and behaviors of an entity. The culture of a business affects its ability to work in teams, to manage change, to innovate, etc. Culture is also reflected in management style and standards of customer service.

**deal breaker.** A deal breaker is a significant issue relating to the proposed acquisition between the buyer and the seller that needs to be resolved in order to close the deal.

**differentiation.** The unique manner in which a business innovates and distinguishes itself from its competitors, in order to increase its competitiveness.

**discretionary earnings.** The earnings of a business enterprise prior to the following items: income taxes, nonrecurring income and expenses, depreciation and amortization, interest expense or income, owner's total compensation for one owner/operator, after adjusting the total compensation of all owners to market value according to the International Business Brokers Association.

**due diligence.** The process wherein the buyer discovers and verifies all the important information on all aspects of a business, especially as it pertains to a purchase. A buyer conducts due diligence in order to confirm that the target company is in the condition it has represented, to uncover any unexpected liabilities, and to eliminate any post-sale surprises. See also: reverse due diligence:

**EBIT.** Earnings before interest and taxes.

**EBITDA.** Earnings before interest, taxes, depreciation, and amortization.

**earnout.** A method of structuring a transaction whereby the ultimate purchase price is dependent in part on the future performance of the business being acquired.

**engagement letter.** A letter that summarizes the terms of the advisor's engagement.

**forecast.** Future-oriented financial information prepared using assumptions, all of which reflect the entity's planned courses of action for the period covered, given management's judgment as to the most probable set of economic conditions. See also: projection.

**fraud.** See irregularities.

**future-oriented financial information.** Information about prospective results of operations, financial position and/or changes in financial position, based on assumptions about future economic conditions and courses of action. Future-oriented financial information is presented as either a forecast or a projection.

**indemnification.** A promise by one person or entity to protect another person or entity from an anticipated or potential loss. For example, a promise by the seller to assume certain potential future liabilities (e.g., tax reassessments, product or health, and safety liabilities, etc.) relating to past activities of the business.

**information package.** A compilation of corporate information provided by the seller to the buyer in connection with the sale of a business. The seller prepares the information or selling package to expose the business that is for sale to interested potential purchasers. Frequently, the seller will prepare two separate packages—one that provides general information on what is being offered for sale, and a second, more detailed document made available to potential purchasers who have shown a serious interest in proceeding with the acquisition. Information packages are good sources of background information and may address the following:

- *information system.* A collection of an entity's resources (people, expertise, facilities, processes, hardware, software, and data) designed to help accomplish business objectives and enable people to carry out their responsibilities. The information system produces reports, containing operational, financial, and compliance-related information that make it possible to run and control the business. An accounting system is part of an information system. The information processed is not only internally generated data, but also information about external events, activities, and conditions necessary to informed business decision making and external reporting.
- *information technology.* The expertise, facilities, processes, hardware, software, and data available to assist in attaining business objectives.

**inspection.** Reading of records or documents, either visually or electronically.

**investment banker.** One who structures and arranges financing for leveraged recapitalizations, mergers, divestitures, IPOs, and private placements of debt; advises on selling strategy; screens buyers; and works as part of the selling team.

**irregularities.** Intentional misrepresentations of financial statements by one or more individuals among management, employees, or third parties. Irregularities may involve manipulation, falsification, or alteration of records or documents; misappropriation of assets; suppression or omission of the effects of transactions from records or documents; recording of transactions without substance; or misapplication of accounting standards.

**LOI.** Letter of intent. Summarizes the principal deal points of a proposed transaction but does not constitute a complete, definitive legal agreement. The term encompasses documents such as term sheets, memoranda of understanding, and commitment letters. Letters of intent can be binding legal agreements, nonbinding summaries of deal terms, or a bit of both.

**M&A intermediary.** A professional who specializes in serving clients and customers who desire to sell or acquire a business or company with a transaction value (selling price) between $1 million and $100 million.

**management.** The individuals in an entity that have the authority and the responsibility to manage the entity. The positions of these individuals, and their titles, vary from one entity to another and, to some extent, from one country to another depending on the local laws and customs. Thus, when the context requires it, the term includes the board of directors or committees of the board, which are designated to oversee certain matters (e.g., audit committee).

**merger.** A transaction where one entity retains the controlling interests and/or operations of another, usually through either a stock or asset sale/purchase.

**middle market.** Those companies that fall into a size range from $1 million to $100 million.

**net economic value added.** Synergy, whereby two entities, when combined, create value greater than the sum of the two parts. This additional value can fail to materialize due to inadequate post-transaction integration planning by the buyer. It is particularly sought after in cases of vertical integration and industry consolidation.

**noncompetition agreement.** An agreement that specifies the period of time during which a seller or departing key employee cannot compete directly with the buyer, and the geographical area covered.

**no-shop clause.** An agreement between the prospective buyer and the potential seller to stop discussing for a defined period, the sale of the business to others.

**offering document.** A document such as a prospectus, statement of material facts, take-over bid circular, issuer bid circular, or information circular provided to investors in order to assist them in making informed decisions with respect to the purchase, sale, or exchange of securities.

**operational integration.** The process of integrating the seller's company into the buyer's ongoing business, including integration of the acquired management and work force and their ways of operating into ongoing operations.

**physical examination.** Inspection of a tangible item, usually other than a document, such as an item of equipment.

**principal role.** A person or company that acts for his own benefit or on his own account.

**projection.** Future-oriented financial information prepared using assumptions that reflect the entity's planned courses of action for the period covered given management's judgment as to the most probable set of economic conditions, together with one or more hypotheses that are assumptions, which are consistent with the purpose of the information but are not necessarily the most probable in management's judgment. See also: forecast.

**prospective financial information.** The financial information that relates to events and actions that have not yet occurred and may not occur.

**published financial statements.** Financial statements, interim and condensed financial statements and selected data derived from such statements, such as earnings releases, reported publicly.

**purchase agreement.** A legal document that records the final understanding of the parties with respect to the proposed transaction.

**rate of return.** The percentage return on invested capital. Often a buyer has, as one of its investment criteria, a minimum acceptable rate of return on an acquisition.

**redundant assets.** Assets that are not necessary for the ongoing operations of the business.

**related party.** A person or entity that has or may have the ability to control or exercise significant influence over the other party in making financial and operating decisions. Accordingly, subsidiaries, parent companies, sister companies, and entities accounted for by the equity method are considered to be related parties, as are principal owners, members of boards of directors, management, and members of their immediate families.

**related party transaction.** A transfer of resources or obligations between related parties, regardless of whether a price is charged.

**representations.** See warranties.

**revenue rulings.** Administrative pronouncements by the IRS. The Revenue Rulings of most significance that relate to business valuations are: 59–60, 65–193, 68–609, 77–287, 83–120, and 92–12.

**reverse due diligence.** The process wherein the seller investigates the buyer. This is especially important where seller financing is involved, where the owner-seller investigates the credit worthiness of the buyer, along with such things as the buyer's business acumen.

**selling memorandum.** A description of the business including its history, products, markets, management, facilities, competition, financial statements, product literature, and a review of its prospects.

**sunk costs.** An unrecoverable cost resulting from an irreversible past decision.

**synergy.** See net economic value added.

**target.** The business, or significant asset (e.g., plant or real estate) being considered for purchase by a buyer from a seller.

**trend analysis.** Analysis of the changes in a given account balance or class of transactions between the current and prior periods or over several accounting periods.

**value chain.** The entire process that transforms raw material, including knowledge and information, into final products and services.

**values.** See culture.

**warranties.** Statements made by the seller with respect to certain elements of the proposed transaction (e.g., financial position of the target at closing date, level of sales achieved, collectibility of accounts receivable, extent of contingent liabilities, exposure to environmental issues) which, if proven to be untrue, may give the buyer the right to make a claim for damages from the seller.

**"what if" scenarios.** The results of analysis of the effect of possible future situations such as economic downturns, loss of key customers, changes in interest rates or price levels, new competitors or technologies.

# Bibliography

Adizes, Ichak. *Corporate Lifecycles: How and Why Corporations Grow and Die and What to Do about It.* Englewood Cliffs, NJ: Prentice Hall, 1988.

Adizes, Ichak. *Mastering Change: The Power of Mutual Trust and Respect in Personal Life, Family Life, Business and Society.* Santa Monica, CA: Adizes Institute Publications, 1992.

Alexander, Charles N. and Ellen J. Langer. *Higher Stages of Human Development.* New York: Oxford University Press, Inc., 1990.

Aronoff, Craig E. Ph.D. and John L. Ward, Ph.D. *Family Business Governance: Maximizing Family and Business Potential.* Marietta, GA: Business Owner Resources, 1996.

———. *Preparing Your Family Business for Strategic Change.* Marietta, GA: Business Owner Resources, 1997.

Bennis, Warren. *On Becoming a Leader.* Reading, MA: Addison-Wesley Publishing Company, Inc., 1989.

Blasi, Joseph Raphael and Douglas Lynn Kruse. *The New Owners: The Mass Emergence of Employee Ownership in Public Companies and What It Means to American Business*. New York: HarperBusiness, A Division of HarperCollins Publishers Inc., 1991.

Block, Peter. *Stewardship: Choosing Service over Self-Interest*. San Francisco: Berrett-Koehler Publishers, Inc., 1993.

Bridges, William. *Transitions: Making Sense of Life's Changes*. Reading, MA: Addison-Wesley Publishing Company, Inc., 1991.

Buchholz, Barbara B., Margaret Crane, and Ross W. Nager. *The Family Business Answer Book*. Paramus, NJ: Prentice Hall, 1999.

Collins, James C. and Jerry I. Porras. *Built to Last: Successful Habits of Visionary Companies*. New York: HarperCollins Publishers, Inc., 1997.

Davis, Stan and Christopher Meyer. *Blur: The Speed of Change in the Connected Economy*. New York: HarperCollins Publishers, 1998.

DePree, Max. *Leadership Jazz*. New York: Doubleday, 1992.

Dyer, W. Gibb, Jr. *Cultural Change in Family Firms*. San Francisco: Jossey-Bass, Inc., Publishers, and London: Jossey-Bass Limited, 1986.

Fein, Adam J. *Consolidation in Wholesale Distribution: Understanding Industry Change*. Washington, DC: DREF/NAW Publications, 1997.

Fisher, Roger and Danny Ertel. *Getting Ready to Negotiate: The GETTING TO YES™ Workbook*. New York: Penguin Books, 1995.

Fisher, Roger, William Ury, and Bruce Patton. *Getting to Yes: Negotiating Agreement without Giving In*. 2nd ed. New York: Penguin Books, 1991.

Fisher, Roger and Scott Brown. *Getting Together: Building Relationships as We Negotiate*. New York: Penguin Books, 1988.

Flamholtz, Eric G. *How to Make the Transition from an Entrepreneurship to a Professionally Managed Firm*. San Francisco: Jossey-Bass, Inc., Publishers, and London: Jossey-Bass Limited, 1986.

Fukuyama, Francis. *Trust: The Social Virtues and the Creation of Prosperity*. New York: Simon & Schuster, Inc., 1996.

Gould, Roger, M.D. *Transformations: Growth and Change in Adult Life*. New York: Simon & Schuster, Inc., 1978.

Heenan, David A. and Warren Bennis. *Co-Leaders: The Power of Great Partnerships*. New York: John Wiley & Sons, Inc., 1999.

Heskett, James L., W. Earl Sasser, Jr., and Christopher W. L. Hart. *Service Breakthroughs: Changing the Rules of the Game*. New York: The Free Press, 1990.

Hesselbein, Frances, Marshall Goldsmith, and Richard Beckhard, editors. *The Leader of the Future*. San Francisco: Jossey-Bass, Inc., Publishers, 1996.

Jaffe, Dennis T., Cynthia D. Scott, and Glenn R. Tobe. *Rekindling Commitment: How to Revitalize Yourself, Your Work, and Your Organization*. San Francisco: Jossey-Bass, Inc., Publishers, 1994.

Lansberg, Ivan. *Succeeding Generations: Realizing the Dream of Families in Business*. Boston: Harvard Business School Press, 1999.

Levinson, Daniel J. *The Seasons of a Man's Life*. New York: Ballantine Books, 1978.

————. *The Seasons of a Woman's Life*. New York: Ballantine Books, 1996.

Maccoby, Michael. *Why Work: Motivating and Leading the New Generation*. New York: Simon & Schuster, Inc., 1989.

McGregor, Douglas. *The Human Side of Enterprise*. New York: McGraw-Hill, 1960.

Mercer, Z. Christopher, ASA, CFA. *Quantifying Marketability Discounts*. Memphis, TN: Peabody Publishing, LP, 1997.

Napier, Augustus Y., Ph.D. and Carl Whitaker, M.D. *The Family Crucible: The Intense Experience of Family Therapy*. New York: Harper & Row, Publishers, Inc., 1988.

Neff, Thomas J. and James M. Citrin. *The Search for America's Best Business Leaders*. New York: Doubleday, 1999.

Neubauer, Fred and Alden G. Lank. *The Family Business – Its Governance for Sustainability*. London: Macmillan Press, 1998.

Olson, Russell L. *The Independent Fiduciary: Investing for Pension Funds and Endowment Funds*. New York: John Wiley & Sons, Inc., 1999.

Paisner, Marshall B. *Sustaining the Family Business: An Insider's Guide to Managing across Generations and Ensuring a Legacy of Opportunity*. Reading, MA: Perseus Books, 1999.

Peters, Thomas and Robert Waterman, Jr. *In Search of Excellence—Lessons from America's Best Run Companies*. New York: Warner Books, 1982.

Poza, Ernesto J. *Smart Growth: Critical Choices for Business Continuity and Prosperity*. San Francisco: Jossey-Bass, Inc., Publishers, and London: Jossey-Bass Limited, 1986.

Reda, James F. *2000 Pay to Win: How America's Successful Companies Pay Their Executives*. Orlando, FL: Harcourt, Inc., 2000.

Renesch, John. *New Traditions in Business*. San Francisco: Berrett-Koehler Publishers, 1992.

Senge, Peter M. *The Fifth Discipline: The Art and Practice of the Learning Organization*. New York: Doubleday, 1990.

Sheehy, Gail. *New Passages: Mapping Your Life across Time*. New York: Random House, Inc., 1995.

———. *Understanding Men's Passages: Discovering the New Map of Men's Lives*. New York: Random House, 1998.

Shim, Jae K., Ph.D. and Joel G. Siegel, Ph.D., CPA. *Handbook of Financial Analysis, Forecasting & Modeling*. Englewood Cliffs, NJ: Prentice Hall, 1988.

Tichy, Noel M. and Mary Anne Devanna. *The Transformational Leader*. New York: John Wiley & Sons, Inc., 1986.

Ward, John L. *Creating Effective Boards for Private Enterprises*. San Francisco: Jossey-Bass, Inc., Publishers, 1991.

Waterman, Robert H., Jr. *The Renewal Factor: How the Best Get and Keep the Competitive Edge*. New York: Bantam Books, 1987.

Zwell, Michael. *Creating a Culture of Competence*. New York: John Wiley & Sons, Inc., 2000.

# Index